Noigandres

VERBAL ARTS: STUDIES IN POETICS

Lazar Fleishman and Haun Saussy, series editors

Noigandres

Poetry Made New in Brazil

Antonio Sergio Bessa

Fordham University Press

Copyright © 2026 Fordham University Press

All rights reserved. No part of this publication may be reproduced, stored in a retrieval system, or transmitted in any form or by any means—electronic, mechanical, photocopy, recording, or any other—except for brief quotations in printed reviews, without the prior permission of the publisher.

Fordham University Press has no responsibility for the persistence or accuracy of URLs for external or third-party Internet websites referred to in this publication and does not guarantee that any content on such websites is, or will remain, accurate or appropriate.

Fordham University Press also publishes its books in a variety of electronic formats. Some content that appears in print may not be available in electronic books.

Visit us online at www.fordhampress.com.

For EU safety / GPSR concerns: Mare Nostrum Group B.V., Doelen 72, 4831 GR Breda, The Netherlands, gpsr@mare-nostrum.co.uk

Library of Congress Cataloging-in-Publication Data available online at https://catalog.loc.gov.

Printed in the United States of America

28 27 26   5 4 3 2 1

First edition

For Edward Yanisch
And in memory of Marjorie Perloff

CONTENTS

	Introduction	1
1	Word as Object	9
2	Sound as Subject	23
3	Mechanics of Composition	46
4	Poetics of the Unpoetic	65
5	Disruption of Style	81
6	Poetry and Modernity in the New World	97
	Acknowledgments	113
	Appendix 1: The Noigandres / Ezra Pound Correspondence	115
	Appendix 2: "Deciphering Semiotics," by Décio Pignatari	137
	Appendix 3: "Pound Made (New) in Brazil," by Augusto de Campos	151
	Appendix 4: "The Aph*freud*isiac Lacan in the Galaxy of Lalangue," by Haroldo de Campos	161
	Notes	173
	Index	201

Noigandres

Introduction

Both a product and an agent of its epoch, concrete poetry came into the cultural scene in Brazil as part of a concerted effort from different sectors of the society to foster a new national identity through the arts. Fueled in great part by the excitement generated by the construction of Brasilia, the monumental project that endeavored to realign the country's infrastructure based on its geographical center, the public debate about the need to modernize the country echoed to some extent the missionary zeal of modernist architecture and art movements in Europe that emerged in the wake of the industrial age. Prominent among all disciplines, architecture led the charge for radical change by adopting a visual vocabulary and processes in tune with the latest developments in Europe spearheaded by movements such as the Bauhaus and theories advanced by radical architects such as Le Corbusier.[1]

In that context, the founders of the concrete poetry movement struck a dissonant note by embracing the strain of modernism promoted by writers like Ezra Pound and James Joyce, thus contributing a highly distinctive voice to the dialogue. Like Pound, the concrete poets were inspired by the possibilities of the Chinese ideogram as a medium for poetry, and from Joyce they borrowed the concept of *verbivocovisual*. Combined, these ideas would inform their conceptualization of concrete poetry and guide their careers throughout the following decades. But nowhere else was the dissonance promoted by the concrete poets more apparent than in the choice of a title for the journal that became their platform throughout the 1950s: the word *noigandres*, borrowed from medieval Provençal poetry, signaled a paradoxical relationship with modernity.[2]

The distinction between different approaches to what it meant to be *modern* at that particular moment in Brazil is important to consider. For one thing, the path taken by the concrete poets, shaped in great part by Pound's idiosyncratic idea of modernity,[3] allowed their work a measure of complexity and depth that has proved relevant to the present day. More importantly, the theoretical essays and translations of canonical works of world literature that they put forth for the most part inspired by Pound's concerns related to a *paideuma*,[4] lent a pedagogical dimension to the concretist poetics. That aspect of the concrete program performed an important reevaluation of the Brazilian literary heritage, a realignment, so to speak, of what Haroldo de Campos called a "tradition of rupture," borrowing from Octavio Paz.

One such consequential examination entailed recognizing the nineteenth-century poet Joaquim de Sousândrade as a precursor of modernism—a claim based on the poet's pioneering use of collage technique in "Wall Street Inferno," a section of his epic poem *O Guesa*.[5] An extraordinary poetic hybrid that collapses fiction (the retelling of a Quechua legend about the sacrifice of a youth to the sun god) with journalistic reporting (the official visit of the Brazilian emperor Pedro II to the United States in 1876), the sequence, according to the Campos brothers, anticipated some of Pound's key innovations related to the use of collage technique and the intertwining of poetry and history. Sousândrade, who lived in New York for a decade over two periods in the 1870s, worked for the Portuguese-language newspaper *O Novo Mundo* as a secretary and collaborator, although there is no indication that he had any role in the newspaper's extensive reporting of the imperial trip. Instead, the events surrounding Pedro's visit provided him fodder for "Wall Street Inferno," deliriously woven into the broader context of the New York political scene at the time, amid echoes of world history and literary references. The sequence is an important marker in two major ways. It signals the point in Sousândrade's epic in which he realized (perhaps for the first time) that his hero, the *guesa*, was a metaphor for the emperor, who as an infant had been abandoned by the Portuguese royal family to the care of a group of elderly councilors. The sequence also signals the moment when the poet seems to lose control of the narrative and the poem becomes truly modern in the sense suggested by Charles Baudelaire of extracting from the everyday "the poetry that resides in its historical envelope."[6] A poetic upheaval, so to speak, that finds echoes almost a century later in Pound's *Pisan*

Cantos, the sequence in which the poet also seemed to lose control of his narrative and is caught up in the machinery of history.

To fully appreciate the significance of Sousândrade in the larger context of Brazilian literary history, it's important to understand the stakes of the imperial visit to the United States, particularly Pedro's presence at the opening of the 1876 Philadelphia Centennial Exposition. For although the visit was conceived largely as a diplomatic mission to introduce the young ruler into the international arena, its implications resonated far beyond the political arena to find echoes in the spheres of literature and popular culture. Taking place barely a decade after the end of the Civil War in the United States, the imperial visit presented a prescient mirror to a monarch struggling to unite a deeply divided population back home made up of three distinctive ethnic groups.[7] In an analysis of the event based on its thorough coverage by *O Novo Mundo*, Krista Brune correctly noted that the exhibition, as well as the presence of the Brazilian emperor, allowed the United States and Brazil to "stake disparate claims to modernity" informed by "Eurocentric visions of progress as a scientific, teleological ideal."[8] And in a short essay on the exhibition's opening ceremony, Brazilian historian Keila Grinberg lamented that the emperor missed the opportunity to meet former slave and illustrious abolitionist Frederick Douglass who was also present at the event.[9]

An important moment in Pedro's visit to Philadelphia was meeting Alexander Graham Bell and being introduced to the telephone. Such was the impact of their meeting that upon his return to Brazil the emperor ordered the installation of the first telephone lines in Rio connecting the royal palace to the residences of his ministers. In the span of twenty years, the telephone network had been expanded to several cities in the country. Although its implementation ought to be seen as an effort to upgrade the country's colonial infrastructure, it should be noted that, for many decades, the telephone would remain a privilege of the elite. For the larger population, the appliance would became the very symbol of class struggle, lampooned in "Pelo telefone" (On the telephone), a samba released in 1917 that wittily subverted the power balance between the bohemian and the police.[10] A celebration of cosmopolitan life, while also a mordant critique of inequity, "Pelo telephone" signaled the challenges of modernizing a nation still grappling with the legacy of colonialism, and whose heterogenic population seemed to deflect any attempt of integration. It's worth noting that like Sousândrade's oddly misplaced sequence, "Pelo Telefone" is a clear product of an era whose newness, to paraphrase Nicolau Sevcenko, required a new diction: "fluid, pointed, plastic, discontinuous and multifarious."[11] The fact that such a quintessentially modern icon was introduced to the larger population through samba is important to consider as it denotes the complex sociocultural moment in early twentieth-century Brazil. Surely, we take into consideration the fact that Oswald de Andrade, one of the founders of Brazilian modernism, ran for a few years a newspaper column titled *Telefonema* (Phone call), but that wouldn't start until 1944.[12] On the other hand, the broad appeal of samba in the early decades of the twentieth century suggests that the modern vernacular in Brazil would no longer be dictated by academics and the elite, but was now being richly affected by the complex makeup of the country's population, a significant cultural renovation that the Noigandres poets were keen to embrace and celebrate.

Regardless of internal social conflicts, the industrial machinery was already afoot in Brazil in the first decades of the twentieth century, and the impact of the world exhibitions was being felt not only through the consumer products released throughout the country on a regular basis, but through the very impact of the eclectic, Babelian nature of the architectures conceived for the exhibitions. Nicolau Sevcenko, in *Orfeu extático na metropolis* (Orpheus Ecstatic in the Metropolis), astutely connected the speedy development of São Paulo throughout the 1920s to the impact of the international exhibitions: "This urban phenomenon is but the visible tip of a deeper cultural matrix," he wrote, and, quoting modernist author Alcântara Machado, he added: "The city exudes the whiff of an international exposition."[13] Indeed, since the Great Exhibition in London, in 1851, the "international exposition" model had become an important stage for fast-industrializing nations to display cutting-edge products and inventions with the promise of a better tomorrow. In its bid to outdo the grandeur of London's Crystal Palace, the 1855 Paris exhibition stressed the inexorability of the modernist program by deeming it *universelle*. As it happened, the event attracted over five million visitors over a span of six months, and two years later, fifteen million visitors went to the exhibition of 1867. These surprising attendance numbers give a measure not only of the success, but also tell something about the objective of the enterprise; i.e., that the exhibitions were not spectacles for the elites, but rather a concerted strategy to introduce the common citizen into a new environment while also creating a market for new products. It's telling, as Walter Benjamin noted, that since the start, the exhibitions became a political ground for workers' delegations.[14] To be sure, nineteenth-century Paris was a convoluted laboratory for urban and social engineering fueled by a succession of political turbulences that gives us a measure of the high stakes at the advent of the modern era.

Brazil initiated its bid to enter the modern era against this backdrop of momentous sociocultural changes in Europe propelled by the fast-paced process of industrialization that was underway. In 1922, the first world exposition was organized in Rio de Janeiro to coincide with the centennial of the country's independence from Portugal. Earlier in the year, a group of artists and intellectuals promoted a three-day event in São Paulo to claim allegiance to modern art. Organized with the financial support of the city's landowner elite, the "Semana de arte moderna," signaled early on Brazil's complicated rapport with modernity.[15] For one thing, the presentation of art and literature as processes independent of the country's social infrastructure was in opposition to the model advanced by the earlier world expositions in Europe, where contemporary art was displayed as parallel events expected to reach a wide and diverse audience. But while such fractured society represented a sharp rebuke to the industrial age's determination to create a new society based on accessibility to communication and consumer goods, it also promoted a kind of parallel modernity in that those alienated from the system of industrial production participated by offering a critical view of the new environment. For if the lyric was to survive in a global industrial society, the new form needed to communicate to everyone. As it were, the lyrical prowess displayed by samba composers, for the most part based in Rio, is noteworthy for its contribution to an urban poetics that immediately responded to new elements put forth by industrial society adapting (modernizing) the Portuguese language to a multifaceted society in the early twentieth century. More importantly, aired throughout the country through radio and made available through recordings, samba culture constituted a formidable corpus of popular culture communicated immediately to large segments of the population through the most advanced technology.

In the essays that follow, I argue that the Noigandres poets fully grasped the complex juncture of time and place in which they arrived in the early 1950s, understanding that if concrete poetry was to succeed, communication was paramount. Their strategy consisted of releasing short essays and manifestos in newspapers and magazines of broad national circulation, while also ensuring that their ideas would be embraced and propagated by artists with a broader audience. As a result, their scholarly research on Sousândrade, for example, found continuity through the work of artists such as Caetano Veloso and Hélio Oiticica who endeavored to transpose Sousândrade's poetics into their own brand of experimentalism.[16] Furthermore, the pedagogical drive to circulate their discoveries were carefully conceived through the release of important translations of works by Stéphane Mallarmé, Ezra Pound, James Joyce, Gertrude Stein, and many others. Bridging the gap between past and present, they delved into forgotten works thus stressing their relevance, while keenly attuned to the popular production of their time. By doing so, they not only promoted the renewal of the poetic craft in Brazil, but also highlighted the complexity of Brazilian culture, often connecting language experiments widely distant in time and space. Consider for example, Augusto de Campos's interest in Provençal poetry, which encouraged a younger generation of poets and scholars to read the work of the *cantadores* in the Brazilian northeast under a new light.

Seventy years after its launching, the legacy of Noigandres still reverberates both in the many reassessments of the movement by young scholars, as well as through new research on Brazilian literature that follows on the paths opened up by founders of the movement. This volume gathers six essays that I wrote over the span of the last fifteen years, and do not aim to constitute a cohesive whole. Inspired by their writings and poems, I thought of a prismatic structure as a means to approach the Noigandres movement from different angles. The first three essays focus on the so-called heroic phase of concretism, while the last three essays follow the paths explored by the Noigandres poets after the 1964 military coup that brought an end to an era of experimentation in the arts in Brazil.

The opening essay, "Word as Object," offers an overview of the main Noigandres manifestos published throughout the 1950s. Its original version was presented at a conference on concrete poetry organized by the Weserburg Museum, in Bremen, Germany in 2011.[17] The next essay, "Sound as Subject," features a close reading of Augusto de Campos's seminal series *Poetamenos* (1954), considered the first example of a concrete poem. The original version of this essay was presented at the Presidential Forum, at the Modern Language Association Conference, in 2006.[18] The third essay, "Mechanics of Composition," examines a series of poems by Décio Pignatari ranging from the early 1950s to the mid-1970s that were influenced by his readings on cybernetics and semiotics. This essay was presented at the conference BOOKMACHINES, organized by Klaus Müller-Wille and Niels Röller, at the Zentrum Künste und Kulturtheorie Universität Zürich, in November 2023.

The fourth essay signals the end of the concretist movement in Brazil, precipitated by the military coup of 1964. Titled "Poetics of the Unpoetic," the essay examines a series of collage poems produced by Augusto de Campos collectively titled *Popcretos*. Despite the reference to American pop art, these poems are highly political and relate rather to earlier experiments in collage such as the work of Hannah Hoch and Kurt Schwitters.[19] The following essay, "Disruption of Style," is an overview of Haroldo de

Campos's book *galáxias*, a sequence of fifty prose-poems that marked the poet's reengagement with baroque literature, a concern that punctuated his entire career and that started before his engagement with Noigandres. An original version of this essay was featured in *Postscript: Writing After Conceptual Art*.[20] The last essay in this collection, "Poetry and Modernity in the New World," features a reading of Haroldo de Campos's late poem "Finismundo, a última viagem" (Finismundo: the last voyage), a modernistic retelling of the *Odyssey* in which Ulysses is transposed to contemporary São Paulo, the poet's hometown, navigating its chaotic urban setting. The essay explores elements of Campos's composition and find parallels with the honorable tradition of samba composers who made a fundamental contribution toward the modernization of the Portuguese language in Brazil. A Portuguese version of this essay was featured in a collection on Campos's translation work in 2019.[21]

The importance of Ezra Pound's ideas in the conceptualization of concrete poetry cannot be minimized; a fact that gains more weight as we consider the correspondence maintained over the span of about five years between Pound and the founders of the Noigandres group. Following the outline of their exchange (Appendix 1), the reader will identify specific aspects in Pound's poetics that—despite cultural and generational differences—attracted the young Brazilian poets. In my understanding, the passion to renew culture through a thorough restructuring of language seemed to be their main drive. That the fervor to "make it new" had a pedagogical basis seemed to be a trait shared by both parties. Consider, for example, that in a letter dated December 21, 1957, Pound suggested that in the event of an official invitation for him to teach in São Paulo, "say Chinese, or any other LITERATURE . . . my presence wd / conduce to the further education of the DeCampos andCo/." Like diligent learners, the three poets set themselves at work on behalf of Pound, promoting his ideas, pleading the support of local intellectuals for his release from St. Elizabeths, and most importantly, publishing a volume of translations of his poems, including a number of the Cantos, in collaboration with other young scholars. Once released from internment, apparently undergoing bouts of depression, Pound's tone shifted and, in a letter, dated January 2, 1959, he wrote sternly: "Adult readers will naturally be more interested in the writing of men who have something to say than in attempts to dress up a cliché in some fancy style that will catch attention." Coming at the end of a decade marked by heated debates and polemics in Brazil, the Noigandres poets' reply is, not surprisingly, sharp and self-assured: "We believe that a new form creates a new content. Or better: that there is a dialectical, isomorphic relation between form & content. The artisanal cycle of poetry is closed with the monumental apex of THE CANTOS. No way out for ersatz products. A new poetry coheres with a new era and its peculiar physiognomy. Ours is a progressively rational and characteristically technical one." Although less frequent and intense, communication with Pound lasted until after his return to Italy, when Haroldo de Campos paid a visit to the aging poet in Rapallo. Despite its brief scope, the correspondence with Pound proved to be an exceptional opportunity for the Noigandres poets, as it allowed them to tap into an international network of like-minded individuals at a time when traveling abroad was not customary in Brazil. Added to the acquaintances Décio Pignatari was able to make during his two-year stay in Europe (1954–1956), the contacts facilitated by Pound opened up a broad field for the Noigandres poets to explore for the years to come. The outline of their correspondence presented here is based on a compilation provided by Augusto de Campos.

In addition, the Appendix section features my translations of three essays by the Noigandres poets that will give the reader further insight into key moments in their careers: "Deciphering Semiotics," by Décio Pignatari; "Pound Made (New) in Brazil," by Augusto de Campos; and "The Aph*freudisiac* Lacan in the Galaxy of Lalangue," by Haroldo de Campos.

1 /   Word as Object

The first paragraph of the manifesto "Pilot Plan for Concrete Poetry," sets off Noigandres' distinctive poetics with an emphasis on graphic space: "concrete poetry begins by being aware of graphic space as structural agent."[1] This renewed attention to the poem's graphic aspect, the manifesto suggests, makes possible for a new "qualified space: space-temporal structure instead of mere linear-temporal development."[2] To Noigandres, space and time has been folded into a new conceptualization of structure that finds in Ezra Pound's notion of the ideogram its ideal formulation, one that will appeal to a "non-verbal communication";[3] a structure that is the poem's very content, an "object in and of itself."[4]

In "Pontos—periferia—poesia concreta" (Points—Periphery—Concrete Poetry), an essay dated a year and a half previous to the publication of "Pilot Plan," Augusto de Campos approached the subject in more detail under the guise of differentiating Noigandres' exploration of graphic space and earlier attempts like those of Guillaume Apollinaire:

> Apollinaire condemns the poetic ideogram to the merely figurative representation of the theme. If the poem is about rain ("Il pleut"), words are displayed in five oblique lines. Accordingly, compositions in the shape of a heart, a clock, a tie, a crown are featured in *Calligrames*. It is valid to question in this context the suggestive value of a physiognomic relationship between the words and the object they represent, a subject to which not even Mallarmé would feign indifference. Nevertheless, it pays to make a qualitative distinction.

In Mallarmé's poem (*Un coup de dés*) the graphic mirages of a shipwreck and a constellation are but barely hinted at, naturally, with the same natural discretion with which two simple traces can configure the Chinese ideogram for the word *man*. The same way, Cummings's best graphic effects, aiming at some kind of synesthesia of movement, emerge from the very words, from inside out the poem itself. In Apollinaire, on the other hand, the structure is clearly imposed onto the poem, foreign to the words that by their turn take the shape applied to them without being altered by it.[5]

Exploration of graphics in Brazilian concrete poetry is thus not a matter of mimicking the poem's subject into a simulacrum of its visual appearance, but rather of concocting a brand new "object in itself" capable somehow of representing the subject's inner workings. Earlier in the same essay, Campos discusses Mallarmé's use of graphics and space in the following terms: "The first corollary of the Mallarméan process is the demand for a functional typography able to mirror with real efficiency the metamorphoses, fluxes and refluxes of thought."[6] While clearly indebted to Mallarmé's typographic experiments in *Un coup de dés*, Campos's insight on the functionality of typography represents a step forward as it also reflects formal developments in the visual arts based on gestalt theories that sought to redefine the way we perceive objects. The perfect balance between literary and visual forms in the work of Augusto de Campos makes it an ideal case to explore the issue of synesthesia referred to above.

In yet another short essay from 1956, "Poesia concreta" (Concrete Poetry), which previews the telegraphic style of "Pilot Plan for Concrete Poetry," Augusto de Campos explored the idea of functional typography further: "The concrete poet sees the word in itself—magnetic field of possibilities—as a dynamic object, a living cell, an organism complete in itself, with psycho-physic-chemical proprieties, tact antennae circulation heart: alive."[7] Like other texts from the period, "Poesia concreta" betrays Campos's fascination with early texts by Ezra Pound, particularly those related to Imagism and Vorticism.[8] One can, however, already detect a visionary quality all his own, as his texts make us believe that the poet *sees* words and considers the eye as the entryway to a complex sensorial experience. Further down in the same text he writes:

> Phono-graphic functions-relations and the substantive use of space as compositional element entertain a simultaneous dialectic of eye and breathing, that, allied to the ideogram-like synthesis of the signified,

convey a sensible totality, "verbivocovisual," such as to juxtapose words and experience into a narrow phenomenological fold, until now unprecedented.[9]

Since James Joyce never provided a full explanation as to how a verbivocovisual text operates, we must again turn to Pound and in particular his concepts of *logopoeia*, *melopoeia*, and *phanopoeia* to which Campos's ideas also seem to be related. A summary of these three poetic modes was offered by Pound in *The ABC of Reading* (1934): "one could charge words with meaning mainly in three ways: You can use a word to throw a visual image on to the reader's imagination (*phanopoeia*), or you charge it by sound (*melopoeia*), or you use groups of words to do this (*logopoeia*)."[10] While Pound considered these three categories as distinct expressions, Campos's nod to Joyce seems to suggest that he sees in concrete poetry the possibility of fusing them into one amalgam. In "How to Read" (1929), Pound affirms that "all writing is built up of these three elements, plus 'architectonics,'"[11] the implication being that a poem entails a *gestalt*, "the form of the whole."[12] He notes, on the other hand, that "in *phanopoeia* we find the greatest drive toward utter precision of word; this art exists almost exclusively by it."[13]

Phanopoeia, or the method of writing through specifics, through the juxtaposition of concrete elements, was indeed a great concern of Pound's, steered in great part by Ernest Fenollosa's study of the Chinese ideogram. In "How to Read," Pound notes: "It is not quite enough to have the general idea that the Chinese (more particularly Rihaku and Omakitsu) attained the known maximum of *phanopoeia*, due perhaps to the nature of their written ideograph, or to wonder whether Rimbaud is, at rare moments, their equal."[14] Tantamount to a collection of images, *phanopoeia* seems closer to fulfill the promise of a universal language: "*Phanopoeia* can, on the other hand, be translated almost, or wholly, intact. When it is good enough, it is practically impossible for the translator to destroy it save by very crass bungling, and the neglect of perfectly well-known and formulative rules."[15]

In 1930, Pound revisited the same themes in "How to Write," an obscure text that rehashes a number of familiar arguments and in which at some point he comically admonishes the reader that "sincere means without wax"; its tone of mock-exasperation as to warn us that before acquiring moral/ethic abstract values, common expressions have a visual, object-like basis.[16] "The ideograph is a door into a different modality of thought,"[17] he maintains, and further down, commenting on Fenollosa's explanation of the Chinese ideogram for *red* (rose / cherry / iron-rust / flamingo) he adds: "Whatever the inconveniences of this form of writing it has for poetry a great value. It is a treasure house of concrete images."[18] Fenollosa tried to explain the process in plain grammatical terms:

> The true noun as isolated thing does not exist in nature. Things are only the terminal points or rather the meeting points of actions, cross sections, snapshots. The eye sees noun and verb in one, things in action, action in things and so the Chinese conception tends to represent them.[19]

Pound's rejoinders on the other hand have an awkward pseudo-historical perspective as he equates "the vividness of Dante," with that of Li Po and the bushman: "The savage to whom the wood or the bend of the river is not a wood or a bend but one particular stretch of wood, one particular bend in that river."[20] As it were, what could pass as merely a call to a "return to the roots" is in reality a rather concerted effort toward purging poetry of unnecessary mannerisms in, as Pound has put it, his "struggle against abstraction."

> I should suggest the following formulation as an improvement or if you like as a sign of where we have got to in our struggle against "abstraction," abstract terms, ideas that are merely "imperfect inductions from fact." A real thought (Leibnitzian monad of thought; ever active, incapable of being compressed out of existence, etc.) as distinct from a mere cliché or imperfect verbal manifestation consists of a pattern or group of related images; and this relation can be either in nature before the thought, or it can be the arbitrary relation thrust on the images by the man thinking.[21]

In this struggle Pound seems to crave the immediacy of a language through which thought becomes apparent without recourses to filters. "Every language," he writes in the same essay, "has absorbed into itself and made common metaphors that were at their origin probably just as startling and fancy as the wildest tropes of our contemporaries eccentrics."[22] And although Marjorie Perloff correctly notes that his "own poetry contains little of such concrete thing-language,"[23] his pedagogical bent on the other hand continuously points toward a future writing of sharp edges and bright colors. As early as 1914, for instance, in an essay contemplating the possibility of an "awakening" in American letters, Pound often recurs to pictorial images to highlight the newness of current trends in criticism (equal to "contemporary search for pure color in painting");[24] or the greatness of those poet-inventors ("one does not copy colors on a palette. There is a difference between what one enjoys and what one takes as proof color").[25]

> Note—I have not in this paper set out to give a whole history of poetry. I have tried in a way to set forth a color-sense. I have said, as it were, "such poets are pure red . . . pure green." Knowledge of them is of as much use to a poet as the finding of good color is to a painter. Undoubtedly, pure color is to be found in Chinese poetry, when we begin to know enough about it.[26]

In reading Pound's poetry, one finds that references to colors bring up a different set of concerns, as their use is often related to his *imagist* pursuits. "In a Station of the Metro,"[27] unanimously considered a prime example of Imagism, offers a good instance with which to analyze Pound's rapport to colors:

> The apparition of these faces in the crowd;
> Petals on a wet, black bough.

Black, which is not to be considered a color in the physical sense but actually the absence of any color, works here to anchor the myriads of colors implicit in the faces/petals metaphor, while at the same time curbing any possibility of ornamentation. Ultimately, it is Pound's precision in defining this (absence of) color (wet, black lumber) that renders the poem a lacquer-like finish, adding to this English haiku another layer of *japonaiserie*. Reminiscing about the chain of events that culminated in that poem, Pound wrote in *Gaudier-Brzeska* that he searched for words that seemed "worthy, or as lovely as that sudden emotion." Words, as it turned out, were not adequate enough:

> I was still trying and I found, suddenly, the expression. I do not mean that I found words, but there came an equation . . . not in speech, but in little splotches of colour. It was just that - a "pattern," or hardly a pattern, if by "pattern" you mean something with a "repeat" in it. But it was a word, the beginning, for me, of a language in colour.
>   . . .
> That evening, in the Rue Raynouard, I realized quite vividly that if I were a painter, or if I had, often, *that kind* of emotion, of even if I had the energy to get paints and brushes and keep at it, I might found a new school of painting that would speak only by arrangements in colour.
>   . . .

> Colour was, in that instance, the "primary pigment"; I mean that it was the first adequate equation that came into consciousness.
> ...
> In a poem of this sort one is trying to record the precise instant when a thing outward and objective transforms itself, or darts into a thing inward and subjective.[28]

For Pound, consciousness is first apprehended through color; a point which is worth exploring further as the issue of "consciousness," according to many Pound exegetes, is central to "In a Station of the Metro." Hugh Kenner, for one, points out that the use of the word *apparition* in the poem "reaches two ways, toward ghosts and toward visible revealings."[29] A more technical explanation is given by Ralph Bevilaqua, who proposes that Pound had in mind the French use of the same cognate, which carries "the special meaning of the way something appears to a viewer *at the precise moment it is perceived.*"[30] Perception and all the senses involved in its apparatus is thus at the very basis of Imagism.

In *Sense and Sensibilia*, J. L. Austin refutes the branch of philosophy that affirms that "we never see or otherwise perceive (or 'sense'), or anyhow we never directly perceive or sense, material objects (or material things), but only sense-data (or our own ideas, impressions, sense, sense perceptions, percepts, etc.)."[31] Austin cautions against the imprecise use of the expression "material things" and points out that color and sound are invoked by many thinkers as pre-"material reality" phenomena that can be misread by the senses. That senses can be deceived by phenomena such as refractions, mirages, double visions, and hallucinations, Austin contends, is a question not "*factual but linguistic.*"[32] "Why shouldn't we say," Austin asks, " that material things are much spryer than we've been giving them credit for—constantly busy, from moment, in changing their real shapes, colors, temperatures, sizes, and everything else?"[33] We find in Austin's views on "material things" and our perception of them something akin to Pound's "struggle against abstraction." For both men, it was less a matter of senses deceiving than about our inadequate power to describe them:

> A painter, or at any rate a certain kind of painter, may well see a scene differently from someone unversed in the techniques of pictorial representation ... they may be due to the fact that what is seen is seen differently, seen in a different way, seen *as* this rather than that. And there will sometimes be no one right way of saying what is seen, for the additional reason that there may be no one right way of seeing it.[34]

Doubting the power of language to convey the object, both Austin and Pound delegate to the painter what the writer is unable to put into words. Hence the problem of *phanopoeia* and its improbable challenge to merge two different systems: "sense-datum language" and "material object language." Austin's text is basically an argument against George Berkeley's theses that material objects are but a "collection of ideas," and criticizing another proponent of the "sense data" theory, he writes: "(Ayer) sometimes speaks as if only sense-data in fact existed and as if 'material things' were really just jig-saw constructions of sense-data."[35] Perhaps the difficulty associated to *phanopoeia*, even our difficulty to define it properly, relates to this fundamental chasm between object and idea. In *phanopoeia*, the words conjured to convey an image of the object are often related to our perception, our senses, and thus utterly abstract and subjective,[36] as in Pound's poem under the same rubric.[37]

Phanopoeia

I
ROSE WHITE, YELLOW, SILVER
The swirl of light follows me through the square,
The smoke of incense
Mounts from the four horns of my bed-posts,
The water-jet of gold light bears us up through the ceilings;
Lapped in the gold-coloured flame I descend through the aether.
The silver ball forms in my hand,
It falls and rolls to your feet.

Is the first part of the poem "Phanopoeia," and for what it is worth *phanopoeia as* a method, merely the arrangement of sense-data? From the very first line, what strikes us in this poem is its high degree of abstraction, and as we scan the lines downward little is offered to anchor the accumulation of effects into a cohesive whole, giving the impression rather of the transcription of a painting, as in an ekphrasis. But this seemingly random composition is not entirely without a tradition, and we find in Pound's 1917 translation of a song by Arnaut Daniel ("Er vei vermeils, vertz, blaus, blancs, groucs / Vergiers, plans, plais, tertres e vaus" [Vermeil, green, blue, peirs, white, cobalt / Close orchards, hewis, holts, hows, vales])[38] the same sense of condensed abstraction. It's as if Daniel's sharply edited depiction of a Provençal landscape had been transposed by Pound in "Phanopoeia" onto the confines of a chamber.

Note that much of the little "concrete thing-language" that Perloff refers to in Pound's work emanates from his rapport to color. His pictorial eye would lead to exquisite formulations like *azure ≠ usura* ("Azure hath a canker by usura");[39] or to obscure words like *glaukpis*, the Greek adjective that qualifies Athena's gleaming eyes;[40] and *brododaktylus*, another Greek term reserved to the gods and recalled with poignancy in the first of the *Pisan Cantos*:[41]

> Time is not, Time is the evil, beloved
> Beloved the hours βροδοδάκτυλος
> as against the half-light of the window
> with the sea beyond making horizon

Transposed to a Latin American context, Pound's ideas on imagistic writing took a radical swerve in the early 1950s. When the first Noigandres manifestos started appearing in Brazil, they played a central role in spearheading a renaissance of sorts throughout the entire country of the kind Pound dreamt for America. Close connection to both the emerging music and visual arts avant-garde in Brazil provided concrete poets circumstances entirely diverse from those Pound encountered in Europe in the early decades of the twentieth century. While Pound was looking for inspiration in anachronistic painters like Burne-Jones, for instance, concrete poets like Augusto de Campos found counterparts in the work of artists from his own generation, like the constructivist painter Waldemar Cordeiro, whose artistic development shared the same foundation. Cordeiro's abstract compositions often hinted at effects of synesthesia like in *Movimento* (Movement), for instance, a painting from 1951 whose ambiguous title refers both to physical motion and musical structures. It is highly significant thus that *Movimento* appeared around the same time that *Poetamenos* was published. Campos has often cited Piet Mondrian as a model for his micro-series, but Cordeiro's arrangements of horizontal bands of colors seems a much more apt equivalent. More importantly, a comparison between the two works makes evident not only their formalistic bond but the pitch-perfect synchrony these two artists shared with the ideals of their time.

Other poets associated to concretism produced new equations in "little splotches of colour" of outstanding effect, and the visual similes were equally contemporaneous. Consider for instance the neo-concretist experiments of Ferreira Gullar, a poet-theoretician with a brief albeit polemic relationship with Noigandres. In "mar azul" (blue sea), five nouns compose a landscape entirely tinted blue, and the diagonal created by the staggering of the word couplets emulate the stylized shape of a rising tide in the sea ("mar") in which a sign ("marco"), might suggest a boat ("barco"), a vision that finally dissolves into the air ("ar"): ("mar azul / mar azul marco azul/mar azul marco azul barco azul/mar azul marco azul barco azul arco azul/mar azul marco azul barco azul arco azul ar azul"). "mar azul" displays Gullar's sharp eye to the geometric compositions produced at the time by Brazilian painters like Willys de Castro and Luís Sacilotto.

In "branco" (blank, see figure 1), a poem from his micro sequence *fome de forma* (hunger for form), from 1955, Haroldo de Campos complicated the rigidity of concretist rules by introducing baroque references onto the structure of the poem. The first line translates Daniel's multicolored landscape into an austere, undetermined setting where the word "branco" can stand either for the color white or for the absence of everything (blank); references to "vermelho" (red) and "espelho" (mirror) in the ensuing lines reminds us, on the other hand, of Pound's lush atmosphere in "Phanopoeia."

These poems are classical enactments of one of Noigandres' fundamental tenets: the call for the isolation of vocables independently from the rule of grammar. This process of word isolation suggests an objectifying view of language, as words are no longer strictly subject to the roles ascribed by grammar. Words are seen as rather opaque icons that, like in the Chinese ideogram, accrue different meanings depending on

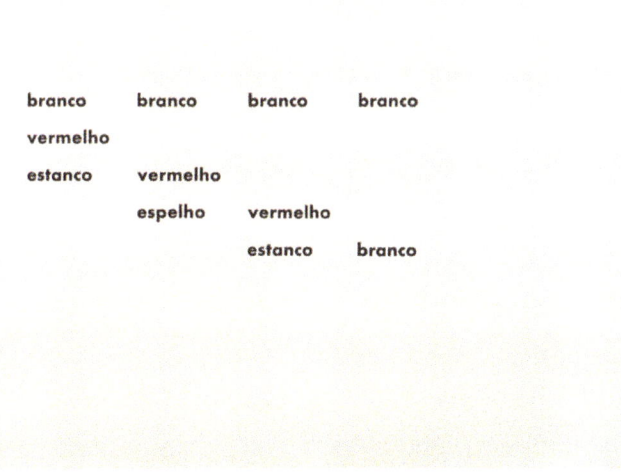

FIGURE 1. Haroldo de Campos, "branco," 1955

juxtaposition and order. Augusto de Campos considers the tendency to blur the distinction between nouns and verbs a "dominant characteristic" in concrete poetry; one that must be employed as "a vector rather than a directive." In "The Concrete Coin of Speech" Campos finds corroboration for the notion of ideogram proposed by Fenollosa and Pound in the language theory of Edward Sapir:

> Sapir has demonstrated that the idea of quality can be turned into a "verb," for instance in cases like "it is red," which could be replaced by "it reddens" and that we should be able to express as "it reds," were not the peculiarities of the English language. He also demonstrated how we can present a quality as a THING.[42]

As for adjectives, Campos is also able to find concrete use as long as they do not tend to the ornamental. Writing about Gullar's "mar azul" he notes that: "The adjective *azul* is incorporated into the poem to such a degree that it acquires a noun-like vitality." In regard to "branco," on the other hand, he writes that "the noun function is superposed to the adjective, for it is precisely the colors white and red that the poem addresses." And he adds:

> Like in Chinese, the tendency is to ignore certain secondary concepts of relation: hence verb tense tends toward infinitive, or rather, to the totality of action. The verb *estanco*, in "Branco," appears as in a psychological infinitive. Concepts of relation (tense, number, person) are therefore deactivated, the subject is practically the poem itself.
>
> . . .
>
> We see then that the noun, the verb, and the adjective are too irreducible a concept to contain the concrete poem's dynamics, which overruns all these categories without attaining the flexibility of the Chinese.[43]

Compared to Noigandres' extreme tactics, Pound's experiments with notions of ideogram and Imagism feel somehow tentative. One major factor may be attributed to their incorporation of different views on the Chinese ideogram other than Fenollosa's; like those of Sergei Eisenstein, for instance, who saw in the ideogram the basis for a revolution in film editing. Given this new context, the practice of writing is conceived by Noigandres no longer in terms of a composition of linear sentences but as the juxtaposition of independent images relating to each other in various degrees of possibilities. It is the method of "thinking through images" that renders concrete poetry its object-like quality and that brings it close to the visual arts.

Augusto de Campos, among the concrete poets, has been able to further the bond between writing and the visual arts to a point that the final product becomes a hybrid, no longer pertaining exclusively to one discipline. Poems like "viva vaia," "rever," and "código," for instance, represent a quantum leap compared to the early concrete poems that still held Pound's definition of *phanopoeia* as a model. These poems share a unique rapport not only with the visual art produced by the avant-garde, but also by self-taught painters like Alfredo Volpi, whose working-class roots are filtered in his work through stylized references to vernacular architecture and popular manifestations like street fair decorations. A comparison between "viva vaia" (see figure 2) and Volpi's *Xadres branco e vermelho* (White and red checkerboard), will demonstrate Campos's rigorous eye for formal solutions in addition to his keen ear for the slipperiness of the Portuguese language.

FIGURE 2. Augusto de Campos, "viva vaia," 1972

It is worth pointing out that Augusto de Campos's experiments in merging poetry and the visual arts are not of the kind Wendy Steiner explored in *The Colors of Rhetoric: Problems in the Relation Between Modern Literature and Painting*, although she sums up her study by commenting on the work of several Brazilian concrete poets. For one thing, Campos did not seem so much invested in the central question in Steiner's book, i.e., the "likeness between painting and literature,"[44] as he is in understanding how mind and emotion mediate language. His "anything goes" approach to communication and expression has a new immediacy that is more in keeping with the breaking down of boundaries after World War II. Jean Starobinski notes in *Enchantment: The Seductress in Opera* that "at the beginning of the last century there was great interest in phenomena referred to as synesthesia. People took pleasure in speculating about the perceptual associations between sounds and colors."[45] Pound's interest in *phanopoeia* and Imagism might as well be a result of that environment, but around the time concrete poetry appears on the scene, the stakes seem to be of an entirely new order. One might say, for instance, that Pound's vision of an "equation-like" writing was more fully accomplished by Marcel Duchamp in the notes that would lead to his two major works, *The Large Glass* and *Étant Donnés*. While the resurgence of the comparison between the two arts in the early decades of the twentieth century is undeniable, the motivation for it can hardly be imputed squarely to a "need to discover the mimetic potential of literature." Steiner's study concerns primarily a metaphor "about the resemblance between reality and the systems man has developed to represent it,"[46] and in approaching this metaphor, the question of whether painting is superior to literature as the system that most closely represents reality inevitably arises.

For the concrete poets, once the safety net of grammar was taken out of the picture, the visual arts would provide new resources with which to use words in the most effective way. Summing up his essay "The Concrete Coin of Speech," Augusto de Campos stressed the lessons learned from the visual arts:

> Concrete poetry dissociates itself not from language or communication, but from the formalist armor of discursive syntax. It affirms its autonomy in relation to the latter, thus eliminating the contradiction between non-discursive nature and discursive form. In a later stage of development, it no longer defines itself in function of this syntax, but only in function of language itself, like a painter no longer defines himself in function of figures or perspective, but only in terms of pure visuality. A pure visuality, however, where the adjective "pure"

no longer signifies detachment from reality and nature, for it is from them that we take the pure elements of this visuality. At this moment, any definition of concrete poetry related to a traditional syntax makes no sense. Just as concrete painting no longer defines itself in terms of anti-figure, for "it is now as real as an apple" (Waldemar Cordeiro), the moment has come in which poetry no longer needs to define itself in terms of anti-syntax, or anti-discourse. It rules over based on its own norms, based on its own conditions, settled as they are, no doubt, in the concrete roots of language.[47]

The symbiotic relationship between poetry and the visual arts is of course not exclusive of the concretist movement in Brazil, although the period as a whole provides a formidable instance of how different disciplines can develop in coordinated manner; nor it is a phenomenon proper to the erudite. Consider Augusto de Campos's high regard for the poetry of Cego Aderaldo[48] in his essay "Um dia, um dado, um dedo" (A Day, a die, a digit).[49] Among the greatest poets of the *cordel* tradition, Aderaldo was known for his deft use of paronomasia such as in these verses from around 1916:

Eu canto o quadro quadrado
Quadrado bem quadrejado
Meu quadro é quadriculado
Por causa da quadração
Porque minhas quadras são
De maneira bem quadrada,
Por isto meu verso enquadra
Quadrado quadro e quadrão

(I sing the square picture [octave rhyme]
Rigorously squared out square [octave]
My picture [octave] follows a grid
For reasons of composition
So that my quatrains too
Are well squared off
Hence my verse contains
Square picture and quatrain)

In "Um Dia, um dado, um dedo," Campos addressed a literary style characteristic of the Brazilian northeast known as *cordel*, that has possible roots in the Provençal troubadour tradition, focusing specifically on a performative feature central to *cordel* known as *desafio*, in which two poets (*cantadores*) challenge each other improvising live to an audience.

Campos marveled at the "artisanal ability" of those singing poets to upstage each other in "rhythmic versatility, as well as in lexical and semantic invention." In Aderaldo's ambiguous lyric, he addresses the making of a poem in octave rhyme (*quadrão*), which becomes deftly confused with a picture (*quadro*).

The interplay between the visual and the linguistic was for Noigandres a concern that permeated both their entire production, poetic and theoretic, and in 2015, Augusto de Campos again addressed the theme in a short introduction to his collection of digital poems *Outro*, which he described as "quadros querendo ser clips" (pictures wanting to be [video] clips). As an epigraph to the volume, perhaps as an echo of Aderaldo, he quoted from Portuguese poet Cesário Verde: "Pinto quadros por letras, por sinais" (I paint pictures with letters, signs). A farewell of sort (the title *Outro* standing in opposition to an *intro*), Campos addressed in that short text the technical evolution of writing that he had witnessed throughout his career, from the early experiments with the typewriter to the computer-generated work (or electronic haikus)[50] that he produced later on—an evolution, according to him, predicted by Mallarmé, and summarized by Walter Benjamin thus:

> Mallarmé, who in the crystalline structure of his manifestly traditionalist writing saw the true image of what was to come, was in the *Coup de dés* the first to incorporate the graphic tensions of the advertisement in the printed page. The typographic experiments later taken by the Dadaists stemmed, it is true, not from constructive principles but from the precise nervous reactions of those literati, and were therefore far less enduring than Mallarmé's, which grew out of the inner nature of his style.
>
> . . .
>
> And before a contemporary finds his way clear to opening a book, his eyes have been exposed to such a blizzard of changing, colorful, conflicting letters that the chances of his penetrating the archaic stillness of the book are slight. Locust swarms of print, which already eclipse the sun of what city dwellers take for intellect, will grow thicker with each succeeding year.[51]

2 / Sound as Subject

With a poetic program that strongly emphasized the visuality of language, it would seem that the Noigandres poets embraced design to the detriment of sound. Their effort to render language iconic, one might think, would push concrete poetry to the brink of aphasia. Indeed, the poems from the so-called heroic phase of concretism display a heightened sense of design that seems to overwhelm other aspects of the text. Some of those poems appear on the page like highly modernistic architecture, while others strike the reader rather like graphic riddles that need to be decoded in order to be read: An operation for the eye only, with the ear playing a very small role in the reading process. But it would be a mistake to affirm that sound was altogether out of the Noigandres picture. I suggest that in the work of these poets, sound was submitted to as rigorous a program as the written text. Nevertheless, this rigor, as I hope to make clear in this essay, did not imply the loss of a sense of humor or the negation of pleasure.

In several texts written in the early 1950s by the Noigandres poets, collectively and individually, one finds repeated references to sound, particularly the emerging new music of composers like Pierre Boulez, Guido Alberto Fano, and Karlheinz Stockhausen. These references are telegraphed throughout the cryptic text of "Pilot Plan for Concrete Poetry," the concretist period's culminating manifesto, but other texts explored some of the same themes to a greater extent, and they lay out Noigandres' understanding of the role sound ought to play in poetry. It is curious, among those early texts, how Décio Pignatari astutely connects the explorations of concretism to those of early modernism by quoting Mário de Andrade in "Poesia concreta: organização":

> Mário de Andrade, in "Prefácio interessantíssimo" (Most Interesting Preface), after commenting on the common melodic verse, approaches what he calls the harmonic verse, formed by words without any immediate connection among themselves: "These words, by the very fact of not forming a coherent sequence, superpose over themselves and form, to our senses, not melodies, but harmonies.... Harmony, combination of simultaneous sounds."[1]

Departing from Andrade's proposition of a "harmonic verse," Pignatari traces a formidable micro-compendium of the late nineteenth and early twentieth centuries' great synthesizers, including Lewis Carroll, Stéphane Mallarmé, Ezra Pound, James Joyce, and the filmmaker Sergei Eisenstein. His idea of poetic "organization" is a composite that might include portmanteau words (Carroll and Joyce) arranged according to ideogrammatic principles (Pound, Ernest Fenollosa) spliced together, as in a film (Eisenstein). Eisenstein via Pignatari: "(sonorous!) representations objectively expressed gathering together to create a unified image, other than the perception of its isolated elements."[2]

Haroldo de Campos seems to agree with Pignatari's equation of visual organization and musical harmony. Compare Pignatari's argument with the following quote from "Olho por olho a olho nu" ("Eye for an eye in daylight"), a text by Campos from 1956:

> THE CONCRETE POEM aspires to be: composition of basic elements of language, optical-acoustically organized in the graphic space by factors of proximity and similitude, like a kind of ideogram for a given emotion, aiming at the direct presentation—in the present—of the object.[3]

One senses in these writings a certain hesitancy with regard to addressing sound (or music, or melody) head on. Note how "acoustics" is appended to "optical," and how the word "composition" remains ambiguously undefined: It might equally refer to a musical composition or a piece of writing. Coincidently three decades later, in a 1983 interview with Rodrigo Naves, Campos declared forthrightly that his rapport with the literary tradition was *musical* rather than *museological*:

> Note that both adjectives derive from the same word, *muse* (from the Greek *Mousa*), and that the Muses are the daughters of memory (Mnemosine). I prefer the derivation that ended up in music because

> I like to read tradition as a trans-temporal music sheet, making, at each moment, synchronic-diachronic "harmonies," translating culture's past into a creative present.[4]

Although not entirely without a nod to museum practices, the "translation of culture's past into a creative present" was eventually effected quite literally by both Haroldo and his brother Augusto de Campos in their translation work. But also note how Campos's understanding of the role music plays in his work, as expressed in the two excerpts quoted above, seems to overlap with Ferdinand de Saussure's insight into the structure of the linguistic sign. In his *Course in General Linguistics,* Saussure explains the linguistic sign thus:

> The linguistic sign unites not a thing and a name, but a concept and a sound-image. The latter is not the material sound, a purely physical thing, but the psychological imprint of the sound, the impression that it makes on our senses. The sound-image is sensory, and if I happen to call it "material," it is only in that sense, and by way of opposing it to the other term of the association, the concept, which is generally more abstract.[5]

Saussure's explanation of the "sound-image" in terms of a "psychological imprint" on our senses provides a linguistic basis for Haroldo de Campos's poetic goal of an "ideogram for a given emotion." Although Saussure's name is conspicuously absent from the early manifestos issued by the Noigandres poets, it is worth mentioning that his insight with regard to how language operates is not unlike Mallarmé's *divisions prismatiques de l'idée,* a theme often echoed throughout numerous Noigandres texts—language as an operation that makes ideas visible (and/or heard).

The interplay of visual and sonic values is also one of Flora Süssekind's concerns in her essay "(Quase audível)—Nota sobre 'ão'" ("[Almost audible]—Note on 'ão'"). In it, Süssekind quotes from a rare 1971 interview with bossa nova singer and songwriter João Gilberto, in which he claims that "when I sing, I think of a light-filled and open space where I will place my sounds; it's as if I were writing on a blank sheet of paper." Commenting on this passage, Süssekind adds that "it is, then, on another plane, that of the graphic space, of the letter, and not in the phonic materiality itself, that the vocal image is constructed. It is through vision that we perceive what is directed to the ear, as Barthes has suggested in commenting on acoustic images."[6]

Elaborating on Pound's concepts of *melopoeia* and *logopeia* in yet another interview from around the same period, Haroldo de Campos writes that his collection of poems *Signantia quase coelum* (Paradisiacal Signifiers) was "conceived in the form of music, as a tripartite composition," and explains the poem's minimalist structure as a visual equivalent of the use of rests in music. And at the end of the interview, he quotes from Severo Sarduy, who wrote that in the texts that compose *galáxias,* one finds:

> la exaltación y el despliegue de una región de la dicción, de un espacio del habla vasto y barroco como el mapa de su país: soplo y articulación, aliento y pronunciación: nacimiento del discurso.
>
> (The exalting and unfolding of a region of diction, of a space of speech as vast and baroque as the map of his country: a puff of air and articulation, breath and pronunciation: the birth of discourse.)[7]

With extraordinary precision, Sarduy sums up the entire concretist approach to sound: The vast legacy of the baroque filtered through breathing, articulation, and pronunciation. The concretist project in Brazil should then be seen as an attempt not only to renew a complex tradition, but also to convey it in an entirely new "voice."

Among the Noigandres poets, Augusto de Campos seems to be the one most overtly interested in sound experimentation. He is the author of three important books on music, *O Balanço da bossa—e outras bossas* (Bossa nova in balance—and other trends), and two volumes of *Música de invenção* (Invention music),[8] and ever since the 1950s, his poetry has persistently pursued a kind of writing fused with music. His micro-sequence of sparsely diagrammed poems *Poetamenos* (Minuspoet, 1953) helped launch concretism in Brazil and was admittedly inspired by Anton Webern's use of *Klangfarbenmelodie* (tone-color-melody). Augusto de Campos's musical ideas, as one might expect, were from the start highly unorthodox—a mix of Viennese dodecaphonic theory and Brazilian bossa nova swing. He prefaced *Poetamenos* with a short text that is still striking in its visionary audacity:

> . . . or aspiring in the hope of a
>
> KLANGFARBENMELODIE
>
> with words as in Webern:
>
> a continuous melody dislocating from one instrument to another, constantly changing its color:
>
> *instruments*: phrase/word/syllable/letter(s), whose timbres are defined by a graphic-phonetic, or "ideogramic," theme . . .

reverberation: oral reading—real voices functioning as timbre (approximately) for the poem, like the instruments in Webern's Klangfarbenmelodie.[9]

It is worth dwelling for a moment on Webern's concept of *Klangfarbenmelodie,* because of its deep impact on concrete poetry—a poetics often accused of being too cerebral and devoid of emotion, and, on many occasions, of impoverishing language. To the Canadian pianist Glenn Gould, Webern's music was deeply steeped in emotion, and *Klangfarbenmelodie* was the method that heightened its expression:

> The string quartet pieces of Opus 5 are one of [Webern's] first essays in atonal writing. Though nothing could display a less extrovert emotionalism, there is a strikingly sensual quality manifest not only in the treatment of the strings themselves, but also in the manner by which Webern frequently isolates an individual tone or short interval-group, and, by alternating dynamic levels and instrumental timbres, succeeds in immobilizing a particular pitch level around which the oblique shapes of his half-counterpoints seek to fulfill their evolutionary destinies. It seems to me that the expressionistic qualities of this music such as the above-mentioned isolated tone procedure—(Klangfarbenmelodie) carries to its zenith the very essence of the romantic ideal of emotional intensity in art.[10]

Gould, with his profound understanding of the complexities of twentieth-century music also commented on the visual aspects of Webern's music in his 1974 article "Korngold and the Crisis of the Piano Sonata,"[11] describing his mature work as "occupied with Mondrian-like geometric concerns." Piet Mondrian's paintings were also one of Campos's inspirations for *Poetamenos,* as acknowledged by the author in an interview from 1998: "Music is for me an indispensable 'nutrient of impulse.' Since poetry, as Pound says, is closer to music and the visual arts than literature itself, I find it natural that it is thus. Without Webern, Mondrian and Malevich I couldn't have formulated *Poetamenos* (which also owes to Mallarmé, Pound, Joyce and Cummings)."[12]

Like Pound, Webern aimed to "make new" an entire musical tradition, from Bach all the way through the romantics, and the two men would certainly find much to agree upon as far as the issue of *melopoeia* is concerned. In the *Ricercare for Six Voices,* for instance, whereas Bach originally only indicated lines for no instrument in particular, Webern disperses the notes among the instruments, transforming the sound of the melody and accentuating its melancholic quality. The rhetoric qualities of baroque music and its doctrine of affects (*Affektenlehre*) is recovered by Webern through his use of *Klangfarbenmelodie*.

Freeing music from *themes* and/or *motifs*—his ability to convey "sound clarity" through the pure structuring of musical elements—is generally perceived as Webern's major contribution. According to Boulez, in Webern "the architecture of the work derives directly from the ordering of the series." Composition becomes a system of proportions, of relationships between intervals. This concept can be illustrated by the "Sator Arepo" palindrome found in the ruins of Pompeii, which became a source of great interest to Webern:

SATOR
AREPO
TENET
OPERA
ROTAS

To Webern, this diagram represented the ideal porous structure,[13] as it can be read horizontally or vertically from top left to bottom right and from bottom right to top left. In addition, it uses a minimum of elements (eight letters, five words) to create a greater number of combinations. This kind of structure was referred to by Webern as a "Spiegelbild" (mirror-form), a device that enabled him to structure a musical composition around as few as three notes.[14] The "monadic architect of the mirror-form" is what Herbert Eimert,[15] founder of the WDR Studio in Cologne, called Webern.

The idea of mirror-forms had a great, long-lasting impact on Augusto de Campos's development of a concrete poetics. In *Poetamenos*, despite the fact that it's not addressed in the preamble, mirror-form technique is used to different effects throughout the series, and throughout his career Campos has refined Webern's practice, quite literally transposing it into poetic terms. In "viva vaia" and "rever," for instance, mirroring is used not only as a method, but also as formal solution: In "viva vaia" the font was specifically designed to blur the distinction between the letters *A* and *V* and accommodate their irreconcilable difference (the same character represents both a vowel and a consonant); in "rever" (see figure 3), the suffix "ER" is graphically reversed to underline the fact that it mirrors the word's prefix. What is achieved in both cases is the dissipation of meaning, as exultation (*viva*) is turned into its opposite (*vaia* [booing]), and even of the word itself, as the verb *rever* (to review) is reduced to the letter *V*, a pivot around which fragments (the prefix and the suffix) mirror each other. Despite their extreme economy of means, these poems, like some compositions by Webern, were calculated to exert the greatest possible

REVER

FIGURE 3. Augusto de Campos, "rever," 1970

impact, and, at least in the case of "viva vaia," they have resonated deeply in the panorama of Brazilian culture.

In *Música de invenção,* Augusto de Campos wrote that:

> in Webern we find an unprecedented use of formal concision and of the dialectic between sound and silence (the latter made audible for the first time, and used not merely as pause but as structural element, at the same level as sounds).[16]

Webern's reputation as a difficult, demanding conductor, whose compositions are equally difficult to perform, is a source of great excitement to Campos, who sees in this difficulty the very sign of genius. When a Uruguayan composer visiting São Paulo in the late 1970s tells Campos, "To this day, no one has ever listened to Webern! There are no recordings that can reproduce his compositions with fidelity," Campos seems undaunted, and ponders how Webern's work might be even greater than he has already assumed it to be.[17] This incident stresses some of the issues at stake around the possible influence of Webern's work on Augusto de Campos. In the São Paulo of the 1950s, knowledge of dodecaphonic theory was still incipient, and acquired mostly from rare, imported recordings and their liner notes, rather than from live concerts and lectures. Certainly, there was the figure of Hans-Joachim Koellreutter championing new musical theories, but the dissemination of information was still minimal. Campos's initial exposure to Webern, therefore, seems to have relied more on the composer's legendary conceptual rigor and his pursuit of an ideal structure than on how his compositions actually sounded. On the occasion of a concert of works by Igor Stravinsky, Webern, and Iannis Xenakis at the Festival of Avant-garde Music that took place in São Paulo in 1965, Campos writes that *Six Pieces for Orchestra*,[18] an early work by Webern, already demonstrates an "extremely concise language, the precise dialectic between sound and non-sound, 'an entire romance in one sigh,' *non multa sed multum,* microcosmusic."[19]

This sketchy background is intended merely as an attempt to situate the poet, who was only twenty-two years old at the time *Poetamenos* was written, vis-à-vis the enormous task he took it upon himself to accomplish, namely the translation of Webern's musical language into poetic terms, thus creating something close to an acoustic image. This translation was effected not without some violence, as accommodations needed to be made in order to transform Webern's aural concerns into purely visual ones that subsequently would once again be turned into sound.

Perhaps it will not be too implausible to argue that *Poetamenos* pushed Webern's *Klangfarbenmelodie* to another dimension, bringing to the forefront issues concerning the interconnectedness of sight and sound. One should be reminded of what Theodor Adorno stressed in *Alban Berg: Master of the Smallest Link*, about the composer's "unmistakable gift for the visual arts," noting that his commitment to music was "almost accidental." Adorno added that Berg "retained much of his sense of the visual, most noticeably in the calligraphic appearance of his full scores," and conjectured that his propensity:

> for mirror and retrograde formations may, apart from the twelve-tone technique, be related to the visual dimension of his responses; musical retrograde patterns are anti-temporal, they organize music as if it were an intrinsic simultaneity. It is probably incorrect to attribute those technical procedures solely to the twelve-tone technique; they are derived not only from the microstructure of the rows, but also from the overall plan, as if from a basic outline, and as such they contain an element of indifference toward succession, something like a disposition toward musical saturation.[20]

Mirror and echo, the visual and aural means of duplication that hold central roles in both Webern's and Campos's practice, can here perhaps be used as tropes to their symmetrical relationship, with Campos as the reverse image of Webern, seen through a metaphorical looking glass that encompasses not only contrasting disciplines, but also geographies.

It is ironic, if we allow ourselves to explore this comparison a little further, that *Poetamenos* has proved to be a work as difficult to perform as any of Webern's pieces. More than half a century after its creation, the series has still not received a fully satisfying performance, with the sole exception of Caetano Veloso's arresting 1979 reading of "dias, dias, dias." This is by no means a minor shortfall, as it suggests that Campos might have created a work the performance of which eludes him. This difficulty in performing *Poetamenos* brings forth a central issue in Augusto de Campos's oeuvre, namely, his ongoing speculation on the relationship between self and voice, a concern that dates back to his earlier poetry, even before the formulation of the concretist paradigm, and traverses his entire oeuvre. We find this concern in poems such as "Fábula" (Fable), from 1949, which features a dialogue between a "Powerful Voice" and a "Small Voice"; in "Bestiário—para fagote e esôfago" (Bestiary—for bassoon and esophagus), from 1955; and in more recent poems such as "pessoa" (persona, see figure 4)[21] in which the possibility of attaining individuality is predicated on the ability of the subject ("pessoa") to *sound*. At the most basic level, the poem plays off the sonority of the Portuguese

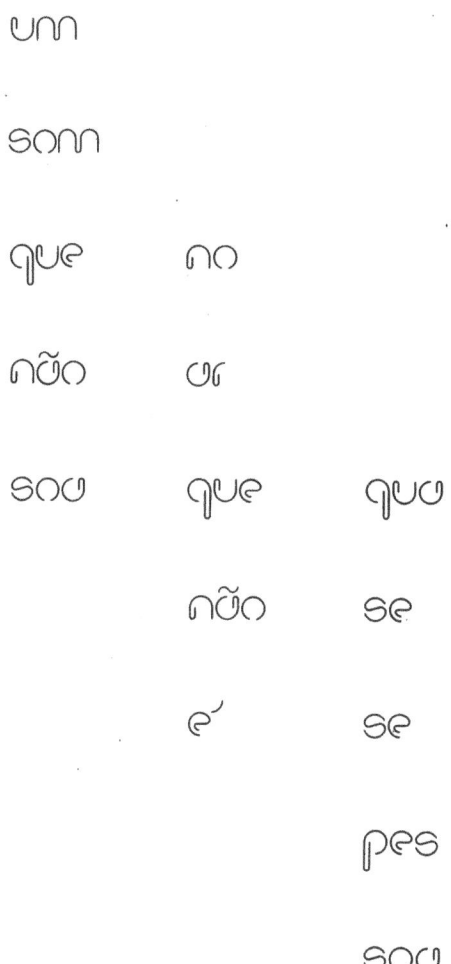

FIGURE 4. Augusto de Campos, "pessoa," 1981

word *pessoa* (person), the suffix of which, *soa*, is homonymous to *soa* (the third-person singular of the verb *soar* "to sound"). Campos's ploy is to suggest that inside each individual (*pessoa*) a sound resonates (*soa*). One should have in mind that the etymology of the word *pessoa*, from the Latin *persona*, suggests the act of "sounding through a mask" in a play; a term that, coincidentally, was used as the title of one of Pound's collections (*Personae*, 1909).

The relationship between sound and subject in the poetry of Augusto de Campos has been approached with great insight by the Brazilian poet and scholar Eduardo Sterzi in "Todos os sons, sem som" (All the sounds, without sound). Commenting on the complexity of Campos's trajectory, Sterzi considers the "progressive emptying of the lyrical subject" in Campos's early poetry, which led to the concretist phase:

> The "I," even if it no longer rules, continues to be the focal point around which the poem is organized, a proposition attested to by the frequency with which it employs the personal pronoun in addition to verbs inflected in the first-person singular. And to organize the poem means above all to organize the lyrical subject's private fictions, its interior monologues and dialogues, its *psychomaquias*. Thus, since it's not yet embodied in a definitive form, the main artifice through which the increasing annihilation of the "I" will be achieved, preparing the ground for the appearance of what is known today as "concrete poetry"—I am referring to the fragmentation or the shattering of the voice—is anticipated in embryonic form.[22]

The progressive "shattering of the voice" in the early poetry of Augusto de Campos, a phase Sterzi defines as *breathless* (ofegante), achieved its optimum moment in *Poetamenos,* wherein the poet organized his "private fictions" and "interior monologues and dialogues" during an important moment in his life: the beginning of his relationship with Lygia Azeredo, who later became his wife. This organization did not so much take the form of an ideogram, which is what the poet seemed to be aiming at in the series preface, as of a diagram, as Sterzi suggests. As for the poet's use of *Klangfarbenmelodie* as a model, Sterzi notes that "it is significant that the fragmentation of the voice takes the form of choral writing," and adds:

> The initial impression that we are listening to the poet's voice mixed with the voices of his beloved and possibly of her relatives, is replaced by the realization that we are witnessing a dialogue between the poet and his own self, questioning the tools of his writing.[23]

The difficulty of determining whose voice(s) speak(s) in and through *Poetamenos* is one of the series' most complex achievements—one that, beyond its debt to Webern's technique of orchestrating echoes, is intrinsically connected to a major cultural shift taking place in Brazil at the time, which deeply affected the country's speech pattern.[24] The reluctance to embrace a voice associated with an outdated model of subjectivity pushed the poet to confront the voice of his own epoch, and in the process acquire new tools for his craft. In Brazil, the *voice* of the epoch was personified by João Gilberto, who, around the time of the publication of *Poetamenos,* was struggling to get his *canto-falado* style recognized by the mainstream musical establishment. Discussing the first bossa nova recordings in *Bim Bom—A Contradição sem conflitos de João Gilberto,* Walter Garcia notes that:

> The kind of singing "that flows in everyday speech" is kept on the threshold between the rhythm of thought, with its chain of ideas, and the rhythm of the body, of feelings and sensations. . . .
> Sound engineering during record production integrates the voice to the instrumental, while still keeping it in the foreground.[25]

Garcia's observation on the role of sound recording in making *canto-falado* possible is a point worth considering, as it relates to core ideas discussed during the formulation of a concrete poetics in the early 1950s.[26] He goes on to elaborate on how technology had made the "big voice" almost pointless:

> One must be reminded that João Gilberto's phonographic oeuvre is comprised of songs whose structure is defined fundamentally by the voice superimposed onto the beat. Much has been said about how the low voice has been adequate to microphone technology, on the evidence that, around 1958, one does not need a big voice to be able to record.[27]

The new technology opened up the possibility of capturing a kind of speech associated with "natural" rhythms, a voice more in consonance with the realm of ideas and hence able to transmit emotions:

> João Gilberto's spoken-singing, by balancing itself on the line between the origin and the disappearance of the very act of singing, conciliates the rhythm of speech—dictated by the chain of ideas that must be understood intellectually by the listener—and the rhythm of music—created by psychosomatic stimuli to reach the listener's body, and emitted in dissociation combined with its beat.[28]

To corroborate, Garcia quotes from a 1960 interview with João Gilberto:

> I think that singers must feel music as aesthetics, feel it in terms of poetry and naturalness. When one sings one should be as if praying: the essential is sensibility. Music is sound. And sound is voice, instrument. Thus, the singer will need to know when and how to elongate a sharp, a flat, so as to be able to transmit the emotional message.[29]

Garcia's discussion about *canto-falado* in *Bim Bom* eventually gets around to considering Augusto de Campos's outspoken defense of a new generation of Brazilian singers in the mid-1960s, known as the *young vanguard* (jovem guarda):

> Augusto de Campos called attention to the singing of Roberto Carlos, Erasmo Carlos and Wanderléia for their "clear, unencumbered" style, condemning the "unfortunate technique of *bel canto*, which bossa nova was supposed to have freed us from forever" and that, according to him, was being reborn at the moment in the "emphatic, rigid interpretation, full of melodramatic effects (including easy stage lighting tricks)" of Elis Regina. Halfway through his argument Augusto de Campos affirmed that Brazilian pop music belonged to a tradition of "effortless, direct interpretation, almost spoken," whose lineage included Noel Rosa, Mário Reis, and João Gilberto.[30]

A recurring motif throughout Augusto de Campos's work, poetry, and essays alike, is his denunciation of "the old," often identified with the figure of the consecrated poet, who becomes an "august bust"[31]—his language, no longer living, petrified on a pedestal. At times, this battle against the old assumes oedipal connotations, as in the poem "ovonovelo" (1954–1960). In that poem, as in *Poetamenos,* the bonds between parents and children are rendered as repressive or even threatening. It comes as no surprise that the *big*, operatic voice would be heard as the "voice of the old," and thus associated with an entire network of authoritarian figures. The issue of diction, then, or the establishment of a new speech pattern thus became paramount to Augusto de Campos, from both an individual and a collective perspective. In *Metaphysical Song,* Gary Tomlinson presents a compelling argument for the perception of the "operatic voice" as conveying "an early modern experience of subjectivity,"[32] from early Renaissance works by Jacopo Peri and Claudio Monteverdi to the dodecaphonic era of Arnold Schoenberg and Webern. In Augusto de Campos's poems, particularly in *Poetamenos,* the voice becomes not only the vehicle through which the poet asserts his individuality, but also, as Sterzi maintains, the means whereby the boundaries of this individuality are overcome, and "the construction of a possible subjectivity is dramatized."[33]

Augusto de Campos is a refined reader, capable of incorporating into his writing the most avant-garde tendencies available to him. In addition to writing poetry, he has dedicated much of his time to an extraordinary translation program that includes authors as diverse as Dante Alighieri, John Donne, Emily Dickinson, Arthur Rimbaud, Mallarmé, Pound, and Paul Valéry. He is also the author of three volumes of translations of Provençal poets. It is interesting to note, however, that despite the great variety of interests evident in his translation work and writings on music, his own poetry is in essence influenced by specific threads in Brazilian popular culture. In an essay in *Balanço da bossa*, for instance, he revealed that *Poetamenos* was written under the influence of both Webern and Lupicínio Rodrigues, a samba composer whose torch songs were popular in Brazil in the 1940s and 1950s.[34] In the same essay, Campos praises Rodrigues's "restrained expressionism" and notes that Webern "gave classical music the physical dimension of popular music."[35]

Campos's fascination with Rodrigues motivated him to track the singer/composer down in his hometown in the Brazilian south,[36] to attend one of his performances and interview him. He admired Rodrigues's soft singing, which was the opposite of the big voice current in the 1940s and 1950s. In addition, he was amazed by Rodrigues's lyrics,[37] which make use of everyday, commonplace language and cliché phrases to the greatest effect. "Lupicínio," he writes, "tackles [the lyrics] with naked hands, with all the clichés of our language, using that which has been discarded to attain greatness, isolating redundancy from its context to achieve the new." Campos marvels at the fact that in popular music, lyric and melody are impossible to dissociate. And in the case of Rodrigues, his very interpretation of the song must be taken as part of the entire gestalt: "The degree of involvement is complete—one would even say 'verbivocovisual'—and cannot be sectioned off without losses."[38] The interpretation of a song or a poem is an issue particularly dear to Campos, one that he regards perhaps as the mark of a true poet. In this context, the fact that only late in his career he was able to perform his poems/compositions on stage is revealing, and one is tempted to see in this reluctance to perform a parallel with Arnold Schoenberg's *Moses und Aaron* ("Meine Zunge ist ungelenk: ich kann denken, aber nicht reden [My tongue is not supple: I can think, but not speak.]), as if the poetry envisioned by Campos would ultimately elude him in terms of sound. It is also through this complementary optic, wherein Veloso plays Aron to Campos's Moses, that Tropicália's rapport with concretism must be considered. Ultimately, the bridge between twelve-tone theory and samba proposed by Campos is what prevents *Poetamenos* from being a mere illustration of a thesis.

The six elegiac poems that compose *Poetamenos* were written as homage to the poet's wife-to-be, Lygia, in the tradition of spousal verse, or epithalamium. Rigorously structured, the series is introduced by a short prelude, followed by three euphoric moments (*"paraiso pudendo," "lygia fingers,"* and *"eis os amantes"*), interspersed by two dysphoric moments (*"nossos dias"* and *"dias dias dias"*). As in Webern, echoes of other works and styles reverberate throughout—Provençal, baroque, and Parnassian poetry. But from within this rigorous structure, the poet's voice emerges to tell us the story of his love for Lygia, full of longing and youthful yearning. Throughout the sequence, words are cut into syllables or letters, with their fragments often interspersed among other words. Different colors indicate different timbres, while the spacing between words and lines dictates the rhythm. Words, syllables, and phonemes mirror each other, creating the effect of an echo chamber. Amid this cacophony other literary works resonate, adding new shades to the poet's erotic reverie.[39]

Poetamenos opens with a lyrical proem (see figure 5), introducing the series' central themes through two felicitous portmanteaux.[40] The first, "*rochaedo*," suggests the figure of a poet (*aedo*, from the Greek *aoidós*), inert like—or with—the rocks (*rochedo* [cliffs]); the second, "*rupestro*," suggests that poetic imagination (*estro*, from the Greek *oîstros*) is a force of nature (*rupestre* denotes vegetation that grows on rocks)—the overall image reminiscent of William Carlos Williams's line "Saxifrage is my flower / that splits the rocks." The voice of the poet seems to be directed to his beloved ("*somos um*" [we are one]), and at the same time unisonous with hers ("*uni / sono*" [uni / sonous, or one I am, or I dream I am one]). Like in Williams's short poem, "A Sort of Song," Campos is allowing that "writing be of words," so that subjectivity is purely an expression of language. Worth noting that the figure of the petrified poet (or the poet buried under rocks) had already appeared in Campos's first book of poems *O Reino menos o rei* (The Kingdom Minus the King, 1949–1951): "*De sob a rocha escuto os finos rios / De mercúrio torcendo-se de frio*" (under the rock I hear the thin rivers / of mercury twisting in the cold).[41]

The second poem (see figure 6) suggests an erotic interlude in a garden, with references to an idyllic setting (first a fig orchard, "*figueiral / figueiredo*" and later a hanging garden, ("*jardim suspenso*"), gradually unfolding into a highly sexualized verbal environment. Nature is first evoked through literature and immediately becomes animated and sexualized. The beginning of the poem is a rearrangement of the first lines of "*Canção do figueiral*" (Song of the fig orchard), a Provençal song from Galicia that

por

suposto:

'scanto

eu

rochaedo

meu

rupestro

cactus

ab

rupt

ao mar: **us**

somos

um unis

sono

poetamenos

FIGURE 5. Augusto de Campos, *Poetamenos* ("por suposto"), 1953

celebrates the rescue of six young women captured by the Moors. Many family names in Portugal are inspired by nature, and according to the legend, after freeing the maidens the young hero took the name Figueiredo. The original song starts thus: "*No figueiral figueiredo, e no figueiral entrei*" (In the fig orchard, in the fig orchard I entered).[42] Whether words break

no
entrei   ah
in pubis figueiral
jardim figueiredo
                    braços
suspenso
          petr'eu mim
          exampl'eu fêmoras a ellla
sus   pênis
          flagrante
     ad nauseam
                    e s p a l (s) m a s   jardim
     caem joelhos debonança
penso
paraiso pudendo

FIGURE 6. Augusto de Campos, *Poetamenos* ("paraiso pudendo"), 1953

("*suspenso*" becomes "*sus pênis*") or unite ("*ah braços*" [ah, arms] can also be read as "*abraços*" [embraces]) they seem to refuse clear definition. For instance, in one line the pairing of "*penis*" with "*flagrante*" (flagrant) might denote exposure, as in the phrase "*pego no flagrante*" (caught red-handed), and once again "*suspenso*" is broken, but this time as "*sus/penso*" [under/I think]. Amid this verbal turmoil, the stonelike poet ("*petr'eu*" [stone I]) is brought out of his torpor ("*exampl'eu*") through the woman's thighs ("*fêmoras*"). Both expressions are complicated creations that contain very little trace of Portuguese. Jacques Donguy suggests that "*exampl'eu*" is "*un néologisme latinisé, au sens de 'ouvrir vers l'extérieur,'* " while " '*fêmoras*' *est une autre creation à partir du latin 'femina,' 'femme' et 'femora,' 'femur.'* " It's worth noting that the Latin root *ampl-* is also present in *amplexus* (embrace) and a possible English translation of the portemanteau would be: "I open up my arms." This convoluted line would thus suggest an inversion of the biblical account of the creation of Eve. The poem features clusters of words highlighted in four different colors—blue, red, green, and yellow—and the overall effect is that of superimposed ideograms. The cluster in red, which starts in the third line and continues up to the last, includes pairings like "*pubis/jardim*" (pubis/garden) and "*paraiso pudendo*" (pudendum paradise).

The name of the poet's inamorata, Lygia, is dispersed throughout the third poem (see figure 7), with the letters rearranged in different combinations ("*digital*," "*dedat illa(grypho)*," "*felyna*," "*figlia*") forming new words until the woman is finally morphed into a "*lynx*." The poem opens with an apparent grievance: "*lygia finge*" (Lygia pretends). But the next

```
lygia        finge
      rs     ser
             digital
             dedat illa(grypho)
lynx lynx                           assim
         mãe felyna     com   ly
         figlia me felix sim na nx
      seja:  quando  so lange so
ly
gia    la     sera    sorella
                      so only lonely tt-
l
```

FIGURE 7. Augusto de Campos, *Poetamenos* ("lygia fingers"), 1953

line ("*rs ser*") moves meaning in another direction, as "*finge*" can now be read as "*finge-rs*." The third and fourth lines confirm this possibility ("*digital*" and "*dedat illa[grypho]*"). In the line "*dedat illa(grypho)*," Campos deconstructs the Portuguese verb *datilografar* (to typewrite) in order to insert his beloved's name within his poetic practice. It could be said that the "ghost" (or presence) of Lygia haunts his writing: *grypho* can be read as both "glyph" and "griffin." One possible reading, then, is that "Lygia's fingers type" (the poem?), or maybe she "pretends to" (*finge*). The poem's final lines play with family bonds: "*mãe*" (mother), "*figlia*" (daughter, in Italian), and "*sorella*" (sister, also in Italian).

The metamorphosis continues in the next poem (see figure 8) where Lygia's name is encoded in the Italian word for shell ("*conchiglia*"). And in the fifth and penultimate poem (see figure 9) differences are finally balanced: This is visually conveyed by the poem's symmetrical layout, in which, as in a Rorschach blot, and with minor distortions, the right side mirrors the left. Hence, we have pairings like "*amantes/parentes*" (lovers/relatives), "*cimaeu/baixoela*" (me on top/she below), "*estesse/aquelele*" (this it/he that). Note that the portmanteau "*estesse*" (composed of two demonstrative pronouns with a subtle difference: *este* [this] and *esse* [this]) can concomitantly be (mis)read as "ecstasy." In this poem, the sexual tension accumulated throughout the series reaches its climax, indicated by another portmanteau ("*semen(t)emventre*"), which unfolds in two alternate readings: "semen inside the womb" and "seed inside womb."

The series closes (see figure 10) with a melancholic tone of departure, or absence, conveyed by a concerted series of signs, fragments, and citations: The lovers are apart ("*separamante*") and incommunicado ("*sem uma linha*" [without a line]); without his muse, the poet becomes a nobody ("*expoeta*") near his last breath ("*expira*"); his beloved becomes enigmatic ("*sphinx e/gypt y g*"); and, looming over the entire poem, there are hints of family strife, through references in the first lines to a sonnet by Luis de Camões ("esperança de um só dia")[43] and, toward the end, to Lygia's family name. At this point Azeredo, the beloved's family name, echoes "*figueiredo*" in the second poem.[44]

Poetamenos is a series that is remarkable, paradoxically enough, for both its concision and its opulence, its restrained formalism concealing a torrent of emotions and sexual longing. In it, Campos's technique comes the closest to uniting in one knot Pound's concepts of *melopoeia* and *phanopoeia*. Each poem is composed as a "lyrical ideogram," to use Jacques Donguy's expression, with express indications for rhythm and tone.[45] Sound—the sound of the voice, that is—is a sign of life, and in

```
                    nossos dias com cimento
                                        conchiglia
        e o menoscabo em cubos
            menoscubos como dias
              men digos  ao cabo    frio
                                ao
                                fim
                       do triste
                              há manchas no assoalho
    mendigos  são  os que sentam
    dois nos  bancos         da praça ao
              vento tão   ventre
              segurando  tant o
                as mãos           s passos
      e em boa noite e  até    per   amanhã
                   t e a té t         e afã
                       bem  guntam  fim?
```

FIGURE 8. Augusto de Campos, *Poetamenos* ("nossos dias"), 1953

Poetamenos, the poet's petrified state returns to life through the presence of his lover. Throughout the series, Lygia is the principle that animates, enlivens, and organizes the world around him. Before her arrival the poet is inert, rocklike. Her presence is both a force of nature ("lynx," "felyna") and the possibility of writing ("digital," "dedat illa(grypho"). She is Echo, or rather Syrinx, channeling the poet's voice onto the page.

In *The Figure of Echo: A Mode of Allusion in Milton and After*, John Hollander notes that the phrase *imago vocis* "comes from the fairly literal Latin use of *imago,* or sometimes *imago vocis,* for echo. It precedes, rather

FIGURE 9. Augusto de Campos, *Poetamenos* ("eis os amantes"), 1953

than tropes, our primarily visual use of the word image."[46] And further elaborating on the signification of the relation of the natural world with a voice, he quotes the following passage from Francis Bacon:

> For the world enjoys itself, and in itself all things that are.... The world itself can have no loves or any want (being content with itself) unless it be of *discourse*. Such is the nymph Echo, a thing not substantial but only a voice; or if it be more of the exact and delicate kind, *Syringa*,—when the words and voices are regulated and modulated by numbers, whether poetical or oratorical. But it is well devised that of all words and voices Echo alone should be chosen for the world's wife, for that is the true philosophy which echoes most faithfully the voices of the world itself, and is written as it were at the world's own dictation, being nothing else than the image and reflection thereof, to which it adds nothing of its own, but only iterates and gives it back.[47]

Hollander adds: "This marriage is one of nature to the true poetry of natural philosophy, the marriage for which he himself claims, in the *Novum organum*, to be writing the spousal verse or epithalamium."[48]

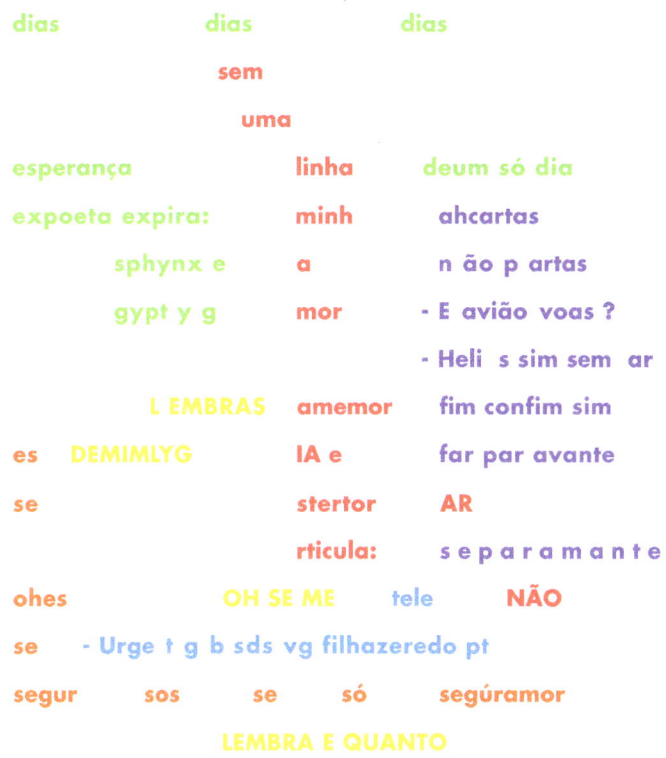

FIGURE 10. Augusto de Campos, *Poetamenos* ("dias, dias, dias"), 1953

The layered, complex material collected in *Poetamenos* presents an opportunity for translators to immerse in one's own culture and assess the transformations that the modern era imparted on specific languages. Since meter and rhyme are of no immediate concern, there is a great deal of freedom for translators to concentrate on and explore the sonorities, dictions, speech patterns, and colloquialisms particular to each language. The dispersion and reassembling of words, as well as the crafting of portmanteaux, will offer many opportunities for invention. Literary references throughout the series might present an obstacle, given the obscurity of their sources. The quotes by Camões and Luis Guimarães Junior, for instance, carry a slightly ironic tone, a literal translation wouldn't capture the irony of the juxtaposition of old and new voices in the original. One solution might be to look for cultural equivalents and replace them with quotes by authors in the translator's language who stylistically share a sense of kinship with the authors cited by Campos. The influence of Lupicínio Rodrigues's singing style is another instance where translators must exert their own judgment and select an equivalent that works for them. Rodrigues's influence is invisible, so to speak, and highly subjective. The equivalent here would be to imagine that a poet like Susan Howe, for example, in addition to her interest in the poetry of Emily Dickinson and the film technique of Chris Marker, was also somehow influenced by the speech patterns of Mississippi Delta blues singers. This very personal choice will not be visible in print but rather guide the decision-making process in structuring the text.

The greatest challenge in *Poetamenos,* however, has to do with what Marjorie Perloff explored in the poetry of Ezra Pound in terms of nominalism. In her essay "The Search for 'Prime Words': Pound, Duchamp and the Nominalist Ethos," Perloff asks, "Why this longing to turn words that have specific meanings into proper names—names that designate a particular person or place and hence restrict the possibilities of reference?" The usual answer, she herself responds, "is that the proper name is a form of concrete image." And she continues:

> If as Pound says in "A Retrospect," 'the natural object is always the *adequate* symbol,' if, as he puts it later in the *ABC of Reading,* 'the Chinese ideogram is the touchstone for poets because, unlike the letter unit of the Western alphabet, the ideogram provides us with the picture of a thing,' then the proper name is essential to a poetics of "constatation of fact," of "accuracy of sentiment."[49]

In the case of *Poetamenos*, a series constructed under the aegis of both Webern and Pound, the presence of the beloved animates everything around the poet, in nature and in literature—a presence made felt by the dissemination of her name throughout the series. Hence, a reference to "figueiredo" in the second poem, for instance, bridges the poet's love for Provençal song and for Lygia Azeredo ("*filhazeredo*" in the last poem). In addition, the wordplay with *aedo* (*aoidós*), which we first encountered in the portmanteau "*rochaedo*," also reverberates in "*figueiredo*" and "*filhazeredo*" and completes the associative chain that links the possibility of poetry to nature and to the beloved. To translate "*figueiredo*" as "fig tree" is therefore to lose an entire chain of meanings and references.

Halfway through her text, Perloff moves away from her line of argument to suggest a kinship between Pound's compulsion to name and

Marcel Duchamp's idea of a "pictorial nominalism," which, according to Thierry de Duve, "turns back on metaphor and takes things literally." Although "pictorial nominalism" might seem an apt term for classifying *Poetamenos*, Campos seems to complicate things further by turning a noun (Azeredo) into a metaphor (the fig tree), thus undermining not only Duve's explanation but also one of the guiding principles of concretism itself. In the end, it is this relentless resistance to conforming (to a given principle, to a given form, and even to translation) that has kept this protean concrete poem/painting/composition vital for over seventy years.

3 / Mechanics of Composition

The paradoxical pursuit of purely abstract forms mixed with utilitarian concerns was a distinctive characteristic of constructivism, one that clearly demarcated a rupture with preindustrial societies. To be sure, the emphasis on usefulness by the early twentieth-century avant-gardes did not carry the moral implications related to Utilitarian philosophy, focusing instead on pressing social inadequacies. As market economy, with its concomitant proliferation of consumer goods, became ubiquitous around the globe, usefulness became a core value, neutral to both commercial and artistic areas. In Brazil this dichotomy was evident in the eclectic production of artists such as Abraham Palatnik and Geraldo de Barros that included commercial ventures in furniture-making and graphic design alongside the pursuit of abstraction. Hinting at the idea that artworks and domestic utensils partake of the same symbolic chain, Palatnik titled his first kinetic sculptures "aparelhos" (appliances), echoing Stéphane Mallarmé's statement half a century earlier that equated the book to an instrument. While both statements seemed to respond to the emergence of new social-cultural habits, it's important to note that Mallarmé seemed to lament the loss of ancient reading rituals,[1] while Palatnik rang a hopeful note about future uses of machines. In this regard, he seemed more in tune with William Carlos Williams who in his introduction to *The Wedge* described the poem as a machine made of words, noting furthermore that the arts have a *complex* relation to society: "poet isn't a fixed phenomenon, no more is his work."[2] As the title of Williams's collection indicates, his poem-machine analogy related to rudimentary devices like the wedge, designed to augment force—the original intended title, *The (lang)Wedge: A New Summary*, suggested that poetry could be a useful tool.[3] Writing as the United States was being pulled into World War II, Williams felt the need to state that the arts are not "a turning away," "it is the war or part of it"; in this sense, his analogy of the poem-machine represented a departure from Paul Valéry's concept of the poem as a machine "for producing the poetic state of mind."[4] Rather than the pursuit of ideas, Williams emphasized process and motion, and saw the task of the poet to capture the subtleties of American speech, proposing the page as an active "field" of composition, a theme he would later develop in his 1948 essay "The Poem as a Field of Action."

The release of *The Wedge* in the mid-1940s passed unnoticed in Brazil, even though Williams's search for a "new form of poetic composition for the future" could have been seen as in step with the aspirations of the Noigandres poets.[5] As it happened, a vision akin to Williams's "machine made of words" would be articulated a decade later by the concrete poets, who like him were concerned with the role of poetry in society. Décio Pignatari's 1954 essay "Forma, função e projeto geral" provides a starting point for an exploration of the mechanistic trope in concrete poetry and how it relates both to then-emerging studies on cybernetics as well as to ideas drawn from design and architecture:

> Faced with the great antagonistic contradiction between industrial and artisanal production—which has opened an abyss between art and public—merging usefulness with beauty has become a necessary step to meet the needs of a new kind of consumer: the "consumer of physical design," to quote Richard Neutra, and to overcome the individualist phase of critical rebellion against the machine that led to Picabia's purely literary "beautiful" useless machines. In this process of awareness, Bauhaus marks a turning point in a positively constructive sense: beautiful useful machines.[6]

Published in the influential architecture magazine *AD*, Pignatari's text addressed a specific audience made up for the most part of the intellectual elite engaged in the heated debate around Brazil's commitment to modernize. In keeping with the context, the essay seemed to validate the widespread view of architects like Leo Ribeiro de Moraes who in his opening address at the IV Brazilian Architects Conference in 1954 noted that modern architecture is a "language that everyone understands."[7] Pignatari breaks down the stakes of such vision thus:

> The visual arts found in architecture and urban planning, as well as in industrial design, cinema, and advertising, a vast field in which to

interact, while, for the need of faster and incisive communication—more economic—our era projected itself under the sign of non-verbal communication. Electronic music is already being introduced in filmmaking, television, and radio as sound effects. Concrete poetry, for being more recent, only now starts to glance the possibility of being applied to advertising, graphics, and journalism.

If the radical project of upgrading the country's infrastructure was to succeed, people from diverse social classes and cultural backgrounds ought to be introduced to the basic codes of constructivism, as well as to the significance of mechanical appliances in everyday life. The task of the poet would be to engage the reader in understanding this new environment, and in the following years, Pignatari would respond to the challenge by producing an extraordinary series of poems that shed a light on the mechanics of poetry. The ambitious breadth of Pignatari's essay was in keeping with the often-polemic tenor of the short texts he published in the years leading up to the publication of "Plano piloto para poesia concreta" in 1958. A restless thinker, Pignatari's distinct contribution to concrete poetry was predicated on his ability to make connections between disciplines such as the ones he mentions in this essay—the visual arts, architecture, urban planning, electronic music, advertising, etc. This penchant for the cross-disciplinary was already evident in his first trip to Europe when accompanied by his wife in 1953, he visited Max Bill at the Hochschule für Gestaltung, in Ulm, Germany, and the young experimental composer Pierre Boulez in Paris.

While Williams and Pignatari might have shared a common ground as to how contemporary poetry ought to relate to new societal developments, it is undeniable that each man was responding to different contexts, and priorities. Equally important to note is the fact that even though Williams developed a refined understanding of the visual arts through the close association he maintained with the New York avant-garde of the first half of the century, his focus turned early on to metric, rhythm, and ultimately to how the poem ought to sound. In Pignatari's poems, on the other hand, the aural seems to give way to the visual, as the ear for everyday speech became supplanted by the awareness of iconic objects newly inserted in the market system. Hence poems on mass-produced goods such as Coca-Cola, and *LIFE* magazine, for instance, experiments that later will lead the poet to incur into advertisement-as-poetry. But it would be a mistake to read these poems as merely textual versions of pop art strategies. If anything, Pignatari's poems work as a primer on how to read a (concrete) poem, and as such they stress the main tenets explored in Noigandres' early manifestos, including Pound's considerations on the Chinese ideogram, Sergei Eisenstein's theory of film montage, cybernetics theory, and Vladimir Mayakovski's foray into agitprop. Created between 1956 and 1960, the series comprises four poems notable for a structural coherence that manages nevertheless to avoid becoming an exercise in style. On the contrary, and truly remarkable, in the span of those four years, Pignatari delivered in these poems a kind of manifesto about the artificiality of language, questioning among other things, the ability of writing to produce meaning.

Starting with "terra," from 1956 (see figure 11), Pignatari radically broke away from established poetic forms based on rhyme, stanzas, and metric proposing instead a text-structure meant to emulate the reading process, whether by the human eye or a word processor. Extremely reductive in its repetitive structure, "terra" enacts the gradual dismembering of the word *terra* into smaller components that at times suggest new meanings or else stand merely as empty fragments. Like the other poems in this series, "terra," does not aim to *reproduce* the real; rather, it seems invested in setting forth a new relationship with the real, one in which the reader becomes an active participant in the poetic production. In this process, the reader is pulled into the mechanics of the text following its play of decomposing and recomposing, No longer a mimesis of real objects (*terra* can be translated both as *earth* and *hearth*), the subject matter of the poem is the word *terra* itself, which, like an Alexander Calder mobile, suggests different forms depending on one's point of view.[8] Notwithstanding Pignatari's reductive approach, it's tempting to read "terra" as signaling a transition from agrarian to mechanized culture, for in the context of Brazil's volatile political climate of the 1950s, a poem that proposes to address the issue of land is bound to be politicized.[9]

The following year, Pignatari stepped up his critique of industrialized society with two poems related to mass-produced goods that could as well be misread as incursions into pop art ("beba coca cola," and "LIFE"), however, as I will demonstrate, both poems perform in ways different from pop strategies. To start, it is important to note that although "beba coca cola" (Drink Coca-Cola, 1957, see figure 12), offers some measure of continuity with the system of movement and replacement that Pignatari so successfully demonstrated in "terra," it also indicates a radical departure by addressing mass-produced objects and the political implication of their circulation in society. "beba coca cola," is a poem not only inspired by, but that asks to be read as an advertisement: fragmentarily, delexically,

```
ra terra ter
rat erra ter
rate rra ter
rater ra ter
raterr a ter
raterra terr
araterra ter
raraterra te
rraraterra t
erraraterra
terraraterra
```

FIGURE 11. Décio Pignatari, "terra," 1956

beba coca cola
babe   cola
beba coca
babe cola caco
caco
cola
       cloaca

FIGURE 12. Décio Pignatari, "beba coca cola," 1957

out in the world. Like "terra" and many of the poems created in those early years, "beba coca cola" did not conform to the book format, and pushed the idea that poetry, the text, is found everywhere. Inspired by the experiments in advertisement that Alexander Rodchenko and Vladimir Mayakovsky developed during the early revolutionary period in Russia, Pignatari raised the stakes by turning the classic tool of consumer society against itself to deliver the anti-advertisement. Mayakovsky clearly understood, as early as 1923, that advertising was an intrinsic element of the industrial apparatus, a language to be co-opted if the revolution was to prevail:

> The bourgeoisie knows the power of advertising. Advertising is industrial, commercial agitation. Not a single business, especially not the steadiest, runs without advertising. It is the weapon that moves down the competition.... But face to face with the NEP, in order to popularize the state and proletarian organizations, offices, and products, we have to put into action all the weapons, which the enemy also uses, including advertising.[10]

Pignatari's take on advertising was more anarchic, even scatological, phonetically debasing the pop icon (Coca-Cola) into a cloaca.[11] Regardless of the differences, the example set forth by Rodchenko and Mayakovsky would have long-lasting impact on Pignatari's understanding of poetic language (particularly regarding what differentiates a literary text from a nonliterary text) and its use as a weapon, as we will explore later in his incursion into commercial advertising.

Pignatari's insight on the mechanics of language reached a new point with "LIFE" (1957, see figure 13), designed in collaboration with Maurício Nogueira Lima, a poem in which movement was no longer conveyed just by running the eyes through the text, but rather the very handling of the poem (leafing through the pages) unveils the message. Reading, the poem suggests, is attained over a span of time, and through the gradual accumulation of abstract signifiers. Like in "terra," elements of the text are randomly mixed-up following a visual morphology rather than a grammatical order: I L F E and only at the end the correct order of letters is reestablished. The first page of "LIFE" shows a thoroughly abstract vertical black rectangle, again reminiscent of Russian suprematism. The rectangle represents the letter "I" which in the next pages will gradually morph into different letters: L, F, and E. The sequence culminates in yet another abstraction made up of the juxtaposition of the previous four letters, before the word LIFE is finally delivered in the final page.

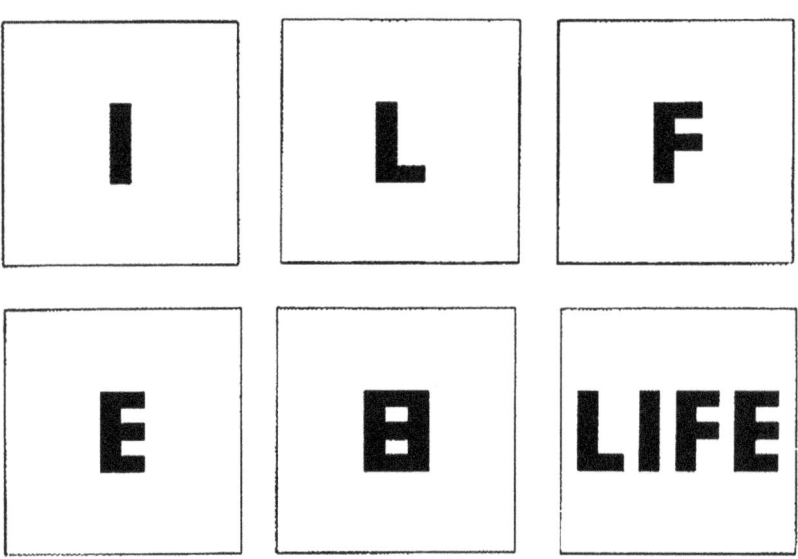

FIGURE 13. Décio Pignatari, "LIFE," 1957

Playing with elements of design and film editing, "LIFE" offers an unnerving meditation on the relationship between language (codes) and organisms (ironically, also articulated by codes), and over the next years, Pignatari would produce two important works that expanded on the same line of reasoning. In 1960, he published the poem "organismo" (organism), and in 1963 he produced an advertisement for Disenfórmio, a medication for intestinal discomfort. At this moment in Pignatari's career, it seems to have become clear that poetic language could no longer be set apart from everyday language. Hence, the same strategies he employed early in the making of his groundbreaking poems, should now be used to reach a wider audience. Like "LIFE," "organismo" (see figure 14) also employs film editing ideas to convey movement and transformation. At a first reading, the poem seems to cast a critical eye on poetic common as it quickly abandons its opening line ("o organismo quer perdurar" [The organism wants to persist]), to zoom in on segments of the sentence. Departing from a general claim (the organism wants to persist), the poet gradually deconstructs the statement to zero in on the letter O of "organism." This inward movement is reminiscent of the right to left movement in "terra," and like in the earlier poem, each subtraction produces new possible meanings. Note in the second sentence ("o organismo quer repet" that instead of "perdurar" Pignatari wrote "repet[ir]" (to repeat) to suggest perhaps that organisms rely on repetition to persist. As the poem mutates further, we are given other variations on the theme ("the organism wants" and "orgasm") until it ends in the ovular-looking letter O, perhaps to indicate that an organism develops from an egg.

In 1963, Pignatari turned his attention once again to advertising, but this time around as a commercial ploy, rehashing ideas first advanced as avant-garde poetry into a catchy visual presentation for a pharmaceutical product. Indeed, the advertisement for Disenfórmio (see figure 15) features some of the techniques related to design and film editing that Pignatari refined in previous works. Like "terra," the text seems to move through the page as in an LED display; like "organismo," the ad aims to represent the organic through elements of language. The most striking difference between these works, however, relies on which audience they were intended to reach: The poems clearly directed to a select group of sophisticated readers familiar with the concrete program; while the ad, released in commercial magazines, targeted the average short-attention span reader hungry for immediate connection. The text consists of seven lines occupying roughly two-thirds of the page. On top, the first line reads "PERTURBAÇOES INTESTINAIS" (intestinal disturbances)

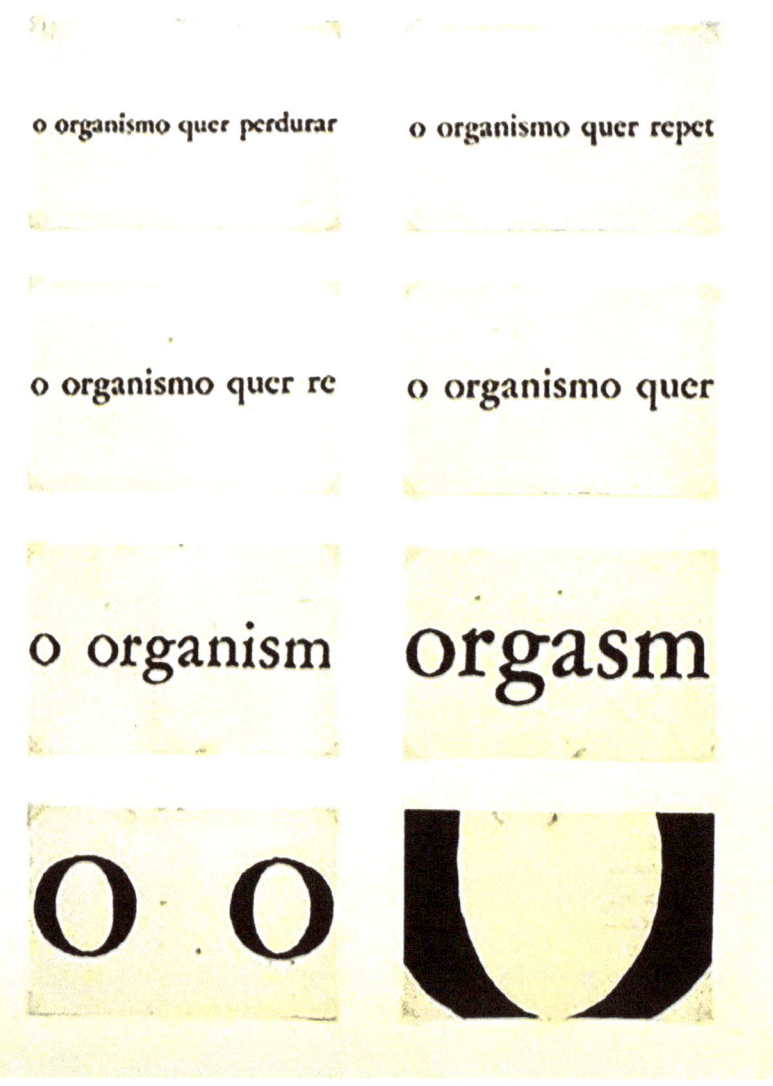

FIGURE 14. Décio Pignatari, "organismo," 1963

in red capital letters occupying the entire width of the page. In the following line, the kerning is tightened so that the original sentence is now surrounded by the black letters "N" and "F" (standing respectively for "DISEN" and "FORMIO") on both ends. In the following lines the red letters progressively move toward the center disrupting the original sentence and ultimately replacing it.

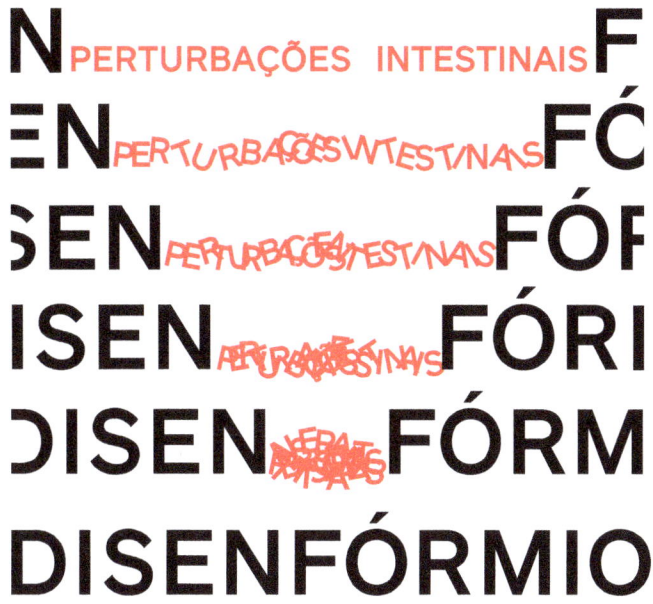

FIGURE 15. Décio Pignatari, Disenfórmio, 1963

Pignatari's advertising for Disenfórmio, designed in collaboration with Ruben Martins, marks a new moment in Brazil when a growing industry demanded a bigger consumer basis, a fact not missed by international advertising agencies that competed for the market. As Walter Benjamin noted, "the possibility now arises that art no longer finds the time to keep up with the tempo dictated by technology and fashion. The advertisement is the ruse by which the dream forces itself on industry."[12] It is worth noting that Benjamin's manuscripts for the Arcades Project only came to light in the early 1980s, and therefore Pignatari couldn't have had access to it when he riffed on the same subject in a short essay published in 1958: "With the industrial revolution, the word started to disconnect itself from the object which once it referred to, alienated itself, and became a qualitatively different object." Earlier in the same essay, he called for "a broader language-based art: advertising, the press, radio, television, cinema, [for] a popular art. The importance of the eye to speed up communication: from luminous advertisement to comics. The necessity of movement. Dynamic structure. The ideogram as the basic idea."[13]

However, although Pignatari's advertisement formally owed a debt to constructivism, one cannot claim that a campaign for the pharmaceutical industry carried the same political weight of the agitprop designed by Rodchenko and Mayakovsky. As it were, the industrial machinery was to devour everything in its path and regurgitate catchy slogans and jingles. However, the crossing of the border between poetry and commercial art that Disenfórmio represented would find a major echo five years later in the advertisement campaign produced by Ogilvy & Mather for the Shell Oil company featuring the emerging pop band Mutantes that included videos, printed ads, and a jingle. The campaign was designed to connect the Shell brand to a younger generation as a ploy to take the market away from Esso, which traditionally pitched to an older audience. The impact that the campaign made throughout the country—with its celebration of youth culture, freedom, and creativity—is worth considering as it was released as the military junta was curbing the common man's and woman's right to assemble and to free speech. To add more controversy to the campaign, Mutantes decided that the jingle they created was a cultural product on its own terms and they included an edited version on their 1969 album, leaving out any reference to the client that had commissioned the work.[14]

The advertising for Disenfórmio marked a pronounced shift in Pignatari's career as he deepened his interest in semiotics and began to collaborate with artists and graphic designers in commercial ventures. The work was created for the advertising agency Metro 3 in 1963, perhaps as a freelance job, and it was also featured in the last issue of the journal *Invenção*, in 1967, as a poem-advertising. Pignatari's interest in design is a development worth summarizing. In 1955, while traveling through Europe with his wife, he visited the newly founded Hochschule für Gestaltung in Ulm, Germany, then under the direction of Max Bill. There he met Bill's young secretary Eugen Gomringer, with whom Pignatari would keep corresponding over the next few years exchanging ideas about concrete poetry. More importantly, it was through conversations with the Argentinian painter and designer Tomás Maldonado that he would become acquainted with the semiotics of Charles Sanders Peirce. Three years later, back in São Paulo, he collaborated with the design group Forminform (ran by Geraldo de Barros and partners) in a rebranding campaign for Coqueiro, a canned-sardine company. In 1960, together with Hermelindo Fiaminghi and Paulo Augusto de Almeida, he founded the advertising agency PDP (Propaganda Direção e Planejamento), a collaboration that lasted until 1963. In parallel to these commercial activities, Pignatari also pursued his interest in design theory and semiotics, and in 1963 cofounded the Associação Brasileira de Desenho Industrial (ABADI). His deepening interest in semiotics would eventually reflect on his poetic work and in 1964, he issued the essay "Nova Linguagem, Nova Poesia," in collaboration with Luiz Ângelo Pinto. This essay coincided with the emergence of a new poetic movement in Brazil known as *poema/processo*, which stressed the poem's information function rather than the aesthetic function, and that considered the reader an equal participant/consumer in the poetic process.[15] Spearheaded by Wlademir Dias Pino, whom the authors graciously acknowledge, and Moacy Cirne.[16] As a matter of fact, the central thesis in this essay was very close to the main tenets espoused by *poema/processo*:

> Every object must be designed and built according to the needs of functions to which they will serve. This basic principle of modern industry is not restricted solely to objects traditionally considered as such, but it also can encompass other objects such as languages. It is in this sense that the poet is a "designer" of language.[17]

The collaboration with Pinto signals a swerve in Pignatari's work toward the writings of Charles Sanders Peirce on semiotics, a passion that he would pursue for the rest of his life teaching classes on semiotics and information theory at several universities in Brazil. In 1973, under the orientation of Antonio Candido, Pignatari defended a doctoral thesis titled "Semiótica e literatura: O signo verbal sob a influência do signo não-verbal" (Semiotics and literature: The verbal sign under the influence of the nonverbal sign). An edited version of his thesis was published the following year as *Semiótica e literatura* (see Appendix 2). In his introduction to that volume, Pignatari stressed the difference between Peirce's semiotics and Saussure's semiology, which he decried as "irredeemably logocentric." Semiotics, on the other hand, teaches us how to "read the non-verbal world (a painting, a dance, a film), and how to read the verbal world in connection with the iconic world."[18] In addition to Peirce's writing, Pignatari also drew from the work of Edgar Allan Poe ("the first *Homo Semioticus*"),[19] and from Paul Valéry's essays on Leonardo da Vinci finding in it a *quasi-method* akin to semiotics particularly in his "relentless pursuit of the relationships, correlations between art and science, between artistic and scientific investigations."[20] Most importantly, however, he would find support for his ideas about the mechanics of reading and writing in a 1888 essay by literary critic and writer Tristão de Alencar Araripe Júnior that defined art as a "machine (to stir) emotion."[21]

Remarkable in its scholarly breadth and philosophical insight, Araripe's essay is a milestone in Brazilian literary criticism centered around the 1888 novel *O Ateneu*, by Raul Pompeia. It is to Araripe's credit to find in Pompeia's *bildungsroman* the subject of his highly informed *treatise* on literary composition. At the start of the essay, after positing his concept of the work of art as a machine, he invites the reader to consider the *interior perspective* that the writer endeavors to reproduce in the reader's spirit through a *superorganic syntax* that does never alter for it is closely related to the laws of morphology. Araripe's understanding of the mechanics of composition made a profound impact on Pignatari, who found in the nineteenth-century scholar a corroboration of his early interest in Mallarmé and Poe. In *Semiótica e literatura*, Pignatari draws richly from Araripe, quoting passages that denote surprising correlations with concepts that he had been exploring over the previous two decades, from the early years of Noigandres to his new interest in the works of Peirce.

Pignatari's discovery of Araripe's critical essays in the late 1960s significantly impacted his understanding of the mechanics of composition, a discovery that might have also led him to reassess his early assumptions on the development of the avant-garde at the turn of the century. In Araripe he found a powerful intellectual with enviable knowledge of late nineteenth-century European literature, whose pointed critique of the then-emerging symbolist movement in France was in opposition to Noigandres' enthusiastic embrace of Mallarmé. To be sure, Araripe's essay on Pompeia dated a good decade before the release of *Un coup des dés*; however, it denotes a sophisticated understanding of the ideas put forth by Mallarmé and René Ghil, particularly in what relates to its emphasis on synesthesia (correspondence among vowels, colors, and musical timbres). In Araripe's view, those ideas did not amount to anything new, and feared that, avoiding Émile Zola's "objective synthesis of the world," the symbolists searched for an adverse synthesis, subjective, not based on observation, but on philosophical categories, a style that would render literature hermetic, addressing only a few adepts. In contrast to this highly abstract "literary Wagnerism," he commends Poe for his "firm, nitid, vigorous" design.

In the essay's second section, subtitled "The Machine," Araripe invokes Vegetius, in his praise of the Roman legion as the "perfect apparatus that conquered the world," and proposes that the work of art resembles this "construction of sociological order," investing against "established schools" on the one hand, while presenting itself as a systemic force destined to counter the anti-art barbarian. Like a Roman general, the artist will lead its legions in every sense, for art is a "work of conquest." The bellicose tone would not be missed by Pignatari who, in 1967, wrote an essay titled "Teoria da guerrilha artística." Araripe maintains that a work of art is similar to this "construction of social order," forced to inveigh against set tendencies, on the one hand, and offer itself as a systematic force, on the other. But the subject of Pompeia's book is not the "work of art," but rather the process of attaining individuality; in the words of Araripe, "the portrait of an individual, of a deeply poetic soul."[22] To close the essay, in a section titled "Psychic Auto-Intoxication: Sense Machines of Objective and Subjective Order," Araripe comments on man's "faculty to grope the invisible and probe the inexpressible; the process through which literary auto-intoxication operates."[23]

> Whoever has analyzed the way through which ideas associate themselves within our brain is not completely unaware of the origins of what propels poetic composition. . . . It is through the senses that the exterior world penetrates us. Fragmented as they are, however, the impressions received from the environment, nature would never reveal itself in our spirit if we did not have the faculty to organize those impressions. Now, this organizing takes place mechanically, fatally, through the redistribution of perception data into groups gathering on one side notions related to beings, and on the other side those related to attributes. . . . The awareness of the universe, or of things, does not integrate until the individual is able to compare and coordinate. And this is what constitutes the integration of knowledge.[24]

Araripe's ruminations on literary composition as it relates to machines were acutely aware of the sociopolitical stakes of a future mechanized society, and in a later essay, he reflected on the *crisis* that Europe was undergoing at the end of the nineteenth century as a consequence of the "replacement of ancient apparatuses by new ones invented by modern democracy; but whose capital machines will not be easily debunked without great shift, and perhaps thunderous subversion of the ground."[25] Araripe's familiarity with European literature and the concomitant societal changes of that period is remarkable, and it is surprising that his highly original critical work was largely ignored after his death in 1911. It was to Pignatari's credit, perhaps under Antonio Candido's orientation, to bring Araripe's writings back in circulation in the same breath as what he saw as seminal contributions by Poe, Peirce, and Valéry. The discovery of Araripe's writings was important for Pignatari in significant ways. For one, it revealed that the ideas on mechanics that he pursued early in his career under the influence of cybernetics studies, had already been sketched out by his compatriot half a century prior. On the other hand, the layered argument set forth by Araripe, enabled him to move ahead beyond constructivism.

That this shift occurred around the time the military was strengthening its hold on civil society through censorship of the press and culture at large is a fact to be considered. As the 1960s was coming to an end, the bright days of early concretism felt like a remote past, and the atmosphere of international dialogue brought forth by the São Paulo Biennial was being replaced by a policy of isolationism. Community-building values related to constructivism, which in the early 1950s had been embraced by a great number of Brazilian architects, visual artists, and poets, were quickly being replaced by antisocial stances inspired by the counterculture movement that was quickly spreading on a global scale. Indicative of the zeitgeist, a major swerve in Brazilian poetry in the 1970s was called "marginal," as if to underline the status of pariah that the country found itself vis-à-vis the industrialized world. Furthermore, the notion that the European constructivist project was at odds with Brazil's stubborn colonial structure was beginning to take hold among detractors of the concrete movement. Nevertheless, despite the reactionary zeal of their critics, the idea spearheaded by Noigandres would find a surprising source of support among the younger generation through short-lived underground publications such as *Flôr do mal, Navilouca,* and *Polem,* to name a few. It was in this new environment, two decades after the launching of the concrete poetry movement, that Pignatari would publish a cryptic but important text in *Polem.*

Organized as a collection of twelve terse, bullet-point musings, Pignatari's text reads like a summary of the themes in poetry and semiotics that he had explored for the past quarter of a century. He writes, for example, that "language is embedded in our DNA," echoing the themes he had approached in his early poems. Continuing the same paragraph, he added: "language is a mutation in human species (Darwin, Freud, Monod). Man is becoming a noospheric and nosferatic sign, as Poe, Peirce, Mallarmé and Pignatari have already noted."[26] This cryptic entry is significant in many ways, not least for offering us a glimpse of the poet's reading list at the time. More importantly, it also indicates that Pignatari was already at work on "noosfera" (see figure 16) a prose-poem that would bring to a close the machinist thread he explored in early poems.

Other entries looked back at the development of concrete poetry and as such it conveyed his concern for a proper assessment of the movement ("before there was 'structuralism,' there was concrete poetry, which proclaimed the end of the verse, a universal historical moment: the new era of icons, recovery of sensibility"), and for a correct approach to the theories of Peirce ("the Marx of language") in statements such as this: "the French diluted Semeiotics into semeiology, just like they diluted Dada into Surrealism. Semeiology is a scam to sell more French books to Brazilian universities." More importantly, Pignatari reflected, albeit obliquely, on the endemic troubles of Brazilian economy by alluding to Delmiro Gouveia (1863–1917), a nineteenth-century entrepreneur whose uninvestigated killing in 1917 put an end to his pioneering effort to industrialize to country.[27] He also praises the aviator Santos-Dumont, "our first industrial designer," whose accomplishments he compares to Piet Mondrian's and Mies van der Rohe's.[28] Pignatari's acknowledgment of Gouveia's and Dumont's contributions to Brazilian industry is important as it indicates a better-informed understanding of the country's persistent colonial structure at the time. The discovery of Araripe's essay on Pompeia certainly represented a turning point in his reassessment of Brazil's complicated path toward industrialization, a development to which not everyone seemed to subscribe if we consider Sérgio Buarque de Holanda's critique of the "lie of utilitarianism," as based on the false association of ideas: "Born of the idea that happiness in life is only attained through an extreme simplification of life."[29]

A surprising tour de force of a poem, "noosfera" has not, to this day, found the reception it deserves. The poem's diagram, featuring irregular spacing between words, suggests a dense modernist cityscape, with tilde accents floating above at irregular heights.[30] On a purely graphic level, the poem seems to suggest that the built environment and language have become one. In this level, the poem is reminiscent of the merging of nature, temple, and language in Baudelaire's "Correspondences"; or else, T. S. Eliot in "The Love Song of J. Alfred Prufrock" ("Streets that follow like a tedious argument/Of insidious intent/To lead you to an overwhelming question . . ."). On another level, the text/city (megalopolis) seen from above mirrors the human brain, with the typographical play now standing for intellectual activity. In an essay discussing "inter-semiotic translation," the visual artist and graphic designer Julio Plaza, a frequent

chanutes   aders   wrights   demoiselles   voi

sins   blériots   fluindo   sedas   tensas   lib

élulas   ouro   onvionleta   no   pôr-de-ar   de

ocre   da   tarde   lá   em   baixo   sôbre   a   calota

megalopolitana   em   olho-de-peixe   sign(

ÕS DECOLANDO PLANANDO CIRCUNVÕLUINDO

SOBRE LOBÕS CALOS QUIASMAS BULBOS VENT

RÍCULOS TRÍGONOS PEDÚNCULOS FENDAS DE

ROLANDO E SYLVIUS SOB UM CÉU PARIETAL)

FIGURE 16. Décio Pignatari, "noosfera," 1973

collaborator of Pignatari's, offered a thorough overview of the poem's structure and subject matter that is worth quoting here in its entirety:

> At the macro-structural level, the poem can be divided into three spaces. First there is the space of the representation of the planetary-atmospheric-aerial medium, through which signs referring to airplanes and names of aircraft builders circulate: *chanutes, aders, demoiselles*, etc. These signs are situated topologically in the upper iconic space of the poem: *voisin—s* (here the grapheme *s* acts as an icon of the propeller). Airplane-signs "flowing" (*fluindo*) light as

"dragonflies gold . . . in the setting of the ocher afternoon—n air" (*libélulas ouro no por de ar de ocre da t—arde*): here the afternoon runs off — which burns or glows (*arde*) economically and syntactically unites *tarde* and *arde* in a single sign. Airplanes flow like "tense silks" (*seda tensas*)—here referring to *asas* "wings," of the airplanes embedded in *sedas tensas*.

Again at the macro-level, there is a phonetic icon of the airplane (*avião*): *onvionleta no*, where there is symmetry of the icon-airplane and its sound.

In a second space, described by "down there over the megalopolitan hubcap in a fish-eye view" (*lá em baixo sobre a calota megapolitana em olho-de-peixe*), there is the topology of the territory (the earth seen from above), with the icon of the city (*calota*—a word with multiple meanings ranging from "skull" to "hubcap" or "polar cap") seen in 360 degrees, as in a photograph taken with a fish-eye lens. Embedded in this second space, there is a third space which represents the brain as receiver. This reception is indexed by "sign (S TAKING OFF GLIDING CIRCUMVOLUTING . . ." (*sign(OS DECOLANDO PLANANDO CIRCUMVOLUINDO . . .*), where the icons of the parietals are coded as brackets () open to signic [*sic*] penetration—i.e. *sign(OS* . . . This gives a typographical difference in relation to the external signs which circulate in the "sky" —*chanutes aders wrights* . . . penetrating and taking off, gliding and circumvoluting inside the cerebral space. [31]

In its exploration of a philosophical concept (the *noosphere*) through the lens of human industriousness (the invention of the airplane), Pignatari's "noosfera" belongs to a category of writings that problematize the complexity of writing, of language; not as an allegory of a future evolutionary stage for humanity but as an exercise on how to read the present moment.

Pignatari's explorations on the mechanics of language should put to rest the contention by historians like Caroline Bayard who saw concrete poetry as "bedeviled by a lingering Cratylism." While it is tempting to relate that tradition to Cratylism, it's worth noting that Pignatari's play with language was never concerned with the relationship between signifier and signified. As most of the examples discussed above convey, his main thrust consisted of zooming into the core of individual words, often dismembering them to a point of eradicating any meaning (or else, suggesting other meanings/readings). In the specific case of "noosfera," we see yet another modality of close reading, perhaps inspired by the textual analyses he performed on works by Poe, Machado de Assis, and Mallarmé as part of his doctoral studies. In many of those works, he realized that fiction often raises from a play with typography. He explored text as semiotic phenomena, looking, as he noted, for the bits of information that extrapolate the alphabetic code while purely phonetic code, saturating itself in typography.

On the other hand, Kenneth Goldsmith's more enthusiastic view of concrete poetry as predicting "the mechanics of the internet," does not seem to fully account for what Pignatari was after in his machine-poems. Neither a classicist nor a futurist in *latu sensu*, Pignatari created works aimed specifically to address the complicated historical moment he lived in Brazil, and thus not waiting for an "appropriate environment in which [it] could flourish."[32] An alternate account for what Pignatari (and concrete poetry in general) was after might be related to the ideas that George Steiner addressed in "The Distribution of Discourse" related to the development of language, and the realization that "verbal exchanges between human speakers construct an informational environment more powerful and dynamic than that of nature."[33] Indeed, Steiner's well-informed essay on the development of thought and speech (relying for the most part on the studies of Lev Vygotsky) echoes some of the themes that Pignatari addressed in his essay for *Polem*, although it's important to distinguish between Steiner's scholarly rigor, and Pignatari's mercurial-intuitive method of reaching out broadly to gather materials for his compositions; a lifelong pursuit that came to a surprising closure in "noosfera," a work whose complex composition allows the reader insight into the poet's trust in human industry.[34]

4 / Poetics of the Unpoetic

Given the impact of Ezra Pound's ideas in the formulation of concrete poetry, it is noteworthy that the Noigandres poets initially steered away from collage as a compositional technique. As has been well documented, the ubiquitous modernist trope promoted by cubism became Pound's *modus operandi* during the decades he studiously composed *The Cantos*, weaving quotes, citations, his own translations (Canto XXVI), and music transcription (Canto LXXV) in the pursuit of a "poem including history." As it relates to a Noigandres chronology, collage will only appear quite literally in the mid-1960s in Augusto de Campos's *Popcretos*, a small suite of poems composed for the most part of clippings from newspapers and magazines. An extraordinary work in an otherwise cohesive career, *Popcretos* lets us into the poet's mind at a moment when Pound's ideas were being reassessed under the light of a recent discovery: The experiments with poetic montage by Brazilian Romantic poet Joaquim de Sousândrade in the last quarter of the nineteenth century. As it were, the reassessment of Sousândrade's forgotten masterpiece *O Guesa*, which Augusto de Campos undertook with his brother Haroldo, seems to have afforded the two poets a chronological revision of sorts in which collage was no longer understood as a twentieth-century invention, but rather a far more remote practice related to language fragmentation. Given these circumstances, it is fair to suggest that *Popcretos* represents a plunging into the roots of modernity, and it can be read as a corrective to a long-standing misperception of how the avant-gardes operate. Hence, a comparative analysis of the use of collage by Sousândrade, Pound, and

Campos offers us an alternative reading of the avant-garde, not in terms of poetic invention, but rather in terms of understanding how cultural changes impact language. That collage became the means of choice for these three poets to address abrupt economic changes in their respective times, regardless of the particulars of each cultural period, offers an obvious starting point for this comparative reading.

In his insightful essay "O Campo visual de uma experiência antecipadora" (The visual field of an anticipatory experience), Luiz Costa Lima asks us to consider Sousândrade as a seer ("in its etymological precision without any tinge of the magicism that leads us to obscure the world and, concomitantly, art" [in the original: "*na sua exatidão etimológica, sem nenhuma mancha do magismo com que nos acostumam a obscurecer o mundo e, dentro dele, a arte*"]), a poet who projected onto the text his visual experience of the world. He suggests that Sousândrade's worldview differed from the ambiguous position of his Romantic peers who were at the same time "beneficiary and non-participant in the socioeconomic circuit" (in the original: "*ao mesmo tempo um beneficiado e um ausente de participação no circuito socioeconômico*"). The son of landowners, Sousândrade experienced nineteenth-century society from a privileged angle, having lived periods abroad and working in New York as a newspaper editor at a pivotal moment when the first generation of the very wealthy was implementing the country's capitalist structure. Costa Lima considers the section in Canto X of *O Guesa*, commonly referred to as "Wall Street Inferno," as perhaps the first aesthetic correspondent of the world of liberal capitalism. Using fragments collected from his daily readings of the news, Sousândrade was able to circumvent clichés of the Romantic tradition to produce a work that lacked unified sequence, of polymorphic character: "it was necessary to abruptly cut off, impart violence and movement to his vision as to avoid the verse to fall back in the commonly current form" (in the original: "*era necessário cortar bruscamente, emprestar violência e movimento à visualização para que o verso não recaísse na forma comunalmente vigorante*"). He adds that the poet needed chaos, "a verse that would whirl around, a violence that would shake syntax to free itself from imminent faking" (in the original: "*ele necessita do caos, de um verso que rodopie, de uma violência que abale a sintaxe para que se liberte do iminente falseamento*"). He also notes that Sousândrade was pressured to establish a form that "attained beauty precisely for being chaotic and apparently distressed. In reality what was being distressed was a false mind operation" (in the original: "*Sousândrade foi pressionado a estabelecer uma forma que alcança a beleza justamente por ser caótica e aparentemente destroçada. Na verdade, o que se destroçava era uma mentação falsa*").¹ Costa Lima's lucid depiction of a poet breaking free from the constrictions of his epoch to become a seer is something important to consider. His notion of visionary does not carry the metaphysical connotations that T. S. Eliot imputed to the term in one of his essays on Dante Alighieri. On the contrary, based on the writings of Lucien Goldmann, Costa Lima means to convey one's ability to detect the *new* at the moment it emerges and to gauge its impact on the social order. More specifically to the scope of this essay, Costa Lima identifies in Sousândrade one of the first instances in which vernacular language contaminated and threatened the poetic norm.²

Richard Sieburth has also identified a "semiological disorder" in Ezra Pound's *Cantos* and stressed the need to read the passages related to economy as a "mosaic of signifiers without signifieds (or, more precisely, of signifiers treated as if they were signifieds)," noting that they "function less as tokens of commodities or signs of value than as sheer inscriptions, sheer traces, the rewritten residue of reading." Sieburth further observes, recalling Michel Foucault, that both money and language are conceived as equivalent semiological systems, and that Pound's writings related to economy, shaped by this assumption, focus almost exclusively on issues of monetary representation, inscription, and circulation, "virtually bracketing the question of economic production."³ The analogy between these two semiological systems is not a modernist novelty, and we can identify its roots in the Middle Ages with the parallel evolution of monetary policy and the development of rhetorical practice and theory. Sieburth also brings up an essay by Eugene Vance which suggests that the evolution of monetary policy and the development of rhetorical practice in the later Middle Ages may be seen as a strengthening consciousness of *media of exchange*, and identifies an art of inflation affecting both the monetary system ("those princes who would devalue gold currency for profit") and rhetoric ("poets who give themselves too easily to the high and noble style").⁴

Faced with an environment in the grips of fundamental change, Sousândrade and Pound eschewed linear narrative in favor of a mosaic-like composition of signifiers newly available in circulation. Collage (or better yet bricolage, since we are here working by means of signs, and not by means of concepts)⁵ then appears as a possibility to provide us an image of this uncharted situation from within. This reasoning, I argue, is applicable to Augusto de Campos's *Popcretos*, a work produced as a new bourgeois class emerged in Brazil following the military coup of 1964. Moreover, the series marked the poet's acknowledgment of a new era as mass media was increasing its presence in the country.⁶ Offering the news of the day as poetry, *Popcretos* is invested of a sense of emergency, and as often happens with art engaged with the moment, the series is pregnant with new ideas and themes loosely outlined. These sketches of ideas are, however, entirely consistent with the line of development pursued by Noigandres as a group, and Augusto de Campos in particular.

It's uncertain whether *Popcretos* was made specifically for the exhibition that opened at Galeria Atrium on December 9, 1964, featuring sixteen artworks by Waldemar Cordeiro, four collage-poems by Campos, and a "collective composition" coordinated by Damiano Cosela. Although the title seems to acknowledge American pop art, Cordeiro's artworks as well as Campos's collage-poems are more aligned with a tradition of assemblage that we find in European artists such as Daniel Spoerri and Kurt Schwitters. In a brief text for the catalog ("brief exposition on an explosition of expoems" [in the original: "*breve exposição sobre uma explosição de expoemas*"]) Campos addressed the exhibition title with a nod to Marcel Duchamp: "caught and chosen / according to the aleatory nature of ready-mades / through a concrete will" [in the original: "*colhidos e escolhidos / no aleatório de ready-made / por uma vontade concreta*"]). Regardless of the specifics of its genesis, the fact is that Campos continued to work with collage for another two years. The exhibition presented four poems (made between August and November, 1964): "ôlho por ôlho" (eye for an eye), "o anti-ruído" (the anti-noise), "goldWeater," and "SS." Three additional collage-poems were realized in the following years: "psiu!" (psst), "luxo" (luxury), and "F(J)(Y)EUX" (fires / games / eyes). In many anthologies "psiu!" (1966) has been added to the *Popcretos* suite; "luxo," however, has often been presented as a standalone work while "F(J)(Y)EUX" was never printed in its collage form but was later used as the basis for "oeilfeujeu" in the 1970 collection *Equivocábulos*.[7]

The exhibition catalog provides helpful explanation for each collage, as to guarantee correct reading of the poet's intention. The first poem, "SS" (see figure 17), addresses the ambiguity of signs (the "physiognomy of letters" [in the original: "*a fisiognomia das letras*"]) that acquire whatever meaning is ascribed to them. The case in point is the acronym SS that can refer to the Gestapo, His Holiness the pope (in Portuguese, "*Sua Santidade*"), and even to the hot topic of the monokini (*sans soutien*). Pulverized around the page, fragments of letters, words, and clippings of texts mean to emulate the chaotic display in the newsstand, with its mixing of political coverage and entertainment. The poem considers the debasement of language (of the sign) as an indicator of societal transformation; printed matter (the news, packaging of mass-produced consumer goods) as an indicator of the dissolution in (of) language in cities like São Paulo

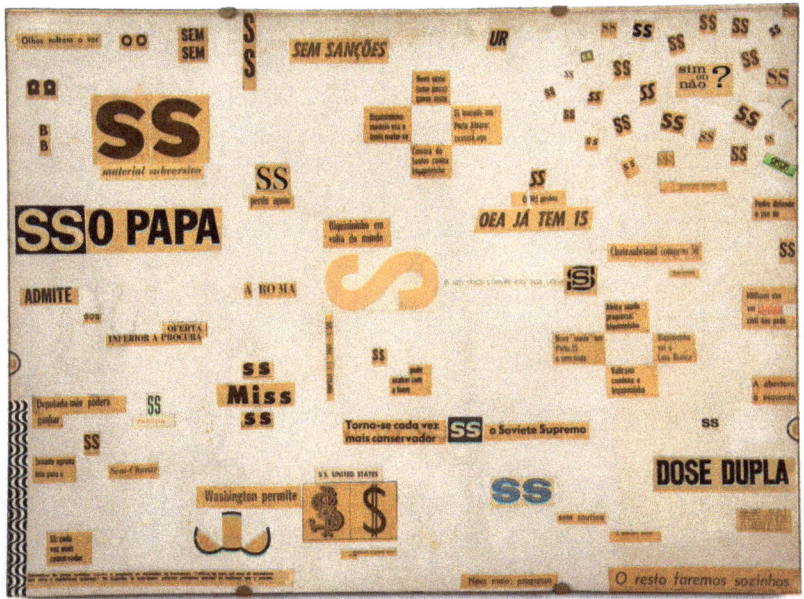

FIGURE 17. Augusto de Campos, *Popcretos* ("SS"), 1964

where it has become signage, advertisement, and merchandise. In another level, the poem telegraphs more immediate concerns hinting at the military coup that had taken place earlier that year: "2 months of rage in the newspapers. clippings. packings. the talk of the tribe. details-detriti of reality. the liberty in letters. the brazilian anthropophagic chaos redestroyed by the titlemania of an anarchitect" (in the original: "*2 meses de raiva nos jornais. recortes. revôlucros. a fala da tribo. detalhes-detritos da realidade. a liberdade em letras. o caos antropofágico brasileiro redestruido pela manchetomania de um anarquiteto*").[8]

The next poem, "o anti-ruído" (see figure 18), is structured around an image inspired by a verse in *Paradiso* ("dal centro al cerchio e sì dal cerchio al centro")[9] in which Dante relates the movement of wise discourse to water circling inside a vase, making waves in the periphery and back again to the center. Campos adds another analogy, that of a "nuclear explosion-implosion," to address the fragmentation of language going on in high-society reporting that abbreviates words to make them more palatable: "*nat*" for *natalício* (birthday), "*deb*" for debutante, and so forth.

In "goldWeater" (see figure 19), Campos evokes Hieronymus Bosch's apocalyptical equation of excrement and money by transforming discarded packagings of cigarettes (Goldleaf) and chocolate coins into

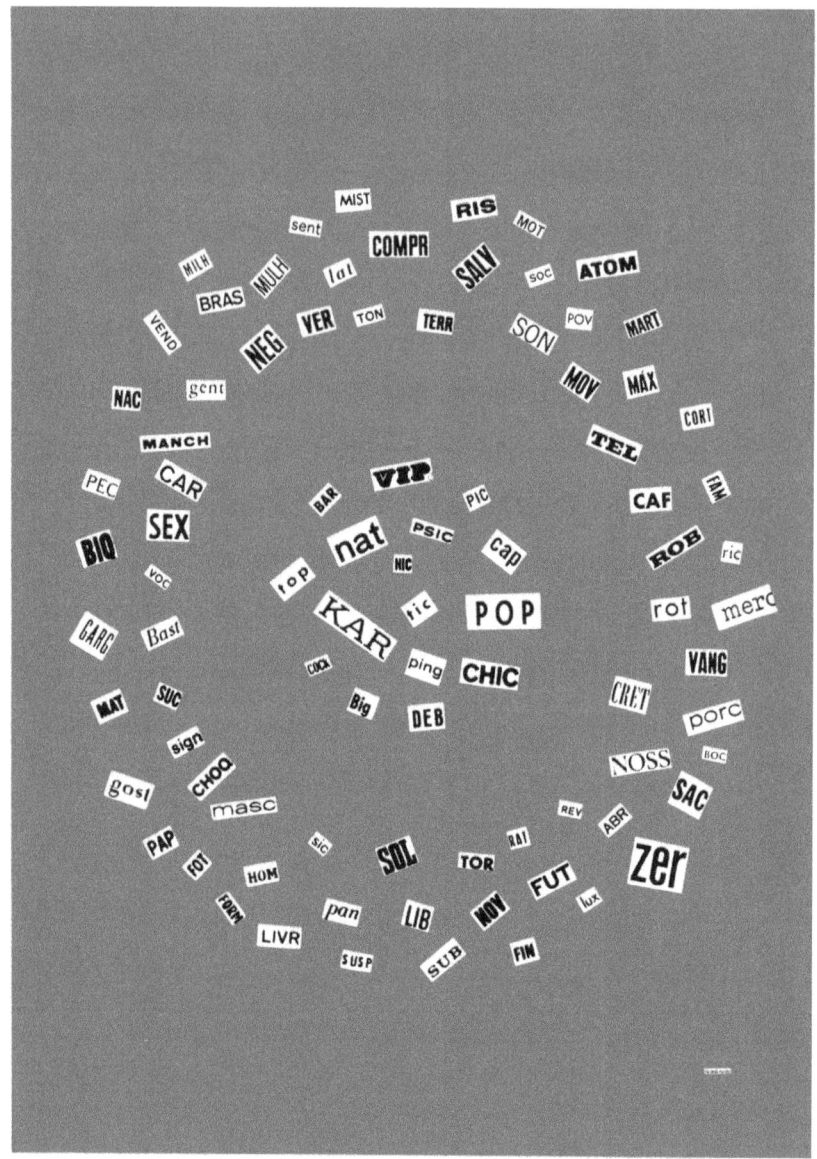

FIGURE 18. Augusto de Campos, *Popcretos* ("o anti-ruído"), 1964

a mock-up of a religious icon. The title is a play on the name of ultra-conservative American Senator Barry Goldwater, who was running for president in 1964 against Lyndon Johnson. In the catalog, Campos describes the collage subject as "*papaouro*," an ambiguous portmanteau that can signify "gold eater" and "gold pope." "gold contamination," he

POETICS OF THE UNPOETIC / 71

FIGURE 19. Augusto de Campos, *Popcretos* ("goldWeater"), 1964

wrote: "from a sign charged with iconicity (gold + color + texture) to the non-sign (white square) semantically contaminated. the maximum and the minimum of redundancy. from the disintegration of the object to a semantic autoantrouropofagia: eaten coins" [in the original: "*do signo carregado de iconicidade (gold + cor + textura) ao não-signo (quadrado*

72 / POETICS OF THE UNPOETIC

branco) *semanticamente contaminado. o máximo e o mínimo de redundância. da desintegração do objeto à autoantrouropofagia: moedas comidas*"]; note that the portmanteau "*autoantrouropofagia*" inserts *gold* (ouro) at the center of anthropofagy.

The last work commented on in the catalog is the most iconic of the series: "ôlho por ôlho" (see figure 20), a pyramidal accumulation of eyes clipped from different sources.[10] Once again, Campos draws from Dante

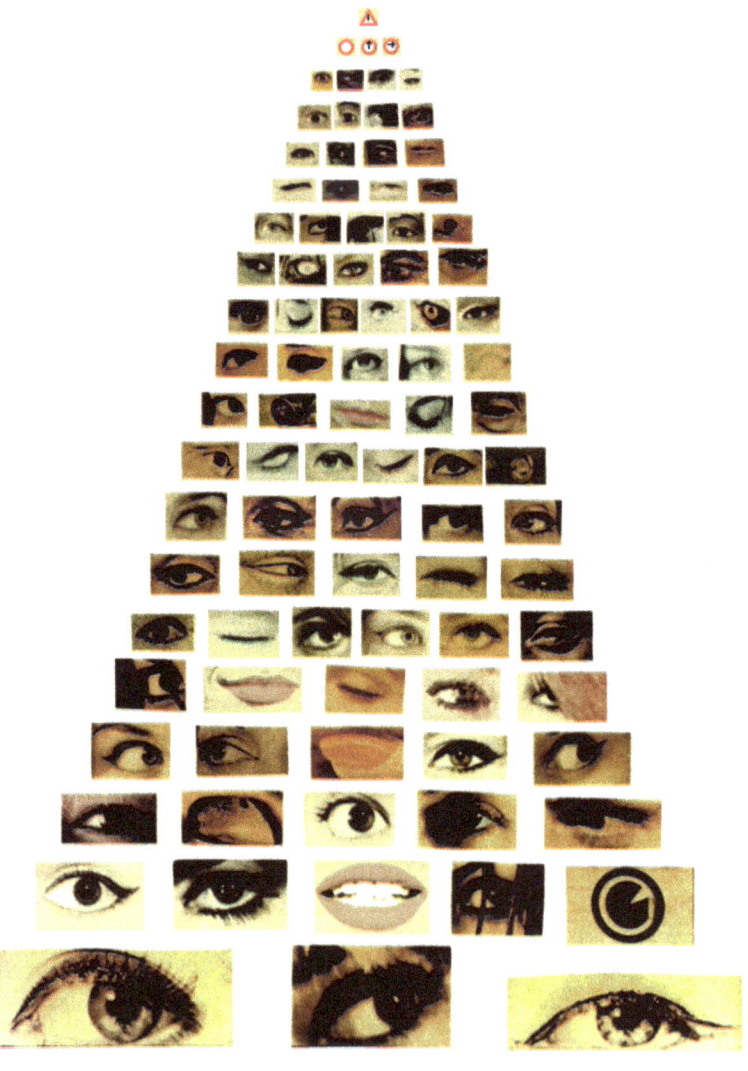

FIGURE 20. Augusto de Campos, *Popcretos* ("ôlho por ôlho"), 1953

("*esto visibile parlare*") to comment on the replacement of text by images in his poem: movie stars, starlets, politicians, poets, beasts, birds, house appliances, and so forth. Notable among the celebrities of the day is the inclusion of fellow Noigandres poet Décio Pignatari, and Joaquim de Sousândrade.

In 1966 Campos created "psiu!" (see figure 21), which since has been added to the suite *Popcretos*. Surrounding a woman's mouth, a carefully orchestrated collage of clippings recycles the news of the past months including the release from jail of Miguel Arraes, the mayor of Pernambuco who had been arrested in the aftermath of the coup two years earlier: "*Saber viver. Saber ser preso. Saber ser solto*" (To know how to live, to know how to behave under arrest, to know how to free oneself).[11] References to the somber political atmosphere is conveyed fragmentarily with words like "ATO" (alluding to the series of Institutional Acts issued by the military junta), and "AME" (referring to the slogan "*Brasil: Ame-o ou deixe-o*" [Brazil: Love it or leave it] promoted under the dictatorship). In an insightful 2017 essay about this poem, João Bandeira called attention

FIGURE 21. Augusto de Campos, *Popcretos* ("psiu!"), 1966

to its actuality contrasting the political events that happened in 1964 to the charged atmosphere of conflicting (mis)information that led to the downfall of President Dilma Rousseff in 2016.[12]

Two additional collages were produced in the following years: "luxo" (1965), and "F(J)(Y)EUX" (year unknown, possibly 1965). In an email exchange with the author, I was informed that "luxo" (see figure 22), was conceived in response to the noticeable capital gains of the upper middle class that supported the military coup.[13] Inspired by a newspaper advertisement for luxury apartments that was published on October 7, 1965, "luxo" effects a powerful critique of rampant consumerism in bourgeois circles and their disregard for the common good. Campos was struck by the typeface chosen for the advertisement meant to convey a sense of lavish bourgeois style, in contrast to the rigorous, clean design promoted by early concrete poetry. Operating simultaneously along micro- and macrostructural levels, "luxo" veers close to the semiotics poetry that Pignatari was exploring around that same time. Essentially a collage of repeated newspaper clippings, its individual elements (*luxo*) are laid out to spell its opposite (*lixo*: trash). This play with micro- and macrostructures evokes both linguistic theory as well as urban planning in that, if one accepts that each icon stands for a "luxury tower" unit, the ensuing composition presents a dismal vision of the city. Campos's ear and eye for the vernacular are ultimately what have made of this poem an emblem of its epoch. Constructed of words (*lixo, luxo*) that in the mid-1960s epitomized in popular culture the dichotomy between high and low classes in Brazil, the poem is nevertheless made playfully accessible in purely musical terms (lee-shoo, loo-shoo). With utmost economy of graphic means, "luxo" sets off a clash of equally conflicting information as the poem takes on the modular vocabulary of modernistic architecture while employing a typeface often associated with kitsch. The title promises a commentary on luxury (*luxo*), while the final product reads like a monument to trash (*lixo*).

Although never published, "F(J)(Y)EUX" (see figure 23) can be considered a liminal work in Campos's oeuvre. In contrast to the poems in *Popcretos*, "F(J)(Y)EUX" lacks any immediate political connotation, and its composition suggests a rather formalistic exploration of typefaces. In that sense, the work seems to announce a new phase in Campos's production free from the restrictions of the typewriter and Bauhausian design (more specifically the Futura typeface). In the decade that followed, Campos would experiment with a variety of typefaces in search of unique solutions for each poem. Consider "Eco de Ausonius" (1977), for example, and his translations of William Blake's "The Sick Rose" (A rosa doente,

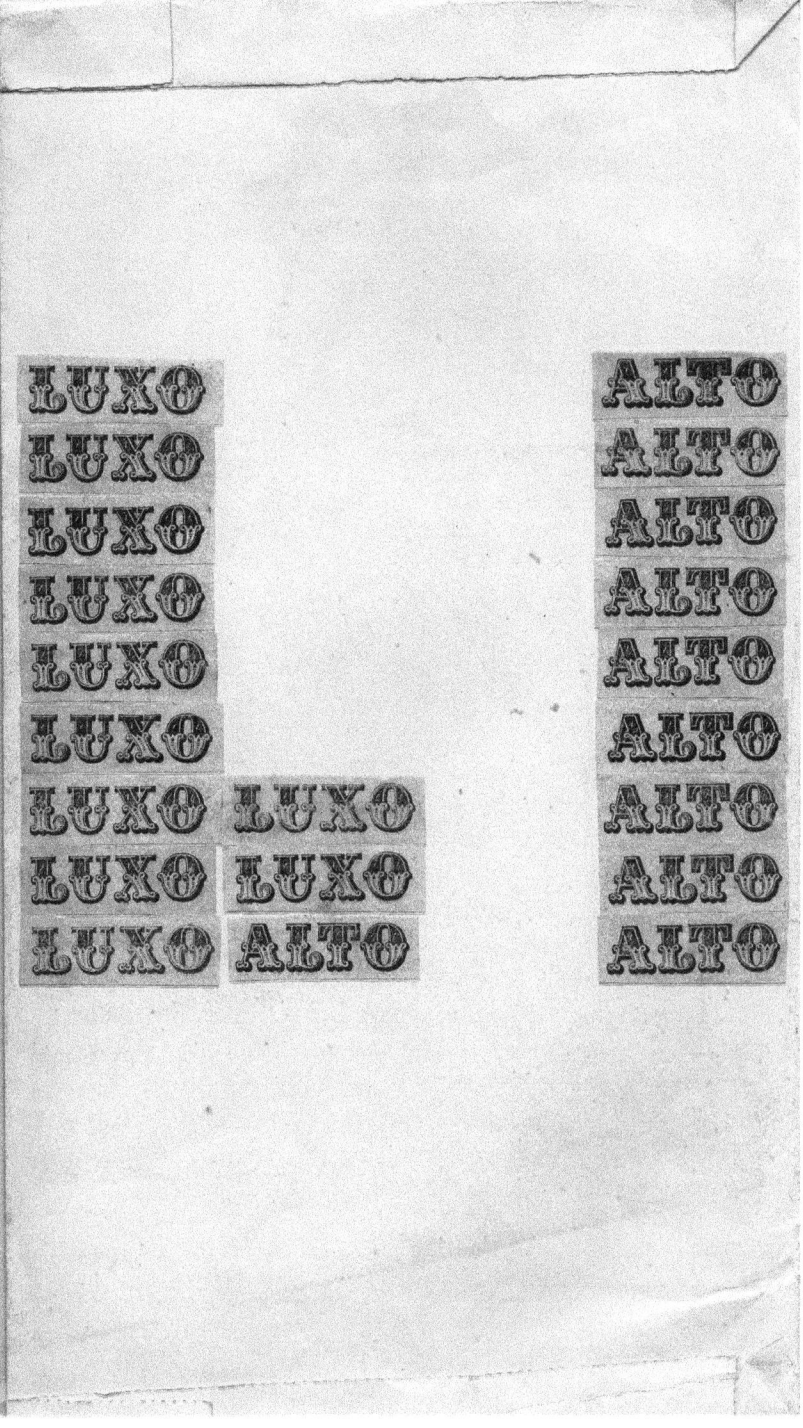

FIGURE 22. Augusto de Campos, preparatory study for "luxo," 1965

FIGURE 23. Augusto de Campos, "F(J)(Y)EUX," 1965

1975) and "The Tyger" (O tigre, 1975). Ultimately, his interest in typeface and graphic design in that period produced iconic works, like "viva vaia" (1972) and "código" (1973). Thus, considered in retrospect, the *Popcretos* suite (and "F(J)(Y)EUX" in particular) triggered an important new phase in Campos's career by allowing him to explore each poem on the basis of their formal aspects.

With its surprising handiwork, *Popcretos* marks a shift in Augusto de Campos's career from the highly conceptual, rigorously diagrammed works from the 1950s composed by typewriter, and anticipates the protean style that since then has become a hallmark of his work. To better contextualize *Popcretos* we must consider its production twelve years after the release of *Noigandres 1*, the publication that launched the concrete poetry movement in Brazil. By the mid-1960s, as their ideas gained international attention, the movement was undergoing an important turning point at home, a shift most clearly evident with the release of the group's second publishing venture, the journal *Invenção* (1962–1967), under the editorial oversight of Décio Pignatari. An editorial note in the first issue of *Invenção* stresses the need for a new basis for the *production* of the artwork: "There is no formal logic, of class [in Brazil], to explain, based on national demand, why we have for example, eight refrigerator factories, nine for television sets, and six for blenders, before having our first tractor factory" (in the original: "*Mas não há lógica formal, classista, que consiga explicar, com base na necessidade nacional, porque tivemos, por exemplo, oito indústrias de geladeiras, nove de televisores, e seis de liquidificadores, antes de têrmos uma só de tratores*").

Although *Invenção* ran for only five issues, it marked a new approach to the avant-garde by championing a deeper engagement with Brazil's literary tradition. To set the tone, the first issue dedicated most of its pages to a comprehensive essay by Cassiano Ricardo looking back at the legacy of the Modern Art week of 1922, followed by an essay by Pignatari on the current state of poetry in Brazil. In the next four issues, the journal documented Pignatari's growing interest in semiology and in the writings of C. S. Peirce; it also introduced to readers Haroldo de Campos's experiments with prose-poetry (the *galáxias*), and Augusto de Campos's growing interest in image (*Popcretos* and *Profilogramas*).[14]

The release of *Popcretos* also coincides with the publication of Augusto de Campos's "Pound Made (New) in Brazil" (Appendix 3), an essay looking back at the time when he, his brother Haroldo, and Décio Pignatari approached Pound, then interned at St. Elizabeths Hospital, in Washington D.C. The key Poundian ideas incorporated into the Noigandres program have been stated many times over, but it is curious how his influence is restated in the context of this essay. Campos argues, for example, that concrete poetry was less interested in the epic form than on addressing discursive language, hence Pound's greatest contribution was the "poetic technique related to montage and the idiomatic mosaic." Another important development instigated by Campos's readings of Pound was a revision of Brazil's literary history based on the principle of *invention*, and in the second half of his essay, he sketches out his approach to the poetry of Sousândrade, which he undertook in collaboration with his brother. Of prime interest to Campos is the section in Canto X of *O Guesa* that deals with the New York Stock Exchange ("the center of financial speculations, conceived as an infernal circle"). According to Campos, in this section Sousândrade's cosmovision touches upon ideas that Pound came to develop in the *Cantos*: "setting aside the extravagant solutions Pound advocated for economic themes and the misguided political affiliations he adopted, we can identify in both poets a common and fundamental aversion to the nefarious power of money. The capacity, to echo Michel Butor, 'de percevoir poétiquement le phénomène de l'économie'" (in the original: "*Postas de parte as soluções extravagantes que Pound preconizou para os temas econômicos de sua obra e as equivocadas vinculações políticas que assumiu, pode-se assinalar em ambos os poetas uma aversão comum e fundamental aos poderes nefastos do dinheiro. Aquela mesma capacidade de 'captar poeticamente o fenômeno da perversão da economia,' para usar de uma expressão de Michel Butor a propósito de Pound* [*Répertoire*, I]"). Campos describes "Wall Street Inferno" as an "atemporal *balmasqué*" that echoes the ups and downs of the American political and financial worlds in the 1870s against a broader international background. Surely this kaleidoscopic description of Sousândrade's sequence, with its "typographic versatility, the graphic physiognomy of newspapers" (in the original: "*a versatilidade tipográfica, a fisionomia gráfica*") could as well be applied to *Popcretos*, but in this essay Campos is most keen on approximating Sousândrade's style to Pound's: "the imagist technique, the synthetic-ideogrammic diction that involves processes such as compression of history, montage of colloquial or literary quotes, or of *fait-divers* of the time, idiomatic *potpourri*, fusion of personae, besides the conversational fragmentation"[15] (in the original: "*a técnica imagista, a dicção sinteetico-ideogrâmica, que envolve processos como a compressão da história, montagens de citações coloquiais ou literaárias ou de 'fait divers' da época, 'pot-pourri' idiomático, fusões de 'personae,' além do fragmentarismo conversacional*"). More recently, in an introduction to a new edition of *O Guesa*, Campos defined Sousândrade's fragmentary style of mixing images of nature with personal experiences interspersed by reflections of clear social tenor as "semantically frayed"[16] ("*esgarçada semântica*") suggesting a relationship between social unrest and semiological disorder. This disorder, he reminds at the end of his introduction invoking Stéphane Mallarmé "*les contemporains ne savent pas lire.*"

Certainly, the gradual insertion into poetic language of elements deemed "unpoetic," such as market brands (see Sousândrade's reference to Pear Soap in "Wall Street Inferno," and Pound's abstracting the logo of the Monte dei Paschi bank into an ideogram in Canto XLII),[17] can be seen as paving the way to more disruptive practices such as Campos's in *Popcretos*, and several other poets thereafter. The implication being that it's no longer about the "rewritten residue of reading," as proposes Sieburth, but a new practice of reading (and incorporating into the text) what is all around; the acknowledgment that a new socioeconomical reality has been established. It is worth reminding that the same year that *Popcretos* was released, Belgian poet Marcel Broodthaers famously proposed to transform his poetry into artworks in order to make a living: "*Moi aussi, je me suis demandé si je ne pouvais pas vendre quelque chose et réussir dans la vie...*," as he explained in the invitation for his first gallery exhibition.

The correspondences Campos establishes between Sousândrade and Pound suggest a more complex understanding of the workings of the avant-garde, now considered not merely on the basis of formal invention but rather in terms of a poet's acute awareness of the changes taking place at his own time. Extrapolating its original militaristic meaning, the avant-garde becomes not simply an issue of aesthetics, but a powerful factor in social activism.[18] In regard to Sousândrade, it's unlikely that he saw himself as avant-garde, a term he used to praise the common American citizen ("young people of the avant-garde" [In the original: "—*Este é o joven povo da vanguarda;/ E na pátria ideal, quanto soffrera, / Pelo quanto de amor e crença houvera, / Sedo o Guesa esqueceu.*"])[19] invested in bringing the republican ideal to modern civilization. As for Pound, his formulation about the great artist as an antenna signaling the future seem equally in tune with an engaged view of the avant-garde. Although highly streamlined and succinct, *Popcretos* ought to be seen along these lines set forth by Sousândrade and Pound. Conceived a decade after the release of *Poetamenos*, fragmentation is achieved in *Popcretos* not through the influence of new (musical) theories, but as direct reaction to a new reality emerging at that moment. Thus, besides capturing an important sociopolitical moment in Brazil, the sequence also reflects on the mass-media apparatus that was in many ways shaping the era.[20]

Popcretos depicts an environment far removed from the romantic worldview disrupted by Sousândrade and even further by Pound. For while Sousândrade, as Costa Lima notes, was a great poet undermined by the colonial structure around him, Campos's experience is of a different order, most tragically marked by the downfall of President João Goulart's efforts to shake up the country's four-centuries old feudal-like structure. According to Costa Lima, Sousândrade had only his "exasperating visualization of a strange world without the conditions to formulate it coherently"(in the original: "*Ele teve de contar apenas com a sua visualização exasperante de um mundo estranho, sem ter tido condições de formulá-la coerentemente*"), hence the discrepancy between the cacophony depicted in the "Wall Street Inferno" section and the book's overall structure informed for the most part by the romantic worldview. As for Campos, under the new climate established by military rule, poetic language seemed to have lost its currency and was debased as cyphers from the marketplace. The elements gathered in *Popcretos* represent the ugly side of the Brazilian press (both in form and content) at that particular moment, in stark opposition to the formal revolution championed by concretism in the early 1950s. By incorporating the ugly, the sequence stands out as a paradoxical work that both acknowledges the failure of the Brazilian constructive project, while at the same time pointing to new possibilities of construction. It might be added that although fragmentation was already present in Campos's work at least since *Poetamenos* (notwithstanding its nod to the atonal theories of Anton Webern and Arnold Schoenberg), the form became an essential feature of his style after *Popcretos*, demarcating a clear transition from early concretism's focus on reason to a dialectical vision of reality as a dynamic whole that progresses through conflict. To paraphrase Lucien Goldmann, any attempt to tone down the paradoxical nature of *Popcretos* and make it more acceptable to common sense would also involve toning down the scandal of the 1964 coup and thus making it more bearable.

By bringing the heroic phase of concrete poetry to closure, *Popcretos* marks an important crossroads in Campos's career as it also hints at the experimental tenor that characterized the years that followed. This new approach culminated in ambitious works like *Caixa preta* (Black box, 1975), the special edition volume designed in collaboration with Julio Plaza that reaffirmed his interest in the fragment. With its allusion to the airplane "black box," essential in identifying the cause of a disaster, the title signals the aftermaths of a tragedy. A retrospective regard is also cast in two important works that appeared in the following decades that take on the form of the epigrammatic fragment to comment on the poet's contribution to the avant-garde: *Pós tudo* (Post everything, 1984) and *Poesia é risco* (Poetry is risk/trace, 1995). The former seems to allude in confessional tone to the early days of concretism and the poet's endeavor to "change everything"; while the latter strikes a bittersweet note on the wager of poetry: The "risk" that paradoxically is only a "trace." In their unfinished form, they seem most apt to convey the unfinished business of the Brazilian avant-garde. As we look back at the development of concrete poetry in Brazil in its sociopolitical context, the words of Lucien Goldmann become highly relevant: "fragment is the expression of a quest for a right order that has not been successful."[21]

5 / Disruption of Style

In November 1985, Haroldo de Campos was invited to address the Biblioteca Freudiana Brasileira, a research group created in 1981 in São Paulo with the goal of promoting the study of Jacques Lacan in Brazil. On that occasion, Campos delivered the first version of "O A*freud*isíaco Lacan na Galáxia de Lalingua" ("The Aph*freud*isiac Lacan in the Galaxy of Lalangue" [Appendix 4]), an essay that he subsequently worked over several times until, in 1998, it was published in its final form in *Correio*, the journal of the Escola Brasileira de Psicanálise.[1] The subject of the essay was prompted by a meeting in Paris in the summer of 1985 between Campos, psychoanalyst Joseph Attié, and Judith Miller at the offices of the journal *L'Âne*[2] during which they discussed an upcoming issue of the journal, which was to be dedicated to style. On the spur of the moment, Campos proposed "Le stylo c'est l'Âne" as the epigraph to the issue.

A short, elaborate text grappling with complex psychoanalytical and literary ideas, "O A*freud*isíaco Lacan na Galáxia de Lalingua" provides a valuable road map for traversing *galáxias*, his masterpiece collection of fifty prose-poems written between 1963 and 1976 and first published in its entirety in 1984. Central to the essay is a concern for *style*, which Campos addresses from the start by commenting on Lacan's gloss on Buffon in the "Overture" to the *Ecrits*: "Shall we adopt the formulation—the style is the man—if we simply add to it: the man one addresses?"[3] With his proposed epigraph, Campos meant to add a further gloss on Buffon/Lacan in which *style* is playfully replaced by *stylo* (pen), and *l'homme* by *l'analyste*. The full passage is worth transcribing here:

> *L'ane* is short for *l'analiste*. *Stylo* (pen) comes to replace *style*, both—*style* and *stylograph* ("*stylo*" for short)—related to the same Latin word, *stilus*—a sharp instrument, made of metal or bone, with which one would write on wax tablets. This is, coincidentally, one of the meanings of the word *estilo* in Portuguese. One is also reminded that, in the same etymological region, the diminutive form of *estilo*, *estilete*, has been lexicalized as a *kind of dagger*, arriving to us via the Italian *stiletto*. It was thus by an act of metonymy—the trespassing of signifiers—that the manual instrument for writing came to designate the scriptural mark itself: the style.

Further down, Campos proposes to "close the hermeneutic circle" by adding a new variation: "Le stylo c'est le style." And in succeeding paragraphs, he traces a succinct diagram of Lacan's interest in style, drawing parallels between the psychoanalyst's famously obscure style and those of Luis de Góngora, Stéphane Mallarmé, and James Joyce.

When Georges-Louis Leclerc, Comte de Buffon, addressed the Académie Française in 1753 to deliver his "Discourse sur le style," he could not have envisioned the implications of such a humble effort, but the fact is, he set in motion a powerful engine that has engaged minds across the world for the last two centuries. One might venture to say that after Buffon's famous dictum "Style is the man himself," style became the embodiment of writing itself, and after this *aperçu* authors have been held accountable not only for *what* they write, but also for *how* they write. It would be hasty to claim that Buffon *initiated* a concern for style, as issues relating to style had occupied the minds of writers (and speakers) since the Greeks formulated the elements of rhetoric. But Buffon's equation of *man* and *style* introduced a new insight on the subject, which subsequently became the focus of writers such as Thomas de Quincey and Remy de Gourmont in the nineteenth century and, most notably, Jacques Lacan in the early 1950s.

At the end of his essay, Campos makes the case for *galáxias* to be inscribed within a tradition represented by Góngora, Mallarmé, and Joyce, and, addressing its innovative style, he suggests a kinship with the idea of the *writerly text* that Roland Barthes developed in *S/Z*: "novelistic without the novel, poetry without the poem, the essay without the dissertation, writing without style, production without product, structuration without structure." His quotation of Barthes continues:

> In this ideal text, the networks are many and interact, without any one of them being able to surpass the rest; this text is a galaxy of signifiers, not a structure of signifieds; it has no beginning; it is reversible; we gain access to it by several entrances, none of which can be authoritatively declared to be the main one; the codes it mobilizes extend as far as the eye can reach, they are indeterminable (meaning here is never subject to a principle of determination, unless by throwing dice); the systems of meaning can take over this absolutely plural text, but their number is never closed, based as it is on the infinity of language.[4]

Barthes's *ideal text*, as a matter of fact, shares many similarities with the mobile-like model that Campos proposed as early as 1955 in texts such as "The Open Work of Art." More, perhaps, to the point is the fact that Barthes's trope of the *starred text* also hints at a much earlier model for Campos: The sermons of Jesuit priest António Vieira, which indelibly shaped the Brazilian poet's vision of language.

The impact of Vieira's writings on Haroldo de Campos was first signaled in 1952 in "The Poem: Theory and Practice,"[5] with a reference to the expression "star chess" (*xadrez de estrelas*), an allegory that Vieira proposed in his "Sermão da Sexagésima" (Sermon of the Sixtieth), as a model of the ideal text. Vieira's image haunted Campos throughout his entire career and was used again in 1976 as the title for his first anthology. In fact, when we look at the titles of many of Campos's major works we immediately become aware of the recurrent trope of celestial bodies: *Xadres de Estrelas, Signantia Quasi Coelum, galáxias,* and even his last major work, *A Máquina do Mundo Repensada*.[6]

The object of many essays and dissertations, Vieira's "Sermão da Sexagésima" is an illustrious page of Brazilian-Portuguese literature and worth exploring here for its relevance to *galáxias*.[7] To start, we must note that Vieira's main argument springs from what he saw as a crisis occurring in language at the time. And the stakes of this crisis are enormous, as the ultimate goal of language for Vieira was its power to convert souls to God ("*Que coisa é a conversão de uma alma senão entrar um homem dentro de si e ver-se a si mesmo?*" [What thing is the conversion of a soul if not man going inside himself and seeing himself?]).[8] The crisis, as Vieira saw it, was the convoluted style of *cultism* or *culteranism* (pioneered by Góngora) that had become popular among missionaries. The opposition Vieira-Góngora problematizes with precision the contrasting forces at play in Campos's writing, most evidently in the *galáxias*: clarity versus obscurity, modernity versus the baroque. Although Campos never directly connected the *galáxias* to Vieira's sermon, he once maintained that the book's fifty fragments are essentially a "defense and illustration of the Brazilian-Portuguese language."[9] It is significant that, to explain his motivation for writing *galáxias*, Campos quoted a famous passage from the great Fernando Pessoa acknowledging his debt to Vieira,[10] but most importantly, the statement conveys the stakes the *galáxias* represented to Campos as he attempted to rally his contemporaries to explore the present possibilities of the Portuguese language.

Vieira's sermon addressed an audience of mostly Jesuit priests, and it argued that in order to be effective, the priest needed to make his style more *natural*. Taking as his point of departure the parable of the sower in Luke 8:5–8 as summed up in verse 11 ("Semen est verbum Dei"), Vieira tells his audience that preaching is like the broadcasting of seeds by a sower. "The style," he says, "must be very easy and natural" (*o estilo há-de ser muito fácil e natural*), "because sowing is an art that has more of nature than of art" (*porque o semear é uma arte que tem mais de natureza que de arte*). He then goes on: "In other arts everything is art . . . . Not so with sowing. Sowing is an art without art; it falls where it falls" (*Nas outras artes tudo é arte. . . . O semear não é assim. É uma arte sem arte, caia onde cair*). At this point in the sermon, Vieira inveighs against the *moderns* and pledges allegiance to the "most ancient preacher that ever existed": the sky. And he outlines his credo thus:

> Words are stars, sermons are composition, order, harmony and their course. See how the preaching style of the sky works, like the style Christ taught on earth. Both are sowers: the earth sown with wheat, the heavens sown with stars. Preaching ought to be like sowing, and not like making a mosaic or setting tile—ordered, but like the stars are ordered: *Stellae manentes in ordine suo*. Every star is ordered, but it is an order that exerts influence, not an ornate order. Did not God make the sky like a star chess game, just as the preacher makes the sermon as a word chess game?[11]

Barthes's rhetoric in comparison sounds no less cosmic and mystical:

> The text, in its mass, is comparable to a sky, at once flat and smooth, deep, without edges and without landmarks; like the soothsayer drawing on it with the tip of his staff an imaginary rectangle wherein to consult, according to certain principles, the flight of birds, the commentator traces through the text certain zones of reading, in order to observe therein the migration of meanings, the outcropping of codes, the passage of citations.[12]

This section in *S/Z* is subtitled "The Starred Text," and although Barthes's textual operations seem far more intricate than Vieira's vision, a case might be made for a shared sense of design, as randomness, or chance, seems to be the basic law of dissemination. "Let us learn from the sky," Vieira proposes, "the sense of design and of words" ("*Aprendamos do céu o estilo da disposição, e também o das palavras*"). And he continues:

> Stars are distinct and clear. Thus ought to be the style of preaching: distinct and clear. And do not fear that [your style when you speak this way] might sound like the low style; stars are very distinct, very clear, and of the highest [order]. Style can be very clear and high, so clear that those who do not know will understand, and so high as to offer something more to those who already know. The rustic finds in the stars directions for farming and the sailor for navigation and the mathematician for his observations and judgment. That is, the rustic and the sailor, who cannot read or write, understand the stars; and the mathematician, who has read all that has been written, can never exhaust that which is in [the stars] to understand. Thus can be your sermon: stars that everyone sees and very few can compass.[13]

Written a century after the "Sermão da Sexagésima," Buffon's "Discours sur le style" shares many basic characteristics with Vieira's text, starting with the fact that it was also delivered to an assembly of peers—the Académie Française. Style, in both texts, is understood as a technical matter to be discussed and shared among like practitioners. Like the *écrits* or the seminars of Jacques Lacan, one might add, these texts deal with a specific linguistic corpus shared by a highly specialized group. Buffon addresses the Académie thus:

> I have nothing to offer you, Gentlemen, save what is already your own: some ideas on style, which I have drawn from your works. It was in reading you and in admiring you that I conceived them; it is in submitting them to your intelligence that I am assured of their appreciation.[14]

The power of language to convert is equally present in Buffon: "In all other times there have been men who could rule others by the power of speech."[15] And while the star analogy is here absent, two other tropes are present: Style as a mirror reflecting nature's elegant design, and the trope of sowing, casting seeds upon the ground:

> Why are works of Nature so perfect? It is because each work is a whole, and because Nature works according to a plan from which she

never departs; she prepares in silence the germs of her production; she sketches in a single act the original form of every living being; she develops this, she perfects it, by a continuous movement and in a time prescribed. The resulting production astonishes us, but it is the divine imprint it bears that ought to strike us. The human mind can create nothing; it can produce only after it has been fertilized by experience and meditation; its acquisitions are the germs of its productions; but, if it imitates Nature in its procedure and in its labor, if it lifts itself up by contemplation to the most sublime truths; if it reunites them, if it binds them together, if by reflection it forms of them a systematic whole, it will establish on unshakable foundations monuments that shall prove immortal.[16]

Buffon, like Vieira, looks at natural phenomena in order to draw a lesson on style, and for both men, it seems, *semen est verbum Dei*.[17] To this tradition we could perhaps read Barthes's formulation "the seme is the unit of the signifier"[18] as a kind of post-structuralist transcreation of the biblical parable. The common ground for these men of such different persuasions, it seems, is their belief in language's power to reveal truth—religious, scientific, or textual—and Mallarmé's coinage "*syntaxier*" seems an appropriate term by which to categorize them. Regardless of personal investments, the concern for "style" in these texts will inevitably outline a textual economy that is highly translatable, whether the goal is to convert souls or to explain natural phenomena or the workings of textuality—or whether it is, as in Lacan's case, an integral part of the psychoanalytical process.

The first fragment of *galáxias*, with its emphasis on beginnings and measurement, makes an oblique reference to the "Sermão da Sexagésima" in that the act of *measuring* ("*meço aqui este começo e recomeço e remeço e arremesso/e aqui me meço*" [I measure here this start, and restart and remeasure and remit/and here I measure myself]) brings up the biblical notion of the Day of Judgment when all acts shall be weighed, *measured*. One might also find echoes of a passage in the Old Testament (Job 38: 4–7), that refers to the creation of earth:

> *Where were you when I laid the foundations of the earth?*
> *Tell Me, if you have understanding.*
> *Who determined its measurements? Surely you know!*
> *Or who stretched the line upon it?*
> *To what were its foundations fastened?*
> *Or who laid its cornerstone, when the morning stars sang together,*
> *and all the sons of God shouted for joy?*

In the "Sermão," addressing fellow missionaries on the responsibility attendant on their travels around the world, Vieira stresses accountability through the trope of measuring: "[Because] on the final day (day of harvest), our sowing will be measured, and our steps will be counted"[19] (*porque no dia da Messe hão-nos de medir a semeadura e hão-nos de contar os passos*). The Portuguese word *messe* means *harvest*, and the *dia* that Vieira refers to indicates the day of the *conversion of sinners*. Thus, there is a parallel here between the poet and the missionary: Both going around the world, measuring every shift in language, bringing their style into harmony with nature, the universe, and, by extension, God, in an attempt to reach men's souls. Note that the proximity between the two texts is also achieved at the homophonic level as Campos's riffs on the alveolar fricative sounds of ç and *ss*—in *meço* (I measure), *começo* (I start), *recomeço* (I restart), *remeço* (I remeasure), and *arremesso* (I throw)—echo Vieira's *Messe*.

It should be noted that despite echoes of Vieira's teachings throughout *galáxias*, Campos never thought of his book in religious terms, much less Christian. And even though he refers to *galáxias* as a "Baedeker of epiphanies" (in fragment 8) his use of the term does not carry the same weight Joyce had in mind when conceptualizing *Dubliners*. While Campos referred to *galáxias* as an *epiphanic text* on several occasions, he did not explain in detail its workings, nor did he make a clear connection with Joyce's use of the same model. In an interview with J. J. de Moraes in 1984, aptly titled "Do Epos ao epifânico (Gênese e elaboração das galáxias," Campos acknowledged that he first "intended to write an *epos* without a 'story,' or a text whose story was nothing and everything at the same time: a pluri-narrative, and the 'degree zero of narrating. From *epos* the project resolved itself as *epiphanic*.'"[20] And in a 2001 interview for the first issue of *Galáxia: Revista transdisciplinar de comunicação semiótica e cultura*, Campos confirmed that initially he planned *galáxias* to be an epic, until he realized that what he was doing was "weaving epiphanies, an epiphanic *tessitura*."[21] In contrast, Joyce approached the subject in his early novel *Stephen Hero* thus:

> This triviality made him think of collecting many such moments together in a book of epiphanies. By an epiphany he meant a sudden spiritual manifestation, whether in the vulgarity of speech or of gesture or in a memorable phase of the mind itself. He believed that it was for the man of letters to record these epiphanies with extreme care, seeing that they themselves are the most delicate and evanescent of moments.[22]

In contrast to the first fragment, which is all about starts and restarts, the final fragment in *galáxias* is about endings. It begins with a nod to Luis de Camões ("*musa nãomaisnãomais*"),[23] indicating the poet's exhaustion and inability to go on, and ends with a quotation from Dante's *Paradiso*[24] (*avrá quasi l'ombra della vera costellazione*) in which the (poet's?) mind attains nirvana (*se emparadisa*) within a "multi-book." In addition, references to Johann Wolfgang von Goethe's *Faust* reintroduce Vieira's "*dia da Messe*," ending the cycle of search (or traveling) initiated in the first fragment. In this fragment, the end of the book collapses with the end of the world ("*no fim do mundo o livro fina*" [the book dies at the end of the world]) and the possibilities of readings are again numerous: is the "*fim do mundo*" the biblical Apocalypse, or is it a geographic metaphor for Latin America? At the moment when the table turns, truth and lies become one ("*a mesa vira verdade é o mesmo que mentira*"), and, he adds in a beautiful succession of sounds: "*ficção fiação tesoura e lira*" (fiction, threading/trust, scissors and lyre). As on several occasions throughout *galáxias*, simple words are carefully chosen so as to defy one-dimensional interpretation, and any translation of *galáxias* must consider the high degree of ambiguity that Campos imparted to the simplest words. "*Fiação*," in this particular position, can be translated equally as "threading" or "trust." The *threading* in this context is in itself an act of *trust*, for in the final hour (*dia da Messe*) one will be measured according to the text(ture) one has produced.

> ... *mas tua alma está salva*
> *tua alma se lava nesse livro que se alva como a estrela mais d'alva*
> *e enquanto somes ele te consome enquanto o fechas a chave ele se*
> *multiabre enquanto o finas ele translumina essa linguamorta essa*
> *moura torta esse umbilifio* ...

> (... but your soul is saved
> your soul washes itself in this book that whitens itself like the palest star
> and while you vanish it consumes you while you lock it with a key it multiopens itself while you end it it transluminates this dead language this
> *moura torta*[25] this umbilical cord ...)

In this passage, the wordplay is as intricate as it is revealing. Through slight alterations in letter placement and/or replacement (*salva/alma/lava/alva/estrela d'alva* [the morning star, or Venus]), Campos sums up in a few lines the stakes of the journey he embarked on in the first fragment. In this final hour, after the death of language, the salvation of the soul is the ultimate reward—and here Vieira seems to meet Lacan, for the work on language, and on style, that both men pursued in writing seems to share a common ground. But while one might be led to read the first and last fragments of *galáxias* as elements of a ritual performance, his intent seems more in tune with the textual operations Mallarmé proposed in *Le Livre*, rather than a simulation of a religious mass.

For Campos, these two fragments that bookend the collection were conceived as *formants*, structural elements that "calibrate the interplay of mobile pages, interchangeable to reading, in which each isolated fragment introduces its 'difference' but also contains in itself, like a watermark, the image of the entire book."[26] In a 1984 interview with J. J. de Moraes[27] about *galáxias*, Campos commented that the work of Pierre Boulez inspired his idea of opening and closing the collection with *formants*. An avant-garde composer informed by atonalism whose career took off in the early 1950s, Boulez was drawn to the same literary influences as Noigandres, and his idea of a musical movement as *formant* is indebted to Mallarmé's concept of the poem as a constellation. In fragment 3, Campos pays explicit homage to Boulez by referring to *Pli Selon Pli* (fold over fold), a series of musical pieces based on poems by Mallarmé composed between 1957 and 1962: *"folha e refolha que se dobra e desdobra nele pele sob pele pli selon pli"* (leaf and leaf anew folding and unfolding itself skin on skin pli selon pli), hinting again at his own textual procedure. The text of *galáxias*, Campos observed in the same interview, has much to do with musical composition, whether avant-garde or popular. With its swirl of styles and citations, *galáxias* finds an equivalent in the sound collages produced by Alban Berg's highly complex and textured *Violin Concerto* (1935), which is written in the atonal style of Arnold Schoenberg with quotations from Johann Sebastian Bach and a Carinthian folk song.[28]

The reference to threading, or weaving in the final fragment, also signals another major theme in *galáxias*—that of writing as texture (Barthes's *tessitura*, in *The Pleasure of the Text*).[29] The theme of text (or narrative) as threading, weaving, is present from the first fragment—*"por isso teço"* (thus I weave); *"me teço um livro onde tudo seja fortuito e/forçoso"* (I weave myself a book in which everything is by chance yet forced)—and this common theme might stand as the leitmotif of the two *formants*. As in Barthes's analogy of the author as a spider that weaves its web (*hyphos*) from a bodily secretion, Campos's weaving originates from the *"umbilifio"* (umbilical cord). And as the text (weaving, web) is being produced, the author disappears, consumed in its production (*"enquanto somes ele te consome"*).

The Baedeker that Campos assembled in *galáxias* amounts to a mazelike structure of unknown cities for the reader to explore, for, despite claims to the contrary (*"isto não é um livro de viagem,"* in fragment 8), *galáxias* is indeed a book of voyages.[30] The idea of the book, as a matter of fact, might have come to the poet sometime in 1959, when, at the age of twenty-nine, and accompanied by his wife Carmen, he left Brazil for the first time to travel through Europe. An autobiographical sketch written in 1985 offers an introduction of sorts for mapping the *galáxias*:

> What has always mattered to me most was traveling. Epiphanies and anti-epiphanies. Ever since my first voyage, in 1959, when I left for Europe on a second-class ticket aboard the Portuguese ship *Vera Cruz* with Carmen, my lifelong companion. We caught a coldish April in Lisbon, traveled by train from Andalusia to Madrid, saw Hemingway and the bullfighter Antonio Ordonez at the Feria de San Isidro, left Spain for France via Irún, Puente Internacional (in the Basque country, the sculptor Jorge Oteiza put us up). Later, Germany (contacts with Max Bense and his group in Stuttgart, and with Stockhausen at the Studio for Electronic Music of the West German Radio (WDR), in Cologne; a visit to the Hochschule für Gestaltung, in Ulm), Switzerland (meeting with Gomringer in Zurich and Frauenfeld), Austria, Italy. We followed the route of Pound's *Cantos*, starting from Merano, then Tirolo di Merano, then Castel Fontana, where E.P.'s daughter Mary de Rachewiltz received us. Finally, E.P. in person and *persona* (still talking: "i punti luminosi"), in Rapallo, Via Mameli 23, interno 4, on a sunny August Tuesday, at 4 pm (*ore* 16). We returned to Brazil via Genoa aboard the *Provence*, stopping in Marseille to visit João Cabral, at the time our consul in the region. Then Recife, Salvador, Rio, Santos. Rediscovering Brazil via the world.[31]

What, one wonders, did these travels mean to the poet? What was their significance? Like the biographical note mentioned above, the *galáxias* are rich in specific references to events experienced by Campos in his many travels. As the unnumbered pages suggest, the reading of *galáxias* is not intended to be sequential (although the texts are displayed in chronological order, starting in November 1963, and ending in March 1976), and the references to places and people scattered throughout the series create a circular narrative. Most of the "information" dispersed throughout the fragments consists of obscure references to personal experiences, and those allusions and references can strike the reader as irrelevant, like the tiny rue Budé on the Île Saint-Louis, in Paris, that is mentioned in fragment 13, for example. Other references, however, memorialize important events for the poet, like "o prédio na via mameli tuesday 4 p.m." in fragment 33, which evokes a meeting with Ezra Pound in Rapallo. The third fragment, which begins with a line from Shakespeare's *Macbeth* ("multitudinous seas incarnadine"), deals most likely with his impressions of crossing the Atlantic for the first time, while other fragments suggest his route through European cities—Granada (fragment 2), Córdoba (fragment 5), Stuttgart (fragment 6), the Basque country (fragment 12), and so forth. His urge to travel, we must emphasize, should not be seen purely as *wanderlust*, but rather as a desire to meet and learn from the "great men of his time," as Pound once urged Hugh Kenner to do. Encoded in these narratives are meetings with Max Bense, Eugen Gomringer, Karlheinz Stockhausen, Octavio Paz, Hélio Oiticica, Marshall McLuhan, and Guimarães Rosa, among others.

Rediscovering Brazil via the world, turns out to be a central theme, as we can gather from fragment 15, often referred to as "Circuladô de fulô," in which Campos pays tribute to the popular art of minstrelsy as practiced in the Brazilian northeast. The text, inspired by a song Campos heard at a state fair possibly on the outskirts of Recife, was written between February 21 and 24, 1965. Its first lines (*"circuladô de fulô ao deus ao demodará que deus te guie porque eu não/posso guiá eviva quem já me deu circuladô de fulô e ainda quem falta me dá"* ['rounded by flowers under god's under the devil's mercy god shall guide you for I myself can't guide god bless those who give me 'rounded by flowers and those who are still to give]) seem to be a direct quotation from the original song, which to my knowledge has never been recorded or printed, nor its author identified. Fortunately, we do know enough about that tradition, for the literature on it is extensive, to infer what triggered Campos's interest. The tradition of troubadours, or minstrels, in the Brazilian northeast is believed to have its roots in the Provençal tradition by way of Portugal and the poet-king Dom Dinis, with his *"cantigas de amigo e de amor"* (songs of friendship and love). Like their European counterparts in the Middle Ages, the Brazilian troubadours are itinerant performers highly admired and respected by the communities that guarantee their survival. Some of the works of the earlier poets, going back to the seventeenth century, still survive through apocryphal texts that to this day circulate as *"literatura de cordel"* (*cordel* is Portuguese for a rope or yarn, and the expression denotes a kind of book that is displayed in street markets hanging from a cord stretched between two poles or hooks). The music of the *cantadores* is highly determined by the text, which is set to a rigorous meter that values cadence. The original excerpt quoted by Campos seems to have been written in the popular *sextilha* style, a verse composed of six lines of seven syllables each. The poet himself emulates the *cantador* in those parts of the text that feature a free flow of internal rhymes. But although he mentions one specific style—the *martelo galopado*, or "trotting *martelo*," named after its inventor, Pier Jacopo Martello, in the second half of the seventeenth century—his free-form style comes closer to the *mourão* ("big Moor"), the style of choice during a *desafio*, or duel between two *cantadores*, for its possibility of wordplay.

Campos's regard for this kind of literature, as a matter of fact, is both affectionate and intellectualized. In a sense, he is "rediscovering Brazil" via Pound. Consider the fact that the Brazilian troubadours are referred to in their area as *cantadores*, and their performances as *cantoria*. One is reminded that Campos's 1960 translation of Pound's *Cantos* (done in collaboration with Augusto de Campos and Décio Pignatari) was titled *Cantares*, although the word "canto" carries the same meaning in Portuguese.[32] He also compares the handmade instrument used by the *cantador* to a *shamisen*, the classic Japanese instrument used in Kabuki. Pound's presence is directly invoked by an allusion to *il miglior fabbro*, T. S. Eliot's famous borrowing from Dante for his dedication of *The Waste Land*. Furthermore, the indeterminacy of the expression "*circuladô de fulô*" also brings to mind the quandary regarding the word "noigandres."[33] Although both "*circuladô*" and "*fulô*" are misspellings, there is no doubt that "*fulô*" means "*flôr*" (flower). But "*circuladô*" can stand either for *circulado*, the past participle of the verb "*circular*," meaning "surrounded," or for the noun "*circulador*," meaning "the spinner." Thus, the phrase might be understood as "the one who makes the flowers spin."[34]

As a counterpoint to the haphazard geometry of the starry model, and the labyrinthian collage of cities and streets, the sea offers another central image for the kind of malleable writing that Campos sets himself to pursue—writing as a texture of shimmering lights and colors, the poem an epic enterprise navigating through unknown seas and guided by the stars. References to the sea start in fragment 3 with an allusion to *Macbeth* ("multitudinous seas incarnadine"), to later return more emphatically in fragment 45:

> mais uma vez junto ao mar polifluxbórboro polivozbárbaro polúphloibos polyfizzyboisterous weitaufrauschend fluctissonante esse mar esse mar esse mar esse martexto por quem os sinos dobram marujando num estuário de papel num mortuário num monstruário de papel murmurrúmor-remurmunhante escribalbuciando você converte estes signossinos num dobre numa dobra
>
> (once again by the sea polifluxbórboro polivoicedbarbarian polúphloibos polyfizzyboisterous weitaufrauschend fluxsounding

this sea this sea this sea this seatext for whom the bells toll sailoring on the paper estuary on a mortuary on a paper monsterary murmur-rumor-remurmuring write-babbling you convert these signs-bells into a toll into a fold)

Inês Oseki-Dépré, who translated *galáxias* into French in close collaboration with Campos, astutely detected a network of references throughout this fragment, starting with the well-known quote from John Donne ("for whom the bell tolls") that Ernest Hemingway used as a book title, and was later made into a Hollywood movie; another strain in the same fragment starts with T. S. Eliot ("these fragments I have shored against my ruins," from *The Waste Land*), slightly transformed by Ezra Pound ("these fragments you have shelved [shored]," in *Canto VIII*), to finally arrive in the *galáxias* as *estes signos você os ergue contra tuas ruínas ou tuas ruínas contra estes signos* (these signs you have shored them against your ruins or these ruins against these signs). Most impressively, however, the idea of networks is conveyed via translation work made throughout history and different geographies:

> Polyspeech [*polipalavra*] designates "polúphloisbos," Homer, but the whole literature in its historical process and development of "translation vowels floating against the mobile springing of consonants." Besides that, this Homeric word works like a touchtone of the text—Ezra Pound (who uses it in his poetics and criticism)—by the phonetic paradigm and also through Joyce's translation ("polyfizzyboisterous") and those of Voss ("weitaufrauschend") and the Brazilian poet Odorico Mendes ("fluctissonante"): all poetic transcreation. It means that the text includes also a theory of translation as poetic medium.[35]

Theoretical concerns aside, fragment 45 is also notable for its weaving of subjective, local material into a network of erudite quotations. (It is important to highlight that the texts that compose *galáxias* were written during a period of great censorship in Brazil that started in 1964 and lasted until 1984; a period when books, films, theater, and music had to be officially approved by the Department of Censorship of Public Entertainment. One of the outcomes of the imposed censorship was a search, on the part of many artists and intellectuals, for ways to communicate political views through highly codified language). Written in the summer of 1970, fragment 45 subtly captured Brazil's ethos during that dark period with a line from "*Cultura e civilização*," a song written by Gilberto Gil in 1969 that became an anthem for the emerging counterculture in Brazil: "*a cultura e a civilização, elas que se danem, ou não*" (culture and civilization be damned, or not). The genesis of the song is particularly poignant as it was written when Gil was in confinement, waiting to be exiled to London. Campos starts the fragment painting a stark scene of what had become of Brazil as the 1960s came to an end, distorting the legendary image of South America as Eldorado through grotesque portmanteaux that allude to *pain, bitterness,* and *death*: "*eldorido feldorado latinoamargo tua barrouca mortopopeia ibericaña.*" The deprecating tone of Campos's wordplay is in keeping with the refrained angst in Gil's lyrics, while also evocative of Lacan's subversive pun in "Lituraterre," which Campos explored in "O A*freudi*síaco Lacan na Galáxia de Lalingua." We could add, paraphrasing his own text, that in sections such as this, Campos's text slides between *letter* and *litter*.

In the previous fragment, also written in the summer of 1970, Campos had already struck a gloomy note about (the state of) language. Whereas in previous works language represented the mother (*idiomaterno*[36]), now he felt being cut loose ("*esta mão que corta um umbilifio*" [this hand that cuts the umbilical cord]), expelled, perhaps reflecting on the many exiled politicians and artists, like Gil, living in different language environments. Evoking Fernando Pessoa's words ("defesa e ilustração"), against the sudden realization of the death of (the Portuguese) language, the fragment opens on a mournful note: "*cadavrescrito você é o sonho de um sonho escrever em linguamarga para/sobreviver a linguamorta*" ("written cadaver you are the dream of a dream writing in bitter language to/survive the dead language"). Death of (this) language, the text seems to imply, has long been announced and Campos obliquely references the Romantic poet and translator Odorico Mendes, whose struggles with the Portuguese language were criticized by his contemporaries as "*macarrônico*" (macaronic): "*destrince esta macarroníada em malalíngua antes que/o portogalo algaraviando-se esperante o brasilisco.*" Impervious to translation, these lines amount to a manifesto of sorts as Campos urges the bard to "untangle this macaroniad in bad language" (a refence to Mendes's poorly received translation of the *Iliad* in the nineteenth century) before the guardians of the area (the portmanteau *portogalos* humorously puns on Portuguese roosters) transform the magical Brazilian speech (*brasilisco* seems to jam together Brazil and the mystic *basilisco* [ouroboros]) into a kind of Esperanto.

What, one might ask, is the style of the *galáxias*—if any—and what is the "defense and illustration of the Portuguese language" it purports to produce? A possible answer would be simply to point to the rich wordplay operating in the texts as a demonstration of the wealth of possibilities in Brazilian-Portuguese. But that assertion does not account for all that *galáxias* proposes to be. I propose that in weaving his galactic fragments Campos purposefully embraced disruption as a strategy—just like Vieira, who while preaching randomness, according to António José Saraiva,[37] structured his sermons like an engine, or a chess game. A more productive way to look at *galáxias* entails an incursion into literary history to appreciate its privileged position at the end of a specific cycle, for *galáxias* represented a radical departure from Noigandres' strict concretist program. With its multilanguage intertextual approach and strong narrative elements, it came at a pivotal moment, when notions of origin, borders, "center versus periphery" were being challenged by deconstruction theory. Following in the steps of concrete poetry's worldwide acceptance, *galáxias* departed from a postcolonialist perspective to defiantly propose a text entirely decentered, global, and polyphonic. In this new environment, *galáxias* reverts the movement of narratives like *Tristes Tropiques*, or for that matter, of Vieira's "Sermão." As Campos noted at the end of "Anthropophagous Reason: Dialogue and Difference in Brazilian Culture":

> To write, today, in both Europe and Latin America, will mean, more and more, to rewrite, to re-chew. *Oi Barbaroi.* The Vandals, long ago, crossed the borders and are crowding the senate and the *agora*, as in Cavafy's poem. Logocentric writers who imagined themselves the privileged beneficiaries of a proud one-way *koine* may now prepare themselves for the increasingly urgent task of acknowledging and re-devouring the differential marrow of the new barbarians of the polytopic and polyphonic planetary civilization.[38]

The disruptive style of *galáxias* ("polytopic and polyphonic") enacts precisely this barbarous moment of crossing borders, of playing on the *other's* field and not following rules. Not quite prose, and not quite a poem, this prose-poem celebrates hybridity on many levels and *affect us with effects* (again paraphrasing Campos on Lacan). No longer beholden to the strict modernist legacy that informed concrete poetry, *galáxias* can be seen as a true postmodern artifact, and as such it inaugurated a new era in Brazilian culture—or counterculture. The very plurality of styles that appeared in Brazil throughout the late 1960s and 1970s and that would later be brought together under the rubric of "*poesia marginal*" owes a debt to *galáxias*. The highly complex lyric of Waly Salomão's *Me segura qu'eu vou dar um troço* (1972), for instance, and the increasingly ambitious texts produced by Hélio Oiticica in the 1970s are post-*galáxias* texts, and perhaps inconceivable without it.[39] As we progress into the new millennium and new technologies continually challenge writing practices and our notions of geography, *galáxias* is invested of new significance as we identify in the work of a younger generation the same concerns that informed Haroldo de Campos's project. Paraphrasing Vieira, Campos's *sowing* found fertile ground, and it is in that sense that *galáxias* can be seen as his defense and illustration of the Brazilian-Portuguese language.

6 / Poetry and Modernity in the New World

Addressing a group of literary scholars at the Center for Brazilian Studies at Oxford University in October 1999,[1] Haroldo de Campos sharply criticized Fredric Jameson's dismissive critique of Guimarães Rosa's novel *Grande Sertão: Veredas* as "that curious Brazilian *high literary* variant of the Western," in his book *The Political Unconscious*. Campos argued that Jameson ignored the Brazilian Portuguese language and had "built a fake, oversimplified image of Rosa's masterpiece." Aptly titled "The Ex-centric's Viewpoint: Tradition, Transcreation, Transculturation," Campos's opening address to the conference was structured around core themes that he had engaged with throughout his career. Before rebutting Jameson, Campos addressed head on thorny issues related to the origins of Brazilian literature, which, he asserted, was born under the sign of baroque: "already born as an adult (like certain mythological myths) and speaking an extremely elaborate universal code—the baroque rhetorical one—in a quite self-assured manner." Given this non-infancy, he went on to say, Brazilians cannot think of themselves as a "closed and finished identity, but rather as difference, as overtness, as a dialogic movement of difference against the background of the universal." One of his final public addresses, Campos's "The Ex-centric's Viewpoint" can be read as the poet's literary *credo*, carefully laying out the role of translation as a process that keeps tradition alive: "Translation as transgressive appropriation and crossbreeding, as the dialogic practice of telling the other and telling oneself through the other, under the sign of difference." As it was, Campos's highly innovative understanding of translation had been masterfully demonstrated in his micro-epic poem *Finismundo: The Last Voyage*, an ambitious late work published in 1990 that considered the transmission of (literary) tradition—namely the myth of Ulysses—and as such can be read as a forceful rebuke to what he saw as the stereotypical views of third-world literature such as Jameson's.

In the same conference at Oxford, Italian scholar Piero Boitani presented a paper on *Finismundo*, placing the poem in a "wider *imaginaire*," as part of an "almost global intertext." Like Campos's, Boitani's view of tradition is generous, and in his essay, he calls attention to Ulysses's "ubiquitous presence in Western literature":

> Slowly, but with growingly significant results, the shadow of Ulysses moves to the Caribbeans and Latin America: Borges, Dário, Harris, Walcott, Carpentier, García Marquez, and many others. There also exists a specifically Portuguese tradition. This begins in classical antiquity and makes Ulysses the founder of Lisbon (Ulixabona). In due course, he becomes the ancestor of Vasco da Gama and Magellan. The names here include none less than Camões, Gabriel Pereira de Castro and Pessoa.[2]

Tapping onto this *global intertext*, Haroldo de Campos constructed a poem that aimed to operate on two registers; one concerning the transmission of tradition (i.e., translation), and another that strives to renew that tradition through procedures developed in the New World. More specifically, Campos meant to address in *Finismundo* the ambiguity of the line *thanatos eks halos*, in Canto XI of *The Odyssey*, which has challenged translators over the centuries due to its obscure syntax, for the line can correctly be translated as a death *far from* the sea, or *because* of the sea. The overall concept for the poem came to Campos via a semiology study by D'Arco Silvio Avalle on Dante Alighieri's attempt to solve the enigma surrounding Ulysses's death, in Canto XXVI of the *Commedia*. Another important source for the poem was Pessoa's "Ulisses," one of the poems in *Mensagem*, concerning the legend that Lisbon was founded by Ulysses.[3] Pessoa's haunting formulation *o mito é o nada que é tudo* (myth, the trifle that holds everything) is therefore a major motif in *Finismundo*, in that myth (as Boitani astutely suggested in his mixing of legendary and historical sailors) is the basis upon which our contemporaneous social structure lies.

Commenting on the structure of the poem in a conference in the mid-1990s, Campos proposed that the first half of the poem pays tribute to a "certain tradition" that he often found neglected in Brazilian literary history. In the broadest sense, Campos meant to address the translation work done over the centuries that has kept alive classics of literature such as *The Odyssey* and *The Iliad*. More specifically, he was referring to the work of Odorico Mendes, the nineteenth-century poet and translator from Maranhão whose Portuguese versions of works by Homer and Virgil were deemed by his contemporaries harder to read than the originals. As for the second half of the poem, Campos revealed that his intention was to put that tradition in question in an irreverent manner: "the same 'cultured' lexicon, some of Latin origin, some proceeding from the Greek, that denoted serious-aesthetic treatment in the first part is, in the second part, focused on a derisory manner."[4]

In 2002 Campos again commented on the structure of *Finismundo*, emphasizing that in the poem's second part a "modern Ulysses" takes over the scene, in "deliberate contrast" to the Hellenic Odysseus: "banal Ulysses made into an 'executive,' a *yuppie*, in a world abandoned by the gods." According to Campos, "this yuppie Ulysses no longer hears the Sirens—the Oceanids, the sea nymphs—but only the mechanical traffic sirens, while being directed by semaphores." This Ulysses is no longer the multitasking *polymetis* but merely a nameless *factotum*, "shipwrecked in the 'fluid green' computer screen that programs his daily disillusion." The poet proposes that, "the contrasting equation of these two moments—the transition of the Greek Odysseus into the contemporary yuppie Ulysses—poses to the reader an existential option and leave it open, without trying to impose a solution." He considers *Finismundo* a "post-utopian" poem: "Satire of a world in which ideologies reached a moment of crisis, and at the same time the celebration of the ceaseless adventure, always renewed, of knowledge and creation. In it, the creative operation is also an operation of translation." Here, Ezra Pound's motto "make it new" seems to overlap with Oswald de Andrade's concept of an "anthropophagic reason," which Campos defined as "the devouring, the mastication of universal cultural heritage, 'to nourish impulse': to renew. To reimagine past data (tradition in its most virtual activity) and reactivate it under the variety of Brazilian difference in vital and problematic instance of the present."[5]

The poem, he noted, is made up of what was "saved from the shipwreck between a past when epic gestures were possible and a present in which the Sirens become sirens, and the obstacles at sea are now turned into traffic hazards." The dilution of a classical tradition into the disconnected fragments of our contemporary era therefore seems to be the poem's main thrust, which Campos dramatizes in musical terms: "It's a poem to be read aloud, to be heard. Because what is behind this poem is the Homeric *melopoeia*, at least in the first part."[6] For the poem's second half, however, Campos aims to strike "a certain ironic tone that is part of a 'colloquial' strand in modern poetry, a certain modern verse that can be traced back to the early Eliot, the early Pound, a verse to be spoken, in certain moments, to be dramatized through some kind of prosodic, oral *mise-en-scène*."[7] The interest in colloquial speech pioneered by modernist poets such as Ezra Pound and T. S. Eliot is a subject important to consider as it suggests the role of the poet as the mediator between the *certain tradition* referred to by Campos, and everyone's usage of language in the great capitals of the industrial era. More to the point, a close analysis of Eliot and Pound's rapport with colloquial forms, and in particular the complicated use of "negro dialect" in their personal correspondence, exposes the very specific racial and social constructs of Anglo-American culture in the first half of the twentieth century.

In *The Dialect of Modernism: Race, Language and Twentieth Century Literature*, Michael North noted that "Pound used a strategy from the popular literature of his youth to create a mask for transatlantic modernism behind which he and Eliot might mock the literary capital they hoped to conquer," and he adds that this dialect became "in their correspondence an intimate code, a language of in-jokes and secrets," thus becoming "the private double of the modernist poetry they were jointly creating and publishing in these years."[8] Black speech—mostly acquired from Joel Chandler Harris's *Uncle Remus and Brer Rabbit* stories[9]—was not entirely reserved for personal exchange and eventually made its way into poetry, most notably in Pound's *The Pisan Cantos*.[10] North is not convinced that the Black characters and voices in Pound's text represent any substantial change in terms of race and class relations as they "function exactly as they did in the most reactionary examples of the dialect tradition to represent a mythical, 'lost' stability in American culture." And he adds: "The 'tradition' evoked by these black voices is the polar opposite of the modern world of jazz with its improvisation and mobility: it is rural, repressive, stratified and static."[11] Faced with the irreconcilable patterns of social-cultural displacements forged during the colonial era, the modernist utopia of an international, multivoiced community seems naïf in hindsight. Hence, any attempt to translate Pound's *make it new* strategy onto other cultural situations is bound to meet with different sets of particulars. In this regard, an analysis of Campos's engagement with Brazilian colloquial forms might help clarify how the conception of modernity in Brazil took a different slant according to local perspectives.

Explaining his personal attempt to rephrase tradition, Campos commented on his translation of Horace's "Persicus odi" which quotes the opening line from a widely popular samba by Noel Rosa and Vadico about an abusive restaurant patron pestering the waiter for cheap fares and free amenities:

> *Seu garçom faça o favor de me trazer depressa*
> *Uma boa média que não seja requentada*
> *Um pão bem quente com manteiga à beça*
> *Um guardanapo e um copo d'água bem gelada...*
>
> (Waiter, boy, please bring me quickly / a fresh cup of coffee, not reheated, / a slice of toast with lots of butter / a napkin, and a glass of iced water . . .)[12]

Campos's operation is an astute conceit as both Horace and Rosa were in a sense addressing the same issue, that is, the defense of a lyric stripped of ornamentation and closer to plain speech. Or, in Campos's words: "There is in the poem that typical Horatian situation of someone addressing the *puer*, the youth, who is pouring the wine, requesting that everything be done with the utmost simplicity, humbly, letting go of any luxury and Eastern fashions, so that all runs with ease in this joyful act of drinking wine."[13] In addition, Campos is also wittily commenting on how words cross geographical barriers (in this case, from the French *garçon* to the Portuguese *garçom*), often maintaining some of the original context. The translation by Haroldo de Campos starts with a nod to Rosa:

> *Garçom faça o favor,*
>   *nada de luxos persas.*
> *Nem me venha com estes*
>   *enfeites de tília.*
> *Rosas, não quero rosas,*
>   *se alguma, ainda esquiva,*
> *Resta da primavera.*
> *Para mim basta o mirto.*
>   *O simples mirto.*
> *O mirto com você*
>   *também combina,*
> *Puer, garçom-menino,*
>   *ministro do meu vinho,*
> *Que o vai servindo,*
>   *enquanto eu vou bebendo*
> *Sob a cerrada vinha.*

While Campos's strategy of renewing Horace by infusing the poem with Brazilian samba might strike as similar to Pound's use of "negro dialect," in reality it carried far different implications. Unlike the characters in *Uncle Remus* that were based on slave plantation folklore, samba mythology for the most part reflected a new social configuration related to the integration of the free slave, or their descendants, into the structure of the newly founded republic. Therefore, in contrast to the Black speech referenced by Pound and Eliot, samba sprung out as a quintessential urban phenomenon, and as such, it grappled with the novelties and mores that were to shape Brazilian modern society. As I have noted in the introduction to this volume, the first recorded samba, "*Pelo telephone*" (Over the phone), celebrated an invention that by 1917 had yet to be popularized in Brazil, while also introducing the figure of the *malandro*, the good-for-nothing bon vivant that will characterize the figure of the *sambista*. In his translation of Horace, it is the figure of the *malandro* that Campos would invoke as a simile of the poet.[14] This trickster figure that survives primarily on his ability to sweet-talk will later be invoked in the second part of *Finismundo* to signify Ulysses, Homer's man of many schemes. Ultimately, by bringing the myth of Ulysses onto the context of the *world's end*, Campos's poem reenacts the original meaning of translation from the Latin *translatio*, which referred to the transfer of relics from one place to another. The task of the translator, Campos seems to say, is to be attentive to the language of his/her time and make the ancient speak anew.

Although the first half of *Finismundo* makes use of collage technique akin to the one Pound mastered in *The Cantos*, channeling and overlapping many voices, and despite Campos's goal of making Greek *melopoeia* "sing in Portuguese," the effect still seems closer to a *graphing* of the voice than the cacophony he aspired.[15] Only in the second half does the poem seem to break free from the strictures of tradition to fully embrace the present and find its own voice. That voice, which Campos wanted to sound derisive, is the voice of the *malandro*, "factotum of chance," drowning amid the icons of a computer screen and the semaphores of the streets of São Paulo. The mood, if not the language, is reminiscent of the lyrics by the great São Paulo *sambista* Paulo Vanzolini that evoke loneliness and longing in the big city.[16] It is significant that in his search for the colloquial in *Finismundo*, Campos did not reference any of the great *sambistas* from Rio. His Ulysses is a *paulista* at heart: To paraphrase Charles Baudelaire, "*son semblable, son frère*." Therefore, unlike the happy *flâneur carioca* depicted by Jorge Caldeira in *A Construção do samba*, ("The discourse of the urban narrator of samba, the carioca *flâneur*, will be that of a happy person in opposition to the worker"),[17] Campos's Ulysses will be a menial worker lost in a double labyrinth of text and traffic.

In contrast, it is worth noting that Pound's years-long effort to translate Aeschylus's *Agamemnon* proved especially difficult, according to Alec Marsh, "because its tone, street-wise and incantatory, dignified yet informal was so difficult to capture."[18] In his informative essay, Marsh comments on a draft of an abandoned essay titled "For the Afro-American Language" in which Pound credited African Americans with the finest American speech: "One race and one race only has fostered in America a speech softer mellower and fuller than the south midland and having a charm not inferior to the 18th cent[u]ry phonetics preserved and tempered in our land."[19] In praising the vernacular, Pound seems to echo Rosa's appreciation for the contribution of the everyman to renew language; more importantly, it reveals the parallel routes taken by Pound and Campos in their pursuit of translating classic literature and make it relevant to contemporary readers.

In *A Construção do samba* (The Construction of Samba), Caldeira examined the figure of the *malandro* with great insight: "Like the fantasy that it entails, the *malandro* is also constituted as an element of language, a metaphor. More than a kind of behavior, it is connected with a certain discourse. Before being a social or historical figure, it is a figure of language, the embodiment of an aesthetic behavior, of style. He is the expression, in human shape, of swing, of the malleability and dynamic of samba itself."[20] Myth (Pessoa's nothing/everything) can only survive in language, and through language, for like in the case of the *malandro*, it is essentially a figure of language. Indeed, in those first decades of the twentieth century, the delivery and attitude in samba seemed to stem directly from language, leading to the perception that its highly original contribution was to create a distinctive speech pattern that would become synonymous with true Brazilianness; the *voz macia* (sweet voice) which, according to Noel Rosa excellent samba "*Sem traducão*" (Without Translation), distinguished the Brazilian language from traditional Portuguese. "*Sem traducão*" inveighs against the sudden invasion of foreign tongues in Brazil through the advent of sound film (the "talkies"). The song opens with surprising candor accusing the emerging technology of spreading new slang (*gíria*) and rhythms (foxtrot) throughout the hills (*morros*) around Rio. Rosa laments that the original vernacular created in the shantytowns, and that had been accepted and used early on by everyone in the city, was now being replaced by new trends.

> *O cinema falado é o grande culpado da transformação*
> *Dessa gente que sente que um barracão prende mais que o xadrez*
> *Lá no morro, seu eu fizer uma falseta*

A Risoleta desiste logo do francês e do inglês
A gíria que o nosso morro criou
Bem cedo a cidade aceitou e usou
Mais tarde o malandro deixou de sambar, dando pinote
E só querendo dançar o foxtrote
Essa gente hoje em dia que tem a mania da exibição
Não entende que o samba não tem tradução no idioma francês
Tudo aquilo que o malandro pronuncia
Com voz macia é brasileiro, já passou de português.

(The *talkies* are at fault for changing / people who now consider a shack more confining than jail. / In the favela, if I make a fuss, Risoleta, / will soon give up the French and the English. // The slang that the favelas invented / was quickly adopted by city folks / but the malandro soon after gave up samba, jumping around / and now only dances the foxtrot // Folks nowadays just want to show off / not understanding that samba does not translate into the French idiom / and that everything that the malandro utters / with sweet voice is Brazilian, way past Portuguese.)

Concocted in the hills surrounding the Guanabara Bay, recorded on vinyl, and aired via radio to the rest of the country, samba offered a radically urban alternative to the early modernists of São Paulo whose program was for the most part still responding to literary models set forth during Romanticism.[21] However, Caldeira notes that Rosa's composition style kept "closely related to the most advanced modernist procedures of the time, mainly with those of Oswald de Andrade's Pau Brasil poetry," in its juxtaposition of elements taken from Brazil's colonial and bourgeois phases, transforming the disjointed product into a "dignified allegory of the country."[22] Ultimately, the modernity of samba relied in its early embrace of emerging technologies such as sound recording and radio that entailed mass communication. As Caldeira keenly notes, recorded samba created a "narrative mode that allowed to account for the complicated ideological game of a society in transition."[23]

In his essay "Anthropophagous Reason: Dialogue and Difference in Brazilian Culture," Campos inveighed against literary critics like Antonio Candido and Afrânio Coutinho for the "logophanic substantialism" of their "models for reading tradition," singling out Candido in particular for his dismissal of our baroque origins in his classic study *Formação da literatura brasileira* (1959).[24] However, in Campos's analysis, Candido's assessment of Brazilian literary history went through a radical revision in 1970 when he published the essay

"*Dialética da malandragem*" (The Dialectics of roguery),[25] about the mid-nineteenth-century novel *Memórias de um sargento de milícias* (*Memoirs of a Militia Sergeant*), by Manuel Antônio de Almeida.[26] In exploring the novel's jarring style and structure, Candido linked it to the openness of Brazilian society during the monarchy, as compared to the highly structured and hierarchical society of other emerging nations like the United States: "Not wanting to build a homogeneous group and, in consequence, not needing to defend it so harshly, Brazilian society opened itself up with more largesse to the influx of dominated or foreign groups. And it gained in flexibility that which it lost in wholeness and coherence." The greatest insight in Candido's reading of Almeida's novel, however, is his analysis of the book's style and use of the colloquial in its depiction of a new social order ("this fact is evident in its style, that moves away from the preferred language of the romance of the era, looking instead for a tonality that has been deemed colloquial").[27] In the "universe without guilt" depicted by Almeida, Candido affirms, "we foresee the contours of a land without definitive or unredeemable evils, ruled by an enchanting moral neutrality. There one does not work, one does not have needs, and everything is remediable."[28] According to Candido, Almeida's antihero is the "first great malandro" to enter Brazilian literature, a kind of character that "would be elevated to the category of a symbol in Mário de Andrade's *Macunaíma*,"[29] and it is into this *derisive* tradition that Campos aims to insert his Ulysses. Also of note is Candido's use as a synonym for *malandro* the English word "trickster," an adjective often used to define Ulysses's character. Ever since its publication, Candido's formulation of a *dialética da malandragem* has become a major model to understand modern culture and society in Brazil. It's noteworthy that in *A Construção do samba*, for instance, Caldeira bases his analysis of the *malandro* character, the samba narrator, in Candido's seminal text. He notes that Candido's *romance do malandro* is characterized by a narrative strategy that "adopts the point of view of free men during the Empire, oscillating between order and disorder, lords and slaves, without taking any moral stand on these transitions."[30]

The transition Brazilian society was undergoing in the first decades of the twentieth century ought to be seen of course in the context of a global realignment in the aftermath of the Industrial Revolution when new technologies were becoming available worldwide. The technology of sound recording—starting with Béla Bartók's pioneering research on Hungarian folk songs around 1904—was a widespread phenomenon that revolutionized our perception of language as evident in the work of linguists such as the Abbé Jean-Pierre Rousselot, founder of experimental phonetics in France. According to Richard Sieburth, Rousselot "occasionally invited poets to his laboratories at the Collège de France to conduct experiments on the phonological analysis of poetic diction."[31] One of Rousselot's invitees was Ezra Pound who around 1912–1913 read his poem "The Return" into Rousselot's phonoscope. Another notable guest of the abbé was Guillaume Apollinaire. The importance of recorded sound and radio broadcast to modernist poets like Pound is not to be underestimated, and in "The Sound of Pound," Sieburth provides an insightful account of the poet's progressive engagement with both technologies, noting that despite his great interest in *melopoeia*, Pound's understanding of sound seemed out of step with his own era, and that ultimately, like in Rousselot's phonoscope, Pound's sound was more easily translated in graphic form.[32] That did not impede him from envisioning the future of writing as "a new medium, something between speech and action (language as cathode ray)." Sieburth also notes that, "as early as 1924, a mere two years after the BBC started regular programming, Pound was already comparing the montage technique of his Cantos to the medley of voices produced by tuning the radio dial."[33]

While *Finismundo* reveals the degree to which Campos was indebted to Pound's montage technique, it also underscores his personal engagement with Brazilian vernacular. Starting with the title, Campos seemed to be in pursuit of a text in dialogue with a complex network of foreign and local references. Note that the word *finismundo* first appeared in Campos' 1952 poem "Claustrofobia" ("In finismundo / the fenixbard awaits the finisnight"),[34] and it might be Campos's creative translation of the expression *finis terrae*, used in the Middle Ages to indicate the western limits of the world. One should note the apocalyptical implications of Campos's *finismundo* in contrast to the more geographically descriptive *finis terrae*. And while it's not certain that Campos had in mind Joaquim Manuel de Macedo's *O Fim do mundo*, a short novel that speculated that the Great Comet of 1556 would collide with earth in 1857, we can certainly associate *Finismundo* with a certain characteristic in Brazilian culture related to catastrophic scenarios. Macedo's earth-shattering anxieties seemed to have found popular support even beyond his time, a topic that was amusingly addressed in 1937 in Assis Valente's samba "*E o mundo não se acabou*" (And the world did not end), recorded by Carmen Miranda:

> *Anunciaram e garantiram que o mundo ia se acabar*
> *Por causa disso a minha gente lá de casa começou a rezar*

E até disseram que o sol ia nascer antes da madrugada
Por causa disso nessa noite lá no morro não se fez batucada
Acreditei nessa conversa mole
Pensei que o mundo ia se acabar
E fui tratando de me despedir
E sem demora fui tratando de aproveitar
Beijei na boca de quem não devia
Peguei na mão de quem não conhecia
Dancei um samba em traje de maiô E o tal do mundo não se acabou.

(The end of the world was announced and certified / Therefore, my folks at home started to pray. / It was also said that the sun would rise before dawn / And there was no music in the barrio that night. // I too believed that rubbish / And though the world was coming to an end / So, I decided to say goodbye to everything / Wasting no time to enjoy myself. / I kissed the lips of those I shouldn't / And held hands with people I did not know / I danced samba dressed in women's panties / And the damn world did not end.)

Toward the end of the 1960s, however, the idea of the *end of the world* deeply resonated with the loss of civil liberties under the military rule. Film director Rogério Sganzerla offered an apt visual translation in the opening sequence of *O Bandido da luz vermelha*, his landmark film from 1968. Against a collage of images drawn from tabloid headlines and semidocumentary scenes shot in the outskirts of São Paulo, a voice announced: "The Third World will explode." The same ethos was also projected that year by poet Torquato Neto in his lyrics for "Marginália II," composed in collaboration with Gilberto Gil: "*aqui é o fim do mundo / Aqui, o Terceiro Mundo / Pede a bênção e vai dormir*" (Here is the end of the world / Here, the Third World / Begs for blessings and goes to sleep). Written twenty years after the release of these seminal works of the Brazilian counterculture, *Finismundo* evokes that explosive cultural moment. But for Campos, "*o fim do mundo*" is São Paulo, the city where he was born and lived his entire life. Perhaps inspired by James Joyce, in *Finismundo* Campos brought Ulysses to the grounds he knew well.

It is worth noting that, considering the strong focus on architectural theory in the early Noigandres essays and that culminated in the 1958 manifesto whose title paid homage to the construction of Brasilia, it is surprising that the city, and specifically the city of São Paulo, was never a central subject for their work. With the exception of a few poems by Augusto de Campos that approached the thematic of the city in highly abstract manner,[35] the main focus for Noigandres remained in the terrain of language. Even Décio Pignatari, who most effectively weaved architectural themes into Noigandres' theory of concrete poetry, avoided approaching the city as a subject until the early 1970s, when he published his poem "noosfera"—perhaps the (concrete) poem that came closest to an image in step with the modernist model of the city as *unreal*. In contrast, Haroldo de Campos's approach to the city as a theme was more complex as it denotes for the most part, a subjective, quasi-autobiographical drive. With the exception of "*A Cidade*" (The City), an allegorical poem from 1951 included in the anthology *Xadrez de estrelas*, one is able to map out a series of personal references throughout his works, like the texts of *galáxias*, for example, or in "Ode (explícita) em defesa da poesia no dia de São Lukács" (1985), a *profession-of-faith*-like poem that situates the genesis of Noigandres in the context of an international avant-garde. The poem sets off restaging a visit Walter Benjamin paid to Bertolt Brecht in his country house on the island of Fin, Denmark, where the two men supposedly discussed the theories of György Lukács. The poem suddenly moves on to other subjects, and concludes celebrating the lifelong collaboration of the three Noigandres poets with humorous wordplay. For instance, the line "joyous mount of partridges" (in the original "monte alegre das perdizes") is a reference to Haroldo de Campos's lifelong address—Rua Monte Alegre, in the Perdizes neighborhood of São Paulo. Campos refers to himself and his brother Augusto as the "siamême twins," hinting to the closeness of their relationship; and add Pignatari as the third head in the formation of Noigandres, the *trigênios vocalistas*. A few lines down, Campos refers to critics of concrete poetry and their attempt to *decapitate* ("tricapitate") the three Noigandres poets. The poem ends with a nod to Noigandres' key contribution of introducing theories related to the ideogram into the poetic discourse in Brazil: "what's the big idea planting / ideograss in our backyard" (in Portuguese, "*grama*" translates as "grass").[36]

Considering the impact of São Paulo's speedy process of industrialization in the first decades of the twentieth century, Nicolau Sevcenko noted that "the city itself would become the source and focus of cultural creation, becoming a dominant theme, explicitly or tacitly. . . . More than a paradigm of order, as the Greek polis was conceived, or the perfect model of civil community, like Rome, the modern metropolis would be characterized as the original locus of an overwhelming chaos, and the matrix of a new emancipatory vitality."[37] In this new environment, Sevcenko suggested, it became necessary to foster a new diction ("fluid, sharp, plastic, discontinuous and multifarious"); echoing Paul Valéry's observation that with Baudelaire, French poetry overcame the stricture of the French language to take its place as the true poetry of modernity.[38] For Sevcenko, the new diction was captured in Brazil by poets like Manuel Bandeira, whose 1919 collection of poems *Carnavais*, "expressed the modern *elán* of total surrender, the blinding passion of intensity as an end, the thrill of belonging to a superhuman collective force";[39] or Rui Ribeiro Couto (1898–1963), whose 1926 collection *O Homem na multidão* (The Man in the Crowd) reunited "powerfully demobilizing poems detached from formulae and indifferent to expectations."[40]

The *demobilizing power* of modern poetry in Brazil would reach a high point in the early 1930s with Carlos Drummond de Andrade's enigmatic "*Cota Zero*" (Point zero), which brutally pitched man against machine as an existential quest ("STOP / A vida parou / ou foi o automóvel? [STOP / Has life come to an end / or was it the automobile?]). However, one must consider that the lyrics that best conveyed a radical image of modernity came from poets disenfranchised from the modernization process and who, although living on the margins of society, best understood the new means of communication production and dissemination. Lyrics like "*Três apitos*" (Three steam whistles, 1933) by Noel Rosa, whose title refers to the three signals that sounded early in the morning to wake up workers living in the surroundings of a factory. Rosa pointedly comments on the stress industrial labor had on the poet's private life: "*Quando o apito / da fábrica de tecidos / Vem ferir os meus ouvidos / eu me lembro de você*" (When the steam whistles / from the fabric factory / hurts my ears, / I think of you); and brings up his jealousy of the impertinent manager who bosses his beloved around: "*ciúmes do gerente impertinente / que dá ordens à você*." An antipathetic view of the modern city pervades most of the samba produced in the early decades of the twentieth century and culminates in the 1970s in lyrics like "Sinal fechado" (Red light, 1970), by Paulinho da Viola, which portrays two friends briefly connecting at a traffic spot: "*Me perdoe a pressa, é a alma dos nossos negócios*" (I apologize for rushing, but it is the nature of the business); and most poignantly in Cartola's "*O Mundo é um moinho*" (The World is a mill), 1975, in which city life is described as a cruel machinery that reduces one's dreams to dust: "*Preste atenção, o mundo é um moinho / Vai triturar teus sonhos, tão mesquinho / Vai reduzir as ilusões a pó*" (Pay attention, for the world is a mill / it will grind your petty dreams, / it will reduce your illusions to dust).

For Haroldo de Campos, the urban experience is best expressed through a mixture of voices, old and new, like in his poem "são paulo,"[41] which strikes a confessional tone at the opening of the second section by evoking Mário de Andrade, and Torquato Neto: The lines "*mas eu / paulista paulistano / confesso que amo*," echo both Andrade's "*sou passadista, confesso*" (I am a confessed nostalgic), the sixth paragraph in his "Prefácio interessantíssimo" in *Paulicécia desvairada*; and Torquato Neto's "*eu brasileiro confesso / minha culpa meu pecado*," from *Marginália II*. Whether the citation was intentional or not, the fact remains that these rather straightforward lines are rich of meaning as they collapse two periods in Brazil—the hopeful years of early modernism, and the frantic era unleashed by the military coup in 1964 that culminated in the counterculture of the 1970s. This juxtaposition further elucidates the trajectory of Haroldo de Campos as a poet trained in the wake of Brazilian modernism, coming into his own during the years of concretism, and witnessing the beginning of a new moment that, to paraphrase Allen Ginsberg, lost its best minds to madness. The city, as evoked by Campos in "são paulo," shows the ugly face of modernity with its clash of viaducts, buildings, and the crowds, and the poem in many ways reads as an expanded version of the second section of *Finismundo*.

Reminiscing about his first visit to São Paulo in 1935, Claude Lévi-Strauss noted that the newly built districts were not integral to the urban scene, "too gaudy, too new, too gay," and compared them to "pavilions of some international exhibition."[42] To paraphrase Mário Pedrosa, São Paulo was "condemned to modernism,"[43] what's more, a modernity that did not have an infancy, as Campos noted of our allegiance to the baroque. Given this particular conjecture, it is not surprising that the reception of Brazilian literature by first-world scholars and writers has often been *oversimplified*. And to be fair, Jameson is not alone in his dismissal of Brazilian literature, as Marjorie Perloff keenly observed in *Unoriginal Genius: Poetry by Other Means in the New Century*, quoting from a letter by Elizabeth Bishop to Robert Lowell: "They are doing something in Rio now called 'concretionism' [*sic*]. It seems like pre-1914 experiments, with a little 'transition' & Jolas, and a dash of Cummings. It's awfully sad." Perloff, who became an attentive reader of Noigandres, noted in the same essay that concretism, "cutting edge as it was vis-à-vis the normative verse or painting of its own day, transformed the Utopian optimism and energy of pre–World War I years into a more reflective, self-conscious, and complex project of recovery."[44]

Commenting on the development of concrete poetry throughout the 1950s and 1960s, Campos wrote that after the 1964 coup, Brazilian poetry "emptied itself off its utopian function (despite, paradoxically, an emerging electronic technology hinted to unforeseen possibilities that seemed to materialize Benjamin-Mallarmé's prophesy of a universal iconic writing)." And he cautioned:

> Without the utopian perspective, the avant-garde loses its meaning. This means that the viable poetry of the present is a poetry post-avant-garde, not post-modern or antimodern, but post-utopian. The totalizing project of the avant-garde, that at its limit can only be sustained by a redeeming utopia, is thus succeeded by a pluralization of all possible poetics. Thus, the hope-principle, turned to the future, is succeeded by a reality-principle. I agree with Octavio Paz that today's poetry is a poetry of the "now," (*Jetztzeit*, a term dear to Walter Benjamin): a poetry of the "present other," that implies a "critique of the future" and of its systemic paradises. This poetry of present time, in my way of seeing, ought not to make possible a poetic of renunciation, nor be an alibi for a regressive eclecticism or to leniency. Instead, the admission of a "plural history" instigates us to the *critical* appropriation of a "plurality of past eras," without a previous determination of the future. Hence, the present "post-utopian" poetry, has, as the present time poetry, an indispensable critical dispositive in translation practice. The translator, as Novalis said, "is the poet of the poet," poetry's poet. Translation—considered as a practice of reflexive reading of tradition—allows us to recombine the plurality of past eras and make them present, as difference, in the uniqueness *hic et nunc* of the post-utopian poem.[45]

Not postmodern, or anti-modern, *Finismundo: The Last Voyage* enacts the shift (the translation) from a past of grand gestures represented by the epic form, to arrive at a poetry of the now.

Acknowledgments

A number of the essays featured in this volume were previously published in various journals and anthologies and I am indebted to the editors who invited me to collaborate and granted permission to reprint: Anne Thurmann-Jajes, curator of *Poetry—Concrete* (Weserburg Museum, Bremen, Germany); Marjorie Perloff and Craig Dworkin, editors of *The Sound of Poetry / The Poetry of Sound*; Kenneth David Jackson, Marjorie Perloff, and André Valias editors of *Augusto de Campos at 90* (Santa Barbara Portuguese Studies vol. 8); Andrea Andersson, editor of *Postscript: Writing After Conceptual Art*; and Andréia Guerini, Simone Homem de Mello, and Walter Carlos Costa, editors of *Haroldo de Campos: Tradutor e traduzido*. Many thanks to Declan Spring and Christopher Wait at New Directions Publishing for their guidance on matters related to the papers of Ezra Pound, and for facilitating the use of excerpts from those letters, and images of letters, drafts, and archival materials in this book. Augusto de Campos has been a generous interlocutor throughout the years and whatever I got correct in these pages, much credit goes to him. I thank him for his guidance as well as for his permission to use excerpts from his writings including his poetry. Raquel Campos has been generous in allowing me to use excerpts from the writings and poetry of Haroldo de Campos. I also thank Elliot Aboutboul and Serena Pignatari for kindly granting permission to use excerpts from the writings and poems of Décio Pignatari. I have benefited over the production of these essays from a sustained dialogue with colleagues such as Lenora de Barros, João Bandeira, André Vallias, and Eduardo Jorge de Oliveira. More recently, the careful review of my manuscript by two anonymous readers has brought many important issues to my attention and for that I am grateful.

I am grateful to Fredric Nachbaur, and his colleagues at Fordham University Press, Kem Crimmins, Thomas Lay, Haun Saussy, and Lazar Fleishman for making this book possible.

Appendix 1: The Noigandres / Ezra Pound Correspondence

This chronology is based on an outline provided by Augusto de Campos to Professor Kenneth David Jackson, director of Undergraduate Studies for Portuguese at Yale University. Additional material was excerpted from letters in the collection of the Beinecke Library (Ezra Pound Papers— YCAL, MSS 43—Box 37, folder 1571);[1] three letters by Pound reprinted in Ezra Pound POESIA, trans. by Augusto and Haroldo de Campos, Décio Pignatari, J. L. Grünewald, and Mário Faustino, 2nd edition (São Paulo: Editora Hucitec, 1985); and a letter by Pound reprinted in Augusto de Campos, "Pound Made (New) in Brazil," A Margem da margem (São Paulo: Companhia das Letras, 1989), 104–7. Images of letters, drafts, and archival materials by Ezra Pound, New Directions Pub. acting as agent, copyright ©2025 by Mary de Rachewiltz and the Estate of Omar S. Pound. Reprinted by permission of New Directions Publishing Corp.

***

1952
Following the release of the first issue of Noigandres, *Augusto de Campos, Haroldo de Campos, and Décio Pignatari mailed a copy to Ezra Pound, the poet whose interest in the Chinese ideogram, among other things, had been an important point of reference for the group.*

1953
Interned at St. Elizabeths Hospital, in Washington D.C., following his release from an Italian prison in Pisa in 1946, Pound received the gift as a

charming homage, and acknowledged receipt in a handwritten letter dated January 26, 1953:

> Thank you
>
> the rhyme is
> perhaps delayed 46
>   years
>   a.d.
>   Spaniard   1906   "Where from"
> young
>   American Traveler:
> "America"
>   Sp. = "del Norte   o del Sur?"
>   Am. Tr.
> "Estados Unidos"
>
>   Sp. (with all ironic contempt
> of Andalusia pre-
> Columbus)
>
>   "Los Estados Unidos
>   de America, Señor, o
>   los Estados Unidos
>   de BraTHil?"
>
> in short travel as prelude to Kulchur
>
> It
> looks lively
> as far as I can make out
>   from the 6
>   lines of Camoens
>   I remember
> best for the coming decade
> Ez. P.
> St. Elizabeths Hospital
> Washington D.C.

Pound's letter was followed two days later (January 28, 1953) by a note suggesting an exchange between Noigandres and Shenandoah.

In an undated reply, the Brazilian poets enthusiastically greeted Pound, and included clippings of an article by Augusto and Haroldo de Campos

("Ezra Pound: A Beleza é Difícil" [Ezra Pound: Beauty is Difficult]) published in O Diário de São Paulo, August 16 and 28, 1953.

>   Doing our best
> to introduce EZRA POUND into a...
>   <u>half savage country</u>?
>
> As to Brasil
>
> <u>My dear</u> E.P. your 1/2 wd. be too moderate
>
> Nobel Eliot very much known here. But we suspect
>   scarcely read.
>
>   E.P. little known and literally not read.
>
>   Joyce not read   cummings not read
>
>   Also working on the translation of a few "Cantos",
>   and "ABC of Reading" and "A Few Donts".
>
>   "E.P.: Beauty is difficult": would you accept it,
>   In spite of all possible errors, as humble homage from
>   the very young?
>
>   Letter, communications, "ORO E LAVORO" received.
>   How can we thank?
>
>   Excuse broken English (The couched Brazilian jaguar)
>   Pity the young.

On November 27, Pound sends an effusive letter to the group (see figure 24):

> Bright Brazilians,   blasting at bastards
> no mais prohundo hundo   das prohundas
> my brazilian wd/ be broken worse than that if I tried to
> continue for more than 3 lines of Camoens
>   cavernas altas dond o mar s'esconde

la dondas undas sahem furibondas
                              etc. p// or
bes linda Ihnes.
no sa
***

Thank you very much. And for PRACTICAL purposes (namely that grandpa OUGHT to be let out of the caleboza SOMEtime /

what with all the damn double crossers getting nervous and

the infiltration etc/ leading to hysteria re/ MacCarthy, who is in voice and on television the calmest and most factual . .

Can you get copies of Diario and send em to

my daughter. Mary de Rachewiltz, Schloss Brunnenburg-Tirolo Merano, Italy.

O.R.Agresti, 36 via Ciro Menotti, Roma, Italy.
Eva Hesse   Franz-Josefstr 7, vi, Munchen 23, Germany

Hugh Kenner, 1415 Bluff Drive, Sta Barbara, Calif. U.S.A.
Denis Goacher, 38 a. Gt. Russel St. London, W.C. 1. England.

** I shd/ have started: thank god that after nearly five decades , or better thank to Rennert for having forced me to do: term in portagoose, contra voglia I can still follow yr/ meaning
          and given six weeks in Sao P/ cd/ probably buy a tram ticket or a cup of coffee.
This damn ribbon seems to be getting
plale.//

On the plane of strict utility. The enemy is Ignorance / black and squalid.
and Sao Paolo, perhaps one of the best places whence
to   smack down both the wop and yank smear.

Note, and NOTE, and continue to note the s.o.b. technique. the LIE reiterated and stuck to. The CONtinual messing of terms. sic. nazi-fascist.
There were NO gas ovens in Italy.
even Ed. Hoover, smacking down the worms, most clearly

27 Nov 53

Bright BRazilians , blasting at bastards

no mais prohundo hundo das prohundas

my brazialian wd/ be broken worse than that if I tried to
continue for more than 3 lines of Camoens

cavernas altas dond o mar s'esconde
la dondas undas sahem furibondas
etc. p/ or

no sa bes linda Ihnes.

***

Thanks very much. And for PRACTICAL purposes (namely that
grandpa OUGHT to be let out of the caleboza SOMEtime /

what with all the damn double crossers getting nervous and
the infiltration etc/ leading to hysteria re/ MacCarthy , who
is in voice and on television the calmest and most factual ..

Can you get copies of Diario and send em to

my daughter. Mary de Rachewiltz , , Schloss Brunnenburg-Tirolo
Merano , Italy.

O.R.Agresti , 36 via Ciro Menotti , Roma, Italy.
Eva Hesse   Franz-Josefstr 7 , vi , München 23 , Germany.

Hugh Kenner , 1415 Bluff Drive, Sta Barbara , Calif. U.S.A.
Denis Goacher , 38 a. Gt. Russel St. London , W.C. 1. England.

** I shd/ have started: thank god that after nearly five decades
, or better thank Rennert for having forced me to do 1 term
in portagoose , contra voglia , I can still follow yr/ meaning
        and given six weeks in Sao P/ cd/ probably buy a tram
ticket or a cup of coffee.
                    This damn ribbon seems to be getting
plale.//

On plane of strict utility. The enemy is IGnorance / black and
squalid.
        and Sao Paolo , perhaps one of the best places whence
to smack down both wop and yank smear.

Note, and NOTE , and continue to note the s.o.b. technique.
the LIE reitterated and stuck to. The CONtinual messing of
terms. sic. nazi-fascist.
                There were NO gas ovens in Italy.
even Ed. Hoover , smacking down the worms, most clearly

FIGURE 24. Ezra Pound, typewritten letter to the Noigandres poets dated November 27, 1953. Copyright ©2025 by Mary de Rachewiltz and the Estate of Omar S. Pound. Reprinted by permission of New Directions Publishing Corp.

1954

A letter from Noigandres to Pound, dated March 22, 1954, humorously referred to a supposed manifesto sent by the latter:
  "thank you very much for your unsigned PAPAFESTO."
  This letter is missing in the holdings of Beinecke Library, but according to the outline prepared by Augusto de Campos, it included clippings of two of his essays ("Poesia estrutura" and "Poema, ideograma") published in O Diário de São Paulo, March 20 and 27, 1954, respectively.

1955

The next letter from Pound arrived a year later. Dated April 7, 1955 (see figures 25 and 26), the text is fragmentary, and includes cryptic references to Stéphane Mallarmé.

> as to me an' Mallarmé getting to Sao Paulo, simult.
> and as to what a small segment of the race runs its KULCHUR,
> it might amuse you to know that in 1897 MMHHm
> an imaginary spectator might have seen a y.m. on bicycle
> rushin that copy of Cosmopolis around London, the same
> known to me later as HH " Bunk " Tucker (Bunk equiv.
> oncle), my wife uncle, and cousin of Lionel Johnson.
>   And as M. Ortmans or wotever he was called left H.T.T.
> I believe " holdin' the bag " or whatever. At any rate
> Bunk havin been left out of pocket and disillusioned
> re/ the nature of belgians or frogs or wh[at]ever, never did
> another stroke of work till come 1914, by which time he
> rolled bandages or did something or other.
>
> Has " Vanni" sent you his wop-lications?
> Alzo, ABC [ROMA woptaly] for 16th March has the most sober
> artl/ yet
> to appear in woptaly / re "Lavoro ed Usura ". AND
> then the Stewed Erection's edtn/ tho cd/ not have come to
> be without the latter.
>
> Also Kenner in the Sewing Circle gazette on 85.
> And TRAXINIAI done at Yale, with what they tell me is
> decent musical setting of Xoroi. (already three
> time transmitted by BBC.)
>
> in fact the lousy radio of Baruchistan under the
> Roosenhauer regime, seemen, to be gittin lonely in
> its boycott. Germany, Woptaly. England, and Australia in

prospect.
Forget if you communicate with Forssell in Stockholm?

AND of course the " timely pubctn/ of the documents
relating to Yalta, shd/ be as balm to the parcched
I suppose it wd/ be tactful, under present circs/
to keep a few pertinent verses inedit for HHH
another few minutes.

Venzuelan consul iib New Orlens has had the bright
idea that the time approaches when it might be useful to
indulge in a little criticism of the BASIC drives,
the " underlying philosophies # of different writers
of our buggared atomic age.
  The really degraded state of a lot of the advertised
Yanks. spewlitzers prize pups etc. OUGHT to supply
food for satire SOMEWHERE.
        Possibly grampa [is] becoming irritated
after ten years in jug, and none of the crablice
coming up with ANY comment whatsodam on the basic
issues raised in the discorsi da Roma.
  It is NOT the real Etats Unisien tradition.
a century ago American writers were not brilliant
technicians / But they were not pussillanimous lice,
scared out of their diapers, mind-conditioned, and
licking the boots of the publishing business.
  Old Whiskers Cullen Bryant beat ø up some
bastid on Broadway for an insult to Andy Jackson, etc.
  The slow degradation under the reign of a cad, liar and
perjurer, has NOT elevated the tone of american letters.
  I wonder if you can send copies of yr/ artl/ to
Dom J.B. de Pina Martins, co/ O.Rossetti Agresti
  36 via Ciro Menotti, Roma, Italy
Swedish and German translations any use to you?
  try Eva Hesse, Franzjosef str 7. vi
    Munchen 13, Germany.

[continuing on verso]

and I shd/ say NOIGANDRES to
    Wm Fleming (poet 1955) 71 Hodgkinson St
            Clifton Hill, Melbourne, Australia
    &   muy simpatico
    Roger Bodart, civilized poet, pre-Mallarmeen
            23 rue Rene Christainens, Auderghem, Brx
                Bruxelles, Belgique.
whether either can translate Belgca Dif/ or present
    Mallarmé / obviouslythe latter shd/ get to
Bodart's review, I forget the name of it, but IT AINT
the journal d.poetes

[another fragment on verso]

    as to the Mexican edtn/ of Cantares Pisanos
    yr/ guess is as good as mine. The nobl
responsibl was hoping to get it printed before he
got the sack.

You do see the Hudson? or not?
    yes, yes, Noigandres v. nicely printed.

        There WAS copy of the original issue of Cosmopolis
in my ma-in-laws flat, which I must have picked up and sent to
Rapallo in 1938 / but I don't remember seeing since then.
Hope it hasn't been LIBERATED

On December 30, 1955, Augusto and Haroldo de Campos sent the following letter, which also included a clipping of Haroldo de Campos's essay "Pontos definem uma periferia" (Points define a periphery) published in the magazine Forum:

Dear Mr. Pound,

    The Brazilian Ministry of Education (letter enclosed), through the Service of Cultural Diffusion, accepted our proposal of publishing a selection of the <u>Cantos</u>, translated into Portuguese, with an introduction, commentaries and bio-bibliography. Cantos I, II, III, IV, VII, XII, XIII, XLV and fragments of Cantos LXXIX, LXXX and L will compose this non-commercial, bilingual edition to be distributed throughout Brazil to universities and individuals interested in receiving it. We are now working on the revision of these Cantos, which are

7 Ap/

as to me an' Mallarmé getting to Sao Paulo , simult.
and as to what a small segment of the race runs its KULCHUR,
it might - amuse you to know that in 1897 MMMHHM
an imaginary spectator, might have seen a y.m. on bicycle
rushin that copy of Cosmopolis around London , the same
know/to me later as HH " Tucker (Bunk equiv.
oncle) , my wifg uncle , and cousin of Lionel Johnson.
       And as M. Crtmans or wotever he was called left H.T.T.
I believ/e " holdin' the bag " or whatever. At any rate
Bunk havin been left out of pocket and disillusioned
re/ the nature of belgieans or frogs or whexar , never did
another stroke of work till come 1914, by which time he
rolled bandages or did something or other.

Has " Vanni" sent you his wop-lications ?
Alzo . ABC for 16th March has the most sober artl/ yet
to appear in woptaly / re " Lavoro ed Usura ". AND
the wop-stone classics (Kung) Pivot is a neater vol/
than the Stewed Erection's edtn/ tho od/ not have come to
be without the latter.

Alzo Kenner in the Sewing Circle gazette on 85.
And TRAXINIAI done at Yale , with what they tell me is
decent musical setting of Xoroi. (already three
time transmitted by BBC.)

In fact the lousy radio of Baruchistan under the
Roosenhauer regime , seemeñ, to be gittin lonely in
its boycott. Germany , Woptaly . England and Australia in
prospect. ale (und) o—
Forget if you communicate with Forssell in Stockholm ?

AND of course the " timely pubctn/ of the documents
relating to Yalta , shd/ be as balm to the parched
I suppose it wd/ be tactful , under present circs/
to keep a few pertinent verses inedit for MHH
another few minutes.

Venzuelan consul ib New Orleans has had the bright
idea that the time approaches when it might be useful to
indulge in a little criticism of the BASIC drives,
the " underlying philosophies # of different writers
of our buggered atomic age,
       The really degraded state of a lot of the advertised
yanks. spewlitzer prize pups etc. OUGHT to supply
food for satire SOMEWHERE.
              Possibly grampa becoming irritated
after ten years in jug , and none of the crablice
coming up with ANY comment whatsodam on the basic
issues raised in the discorsi da Roma.
       It is NOT the real Etats Unisien tradition.
a century ago american writers were not brilliant
technicians / But they were not pusillanimous lice ,
scared out of their diapers, mind-conditioned , and
licking the boots of the publishing business.
       Old Whiskers Cullen Bryant beat ∅ up some
bastid on Broadway for an insult to Andy Jackson , etc.
       The slow degradation under the reing/ of a cad, liar and
perjurer, has NOT elevated the tone of american letters.
       I wonder if you can send copies of yr/ artl/ to
Dom J.B. de Pina Martins , c/o O.Rossetti Agresti
              36 via Ciro Menotti, Roma , Italy
Sweedish and German translations any use to you ?
       try Eva Hesse , Franzjosef str 7. vi
              Munchen 13, Germany.

FIGURE 25. Ezra Pound, typewritten letter to the Noigandres poets dated April 7, 1955, front. Copyright ©2025 by Mary de Rachewiltz and the Estate of Omar S. Pound. Reprinted by permission of New Directions Publishing Corp.

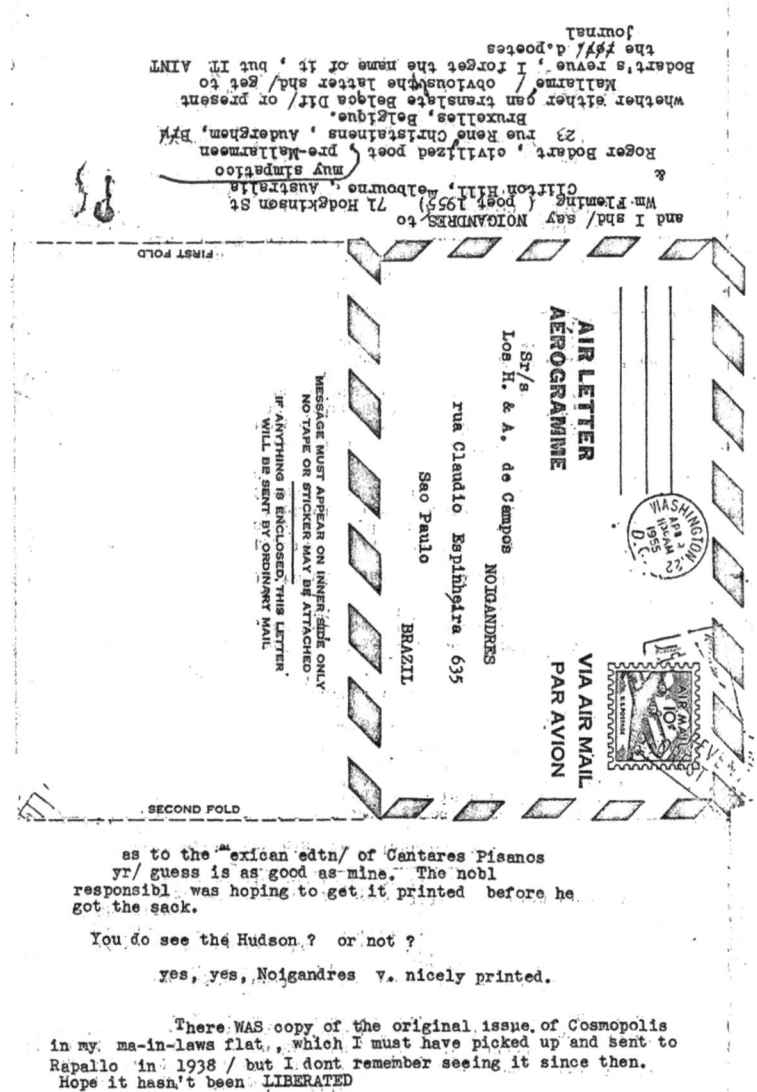

FIGURE 26. Ezra Pound, typewritten letter to the Noigandres poets dated April 7, 1955, verso. Copyright ©2025 by Mary de Rachewiltz and the Estate of Omar S. Pound. Reprinted by permission of New Directions Publishing Corp.

already translated, and so hope the book will be published early in the next year. It is absolutely necessary to us, however, to get an <u>expenseless copyright</u>, since the edition will not be sold, but gratuitously distributed, like all publications from the Service of Cultural Diffusion.

Decio Pignatari, traveling through Europe "in search of Kulchur", has been working with us, and very efficiently, though at distance: some translations, discussion of minor points, etc.. In Munich he met Eva Hesse, who was very helpful to clear some doubts of understanding. Now in Italy (his ancestors' home) Pignatari will try to be with Mrs. Mary de Rachewiltz, whose excellent translations we already know.

CAN WE HOPE TO HEAR OF YOU SOON AS POSSIBLE? MAYBE WE NEED SOME SUGGESTIONS? OR MANY?

We heard about an E.P.'s autobiography. Would be wise to print it? How to get it?

"Vou" (Kaue Kitasono), "Dichtung und Prosa" (Eva Hesse), "25 Dikter" (Lars Forsell), "Tre Cantos" (Mary de Rachwiltz), recd.: points of the periphery.

And "Section Rock-Drill – 85/95 de los Cantares" sent by Vanni Scheiwiller, "per conta di Pound":- How can we thank you?

Brazilian newspapers seems to be mor conscious of E.P.'s case(cage?): "Folha da Tarde", 24-XII-55 – news from Washington (ANSA), under the title "THE GREATEST NORTH-AMERICAN POET LIVES IN A MANICOMY, THOUGH HAVING A SOUND MIND". We enclose, too, "PONTOSDEFINEM UMA PERIFERIA", a blast versus this great crime against Culture.

1956

Pound replies in a letter dated January 16:

"Yes, of course you can have the original text to use with your translation for the bilingual edition selected Cantos, for the Ministero, without charge."

He followed up on June 1:

"Shd/be glad if you can encourage Gordon and Giovannini in their attempt to fumigate the fugg of Edward's etc."

And again, on July 8:

"G's problem with bulletin is: what belongs in it and what shd/ be printed at length in such paper as members of the association can use. I think S's notes in Nuova Anthologia are being sent to you. I suggest that yr/ Mallarmé wedge shd/ go at least 6 members." . . . My wife's uncle was in? 1986 (or approx.) when they printed Jeux de Dés . . ."

1957

On January 29, Pound wrote enigmatically:

"Pignatari's friend or acquaintance Fernando Guedes . . ."

In a letter dated April 5, 1957, Haroldo de Campos sends an update of the group's efforts:

Dear Mr. Pound,

Work done. We delivered the translations (17 Cantos) to the Ministério last month. An exhibit: Canto XXX, published by JORNAL DO BRASIL (whose literary supplement is the best and more read one in the country, presently). Footnote signed by Mário Faustino, a young poet from Pará, North of Brazil, now living in Rio de Janeiro, who, through his page "POETRY – EXPERIENCE" is preaching poundian methods as the only way-out from marasmic literary habits in Brathil.

We are doing too a lot of activist literary job, through exhibitions, lectures, interviews: sanitaris aims. Mental higienics.

Introduction – POUND PAIDEUMA -intended as a blast gegen academic scholastics views of E.P.'s work. The CANTOS – to the young poets – more than ever "an awareness che funge".

Ministry will publish, in the same collection (giant format), e. e. cummings (10 poems translated by a. campos). Working now in some samples of "Finneganswake". Future project: "Un coup de dés" into portagoose. The complete quadrant.
CANTO XXX (the Ignez de Castro & D. Pedro theme) sent to Fernando Guedes, Lisbon. "Graal" mag (Portugal), December 1956 published "CONCRETE OR IDEOGRAMMIC POETRY", by Pignatari, with a note on E.P. Fenollosa study re ideogram & Eisenstein re ideogram/montage programmed for publication in Jorn. do Brasil. Have you received NOIGANDRES 3, AD mag, and the material concerning 1st NATIONAL EXHIBITION OF CONCRETE ART?
Friendly yours, [signed HCampos]

Pound replies in a letter dated April 11, 1957:

"Dear noiGZ/ Thanks for clippings . . ."

Pound sends another letter dated June 20, 1957:

"NOI gandres Have passed on material to W. Watt" . . . Very glad to have 5 more copies of the Jornal with Canto XX. MAGNIFICENTLY done. mes compliments."

Pound follows up again in a letter dated July 1957:

"Three years ago Maverik published the KUANG-TSU"

On August 2, 1957, Haroldo de Campos sent another letter to Pound

Dear Mr. Pound,

Copies of "Jornal do Brasil" page enclosed.
Gomringer, from Ulm, "Hochschule für Gestaltung", will send you his "Konstellationen", and English translation of "Técnica do Poema".

Augusto spent, last month, a week in Rio de Janeiro, and urged the work of impression of translated "CANTARES"; also 10 poems of cunnings in phase of printing. We wait for very soon first proofs.

Prof. Ryozo Iwasaki "Selected Paundo-Poems" received. I am beggining [sic] to study (together ith Pignatari) some Japanese, at S.Paulo's Braziian-Japanese Cultural Cener, aiming at a more definitive knowledge about ideogram (kangi) method and possibilities: Fenolosa & E.P. instigations. It proved impossible to find here, in the moment, a teacher of Chinese. Of course, our rudimentary Jap not reach Prof Ryozo's text.

Spanish Pisanos not received. I have written [a few months ago to J.V. Amaral via Rutgers University, New Brunswick, New Jersey, Box 622 (address supplied by "Pound Newsletter"), but, until now, have no answer. Since this translation is of particular interest to our group, I recur, once more, to your kind help.

Active contact made with Fernando Guedes, whose address reached us through your letter of Jan. 29: Guedes a young portagoose poet really alive and creative. Wrote about our concrete poetry in "Diário Ilustrado", of Lisbon ("A poetic experiment in Brasil").
    Concrete/ideogrammic poetry aroused considerable XXXXXXXXXXXX enthusiasm among young poets throughout Brazil. Besides S.Paulo & Rio, in Fortaleza (capital of Ceará – NE state) an exhibition was held. Pound/cummings/Mallarmé/Joyce discussed on literary supplement of "Unitário" (Fortaleza's chief newspaper). Echoes in Maranhão & Pará (North States), Minas Gerais (center state) asks for a concrete exhibition and lectures.

Fighting for a "new subtlety of eyes" & mind.

Truly yours
[signed H. Campos]

On December 21, 1957, Pound sends another letter:

Dear Noigandres,

        Time has come when IF I had a clear of ficial invitation from SOMEWHERE, say S. Paulo, to come and inhabit and lecture on, say Chinese, or   any other LITERATURE,
    it might just possibly help get me out of quod, i. e. incarceration.
If your Ministero of Education cd. express such a desire, saying they don't regard me as political. either an asset or detriment.
    That given my nature, I wd/ have to be in a country at least ten years before coming to any conclusion re/. what government; what party;   what KIND of government wd/ be or is most suited to the circumstances AND to the nature of the inhabitants /
and that in ten years I will be
82, and UNlikely to want to monkey with any buzz saws.

And that the Ministero thinks my presence wd/ conduceto the further education of the DeCampos andCo/ etc.
and/or the animal life and denizens of   XXX
Los Estados Unidos de braZil

        at any rate worth trying.
All of which cd/ be whispered into the ear of yr/ Ambassador, or sent to ME from Ministero of Educ.

If you know someone there, even if not the Lord GOD and High HEFE, etc.
        cd/ write me and ask me if it wd/ be possible and if I wd/ come and on what conditions.

I suppose they wd/ give me some sort of shack to inhabit. Not a question of high salary, or even of salary.
            anyhow, lets hear what you can do.
    The Min. Educ. wanting Cantos was the FIRST official governmental recognition / The UNIVERSITY of Mexico isn't the STATE,
        though there shd/ be useful to you in talking to Officials.
and so forth.
best of the season

1958

On March 10, 1958, the three poets replied to Pound:

Dear Mr. Pound:

Brazilian edition of "Cantares," although official, means only that in charge of Cultural Diffusion Dept. we find a man of good will and reasonable open mind, who accepted our proposal, making possible the work (he has some autonomy within his field). Of course, this does not implies (*sic*) that Brazilian authorities will take positive initiatives like the invitation you've mentioned.

On the other hand, simple divulgation of your wish to come here and teach literature would certainly arise considerable interest among Brazilian writers, the young specially.

So, as far we can see, the best way of getting some effective results on the matter of yr last letter wd be the following: divulgation, through some newspaper or literary magazine, of a document (the letter you sent us, or any other writing you find more fit to the circumstances) expressing your wish to come and inhabit and lecture on literature.

On this basis, a movement of opinions cd be started, aiming at the invitation on pure cultural grounds – as you too seems to wish. Intellectuals of prestige before Brazilian authorities cd perhaps be enrolled in it.

Though we do not subscribe yr political ideas – but, on the contrary, have fundamental objections to them – we do not think they can be judged by slogans, and refuse to admit they can be used as pretext to ignore the capital importance of your work and aesthetical views and actions. Your presence in Brazil – at this moment, when a new formal awareness of poetry is in progress – wd be of the greatest pedagogical relevance: to no other living poet the pragmatics of a new poetic making owns so much.

Of course, we'll await for yr agreement, before taking any initiative.

s. paulo, 10/3/58
[signed by the three poets]

PS: The publication of some translated Cantares, via Jornal do Brasil, our activities around the aesthetic ideas, as well as the paralell [*sic*] work of Mário Faustino, a young poet, friend of ours, who directs poetry page of J. do Br., created a considerable interest on your work and situation. Yet, recently, an interview, originally published by Il Tempo, was reprinted here, with negative repercussions, because of some ideas, attributed to you, concerning the negroes. Esquire - September 57, has something about John Kasper, racist leader, who claims for connections with E.P.. cd you send us a word about all this matter?

Pound replied in a letter dated March 16, 1958:

"Do whatever you think useful. But start with a declaration of RIGHT."

After being discharged from confinement on May 7, 1958, Pound left the United States for Italy, arriving in Naples on July 9, 1958. On November 26, that same year, he again communicated with the Noigandres poets, now writing from the Schloss Brunneneburg, in the South Tyrol near Merano, Italy.
In August 1958, the Brazilian poets wrote to Pound enclosing a clipping of the open letter, published in Jornal de Letras, in favor of his release.

Dear Mr. Pound:

We are sending you, enclosed, a clipping of the manifesto we made, concerning yr release and yr possible visit to Brazil." The stuff was already composed and about to be published in "JORNAL DE LE-TRAS" (nation-wide literary monthly), when reached us the good news. So, the main goal of the manifesto was attained, even before its issue. Possibilities
of invitation remained: but the Ministry of Education & official intelli-
gentzia kept silence. On the other hand, the fuss around all the matter gave fresh impulse to translated CANTARES' edition – we received, promptly, third proofs we were almost despairing to dig out (buried under bureaucratic dust...).
More we were not able to do, mostly because we've lost our main vehicle
of action, i.e.: "JORNAL DO BRASIL", on account of ethic-aesthetic disagreements (including sudden asinine attacks on E.P.'s work, from J.B.
Literary Supplement's editor). Yet, Mario Faustino still holds his position ("POETRY/EXPERIMENT" page), - now publishing his eighth article on Pound's achievement, as antidote gegen editor's squalor (in the same Supplement).

NOIGANDRES 4: concrete poetry now reaching its precise definition. Kanji-fication of thought. How does E.P. receive our radical-personal use ("vision in motion") of ideogram concept – esto visibile parlare – against discorso? Besides word-key to the poems, we tried to do some tentative arrangements, hoping to give you a more definite idea of our experiments.

Recently, KITASONO KATUE, answering to NOIGANDRES 3, sent us his "tanchona kukan" ("monotony of the void space") – VOU, n.58/ November 57, which presents greater affinities to our work than any other poet's experiments, except

young Eugen Gomringer's "KONSTELLATIONEN". An anthology, "KONKRETE POESIE" is about to be issued, by Gomringer (now living in "Hochschule für Gestaltung", ULM), including poems of all "Noigandres".

                As far as space intervenes –
E.P. joins le JEU DE DES. – Have you heard of 75 Stravinsky paying his tribute to WEBERN (Anton), the Mallarmé of Viennese-trinity? – 'Lors
d'un périple en Europe, après la fin de la guerre, qu'il a passée en
        Amérique, Igor Stravinsky est allé en Autriche, se recueillir sur la tombe de Webern, le plus mystérieux,
        le plus secret, le moin connu des disciples de Schoenberg"

Or: (Boulez dixit)- "Stravinsky est à genoux devant Webern" (6 pieces by Webern precede Stravinsky' AGON première, 11/10/57, salle Pleyel, aux concerts"Le Domaine Musical", - for neo-classical despair of Stvsk's morthodox epigones &/or"acolittles"). The arrow has not 2 points –

                        Such a dialectical power of making new, cd not induce us to figure – "sans présumer de l'avenir. . ." . . . "since a positive evidence is not possible" — E.P. throwing dice with Mallarmé? Lawrence Ferlinghetti (from Frisco "Bitch" -generation), in Pound Newsletter 10, pg. 17, got the right problem ("This is where Pound comes in; or, rather, where he goes out. He ventriloquized history in the Cantos, with Rock-Drill in particular; and poets who have followed Pound down the years now find themselves in an impasse. For Rock-Drill is incapable of being spoken comprehensively. The Cantos end as a complete palimpsest of ideographs. And the ideograph must be seen to be heard."),

>drawing the wrong conclusion (a regressive, <u>melodorous</u> one) / for concrete poetry, precisely, also wants to be (consequent and prospectively) a poetry that must be seen to be heard.

>space + gists & piths (reductions form reductions, iris of light, lumina / the matter of yr Paradiso) = CANTAR BASICO and <u>therefore</u> <u>tending</u>

>[sketch of three geometric shapes]

>akiraka
>crystal / clear things
>3 times SUN

>CODA:
>Watching ole Ez do a Basic Canto

>[signed by the three poets]

A copy of Noigandres 4, was also sent in August 1958. The accompanying card reads:

> for gramps   una poesia 'che si puó mangiare

Pound's response, dated November 26, 1958:

> Dear Campos /no one to correlate effort, save time to send you this (alas my only Carbon, to Terres) Various semi centennial celebrations here. Vide Scheiwiller, extracts."

1959

On January 2, 1959, Pound sent the following letter:

> Adult readers will naturally be more interested in the writing of men who have something to say than in attempts to dress up a cliché in some fancy style that will catch attention.

> In view of guidance departments, the infamy of the press in the occident, the almost total aMEMMH success h in obscuring history, as from 2000 b.c. down to the Nurnberg Trials, and thence onward, there would appear to be
> greater need of clear statement of the 17
> historic facts which the sons of hell ane the eMHH

employers of ROoose and OOZEfelds,   , W.C8s etc, spend
billionsof $ to hide,
than in continuation of experiments,
started ably by Mallarme with a pure heart, but
gone to seed and epigoneity in the later wanderings of
J. Joyce, to say nothing of the snohism and trash   that
Clotted about his declining years in the decaying
Centre of a France that had betrayed Tallyrand and Thiers.

(fold)

Dear h.deC.   hope this is tough enough

am sending the Amaral Cantares, registered, slow.

am fore   forwarding yr/ letter to Harald.
1 Berkeley House, 67 Belsize Rd.
London   n.w. 6
Eng;and.

makewhat you   can of the epigon of Frobenius, Heidegger,
etc. but don't mistake it for the most NEEDED   kind of
writing at this time.   Experiment is useful and has its place
AND TIME.

A new content will (ref/ R. de Gourmont)   impose a new form.
the new form cannot rise without it. Nothing tainted with
Freudand co, can be of the least bloody use.

Brain wash, tosh, N.American universities, all   beneath
human contempt.

Impossible to remember what I may have read/in Washington.   and no

time to examine aesthetic experiment with

Brunneneburg, Tirolo, Merano, ITALIA, January 2, 1959. (YCAL 43
37/1571).

A response from the Noigandres poets followed:

Dear Mr. Pound:

Thank you very much for yr last letter. Indeed we prefer to engage
ourselves in a fighting dialogue rather than ventriloquize before a
living Buda.

Orthodoxy is a kind of hypnosis (all the dilutive "he said" young american amoeboid poets from Origin, Evergreen Review, and so on). We believe that a new form creates a new content. Or better: that there is a dialectical, isomorphic relation between form & content. The artisanal cycle of poetry is closed with the monumental apex of THE CANTOS.

No way out for ersatz products. A new poetry coheres with a new era and its peculiar physiognomy. Ours is a progressively rational and characteristically technical one. Concrete poems operate in various levels:- in the linguistic level, criticizing the "morose delectation," the mannerism of verse; rescuing so-called semantical clichés from the hibernation of habit; bringing words to new ways of action and interaction; - in the psychological one, rejecting subjective catharsis ("the swarms of inarticulate feelings") and promoting objective, immediate communication, direct apprehension of structures (there can be, also, even a participating level, with greater efficiency and contension [*sic*] than cd afford the consuete [*sic*], oratorial routines: coca-cola is an exhibit, aiming at realization of Mayakovsky's claim for a kind of propaganda that cd be, at the same time, poetry in a high degree). To fight for order, against subjective mystic-hedonistic alienation, the luxuriant extremes of individualistic metaphor, the diarrhoea [*sic*] of rethoric [*sic*], the refined ceremonial of verse (free-verse included), - against all forms of entropy, this is our way of being engaged in the language and with our era. Construction is the message and the task of the young. And a new form, a drastic condensation of means, plus the ostinato rigore of control working upon the data of sensibility conveys it. Whatever the parcels of truth in yr most peculiar culturvision, the fact is we acknowledge it not by its trueness, but by its form. So, as we firmly believe, the greatest, permanent message of THE CANTOS' major poetry is its own way of dealing with language, its ending in a "progressive palimpsest of ideographs," - an artizanal [*sic*] monument, filled with fragments of discursive thought, but, nevertheless, a monument to ideographic understanding. And here, by a commodious vicus of recirculation, LOS CANTARES join forces with UN COUP DE DES, and Mallarmé's premonition – qui sortira d'ici, rien ou presque un art – becomes an actual program.

2

Have you heard about Stravinsky's "Canticum Sacrum"? about his "Threni / id est: Lamentationes Jeremiae Prophetae"? His "Variations sur un choral de J.S. Bach"? – Webern, yes, Webern moves in the background. And Boris de Schloezer presided with open mind at La Première Décade Internationel de Musique Expérimentale (1953), where the main theme was the concrete-electronic music, which undoubtedly wd interest the Antheil from Ballet Mécanique (now, unfortunatdely [sic] lost in a commercial phase of neo-classic vulgarization) and, of course, a Varèse, this rare example of faithfulness to invention in American music.

The experiments in colour of the last Matisse (some papiers collés en couleur of the last-years, see – VERVE, number devoted to the painter) emulate Josef Albers' concrete "Homage to the Square" series. An active handling of visual problems, not a mere delivering of new-faced Madonas and pseudo-chinese-egyptian masks, as, for instance, by a vague, almost academic La Martinelli. And Max Bill's sculpture maintains the living tradition of Brancusi's eggs and columns, that "approach to the infinite not by hypnosis, but by form, by precisely the highest possible degree
of consciousness of formal perfection".

---Alan Neame wrote to us, from London, sending poems (plain rerendering [sic], at his best, of Laforgue's via E.P & Possum colloquial-ironical vers de
societé). We received, too, the Spanish Pisanos: many thanks. ---By the way, Gillo Dorfles ("Discorso tecnico delle arti", Trieste University) has made a fine rendering of the spatial dimension in yr CANTOS—

/ But Kitasono Katue gave us a living response – tanchona kukan / monotony of void space

[poem by Kitasono Katue, published in VOU 58 / november 1957]

/ and wrote about a new efficacy to visual intelligence in NOIGANDRES 4. And the leader Pequim's [Beijing] theatral troupe travelling through Brazil (cultural excursion), a poet of the New China, has found NOIGANDRES 4 in the hands of a young Brazilian writer, from Minas Gerais (middle west) and made his interpreter to copy some poems and the pilot plan, and to translate them for him. His training in ideographic reading has provided the exact semantic reactions to analogous structures in an occidental language he didn't know. Hence his interest in our concrete products. Hence our interest in his concrete approach.

Admiration is a form of action, not of contemplatio [sic]. You have taught our generation (the living part of it) to believe this.

> Faithful yours,
>
> noigandres
>
> [signed by the three poets]

At the end of a trip through Europe, Haroldo de Campos reached out again to Pound through a handwritten note sent from Pisa on August 8, 1959:

Dear Mr. Pound:
I have been at Schloss Brunneneberg
to visit you, and to present you per-
sonally the homages from Noigandres group.
yr daughter, Mrs. De Rachewiltz
has told me, you hav departed to
Rapallo.
I am now in my way back to
Brazil, after a 4-months trip
through Europe, and I shd like
very much to meet you before re-
turning to my country.   I have to
get my ship at Genoa the 26-8;
may I visit you he 25-8, at Rapallo?" If it will possible cd you
let a message to me with the con-
cierge of Albergo Grande Italia-Lido?
I shall be there, next 25, looking
for it.
        Yrs. Friendly
        [signed Haroldo de Campos]

Pound replies:

H Campos
O.K. Via Mammeli – 23 int 34 Tuesday 4 p.m. (ore 16)
[Albergo Gran Italia & Lido, Rapallo]

Appendix 2: "Deciphering Semiotics"
Décio Pignatari

Written originally as a chapter for his 1973 doctoral dissertation *Semiótica e Literatura: O Signo Verbal Sob a Influência do Signo Não-Verbal* (Semiotics and Literature: The Verbal Sign Under the Influence of the Nonverbal Sign), Pignatari follows in this essay the semiotic clues dispersed throughout the structure of several works of literature, in pursuit of revealing the encoded messages that subvert the work's perceived narrative. This translation is based on the 1974 version published in São Paulo by Editora Perspectiva and later reissued by Atelier Editorial.

***

If Edgar Allan Poe is to be considered the "master in writing backwards," a "deliberate experimenter in anticipatory, regressive modus operandi," to use the words of Roman Jakobson,[1] that is due not only to his considerable knowledge of mathematics and science, as well as of the mechanical possibilities of his time, or to his ability to put together "machines" (both in the sense of *constructing* poems and tales, and of manipulating weaponry as a cadet at West Point), but rather for his understanding of written language in terms of *codes* (the Morse code was invented in 1832 and the first telegraphic line was launched in 1844), as well as his close experience, as a newspaper writer, with typography and printing techniques.

In his work on secret or ciphered language, he expressly stated:

> The reader should bear in mind that the basis of the whole art of solution, as far as regards these matters, is found in the general principles

of the formation of language itself and thus is altogether independent of the particular laws which govern any cipher, or the construction of its key.[2]

This realization, added to his knowledge of cryptography are implicit in many of his works in prose and in verse, and explicit in "The Gold Bug," where he declares: "In the present case—indeed in all cases of secret writing—the first question regards the language of the cipher; for the principle of solution, so far, especially, as the more simple ciphers are concerned, depend upon, and are varied by, the genius of the particular idiom."[3]

Just like the letterpress typographer composes words and phrases in reverse on the composing stick, Poe stresses the poetic function of language through anagrammatic and hypogrammatic processes, a heuristic method already problematized in his own name (Poe / poetry / poet / poem). After Jakobson's extraordinary discovery in his analysis of "The Raven"—in which the "*raven* is simply an inversion of the sinister *never*,"[4] the bird telling itself, or rather *being* that what it says—it is not difficult to track in Poe's oeuvre cases that illustrate his peculiar anagrammatic, hypogrammatic, and anaphonic method as long as we keep in mind that *semiotic trans-codification*:

- a) presents elements that configure a parameter non-susceptible to be apprehended by purely linguistic instruments, requiring approaches equally applicable to other systems of signs, i.e., semiotic approaches proper;
- b) is a process of saturating the code so that the message spreads to another code, a pansemiotic or intersemiotic operation that is at the same time a metalinguistic operation revealing of the nature of codes and language in the broad sense;
- c) it interrupts the linearity of discourse, for the ambiguity of the poetic sign relies in it being a sign at the deepest level—a sign that moves away from verbal automatism, a vertical sign whose density stems from the levels built-in in palimpsest, generating simultaneity of information and tending to become an ideogram— an icon;
- d) it reveals the iconic nature of the poetic sign in opposition to the predominantly symbolic nature of the verbal sign (Jakobson's *poetic function* becomes nothing but the icon-ization of the symbolic sign), which reveals in fact the "palpable side" of signs. For it is the quasi-sign that comes closest to the object, regenerating it and wishing to be the object it is, since the poetic

sign is isomorphic to a referent generated by itself, a *language being* ("*E a alma canta sem entrave/pois que o canto é que faz cantar*" [and the soul sings unencumbered for it is the song that makes her sing], Fernando Pessoa). On the other side, the conflict between the sign and its referent is unsurmountable, at least at the level of *denotatum* (Poe's "The Oval Portrait"), for the iconic model, bi or tridimensional of a molecule is not the molecule-referent in question (which cannot be known if not in function of its model). This is, in sum, the fundamental ambiguity of the poetic sign that tends, or pre-tends, to be its referent without stopping to be a sign.

Process of Discovery

Among the tales by Poe to which I constantly return, one stands above the rest for being the strangest, most intriguing, and fascinating. Only recently I discovered what I believe to be the master key to its ciphered message, but that does not change (if anything, it confirms), in a startling manner, the magnitude of Poe's reputation as promoted by Charles Baudelaire, Stéphane Mallarmé, Paul Valéry, and many others who analyze this literary phenomenon at the level of language structure.

The short tale in question is "Berenice," published in 1835 when Poe was twenty-six years old. The narrator, one of the tale's characters, insists on giving only his first name, Aegeus. Ancestor of a noble house, his castle features many notable traits, including "the very peculiar nature of the library contents." Believing that he has awakened from another existence, after a long night that "seemed nonentity," Aegeus finds himself immersed in a wonderous place "into the wild dominions of monastic thought and erudition." Not surprisingly, he wasted his infancy amid books and squandered his youth with dreams that obscured the sources of his life and that provoked a radical inversion in his vision of the world. Reality became dreams and dreams became the very fabric of his existence. Berenice, his cousin—"Oh, gorgeous yet fantastic beauty!"—by all accounts his opposite, was once a student of life, but struck by an ailment became physically unrecognizable; meanwhile he is attacked by a sort of monomania characterized by obsessive attention to meaningless details. For example, he spends hours admiring the typography of a book, or repeating a word until the monotonous chant empties the word of any meaning. Although he never loved Berenice—not even in the days of her "unparalleled beauty," because "feelings with me had never been of the heart, and my passions always were of the mind"—he proposes marriage to her for the love she devoted to him. In an afternoon, the day before the wedding, in a room at the library, she comes to him by surprise. "She spoke no *word*, and I—not for *worlds* could I have uttered a syllable," but opened her lips in a smile, showing her teeth, a truly spectral vision. Berenice's teeth trigger Aegeus's monomania to the point of lending sensible and expressive virtues that culminate in him believing "*que tous ses dents étaient des idées.*" After a nightmarish night, a servant comes to announce Berenice's death from an epileptic attack. Back at the library, vague signs of some horrible happening occupy Aegeus's mind, which he tries to decipher. At last, a servant comes to tell him in a tremulous voice that Berenice's grave had been violated and her body disfigured. The servant points to his master's muddy garments, his hands "indented with the impress of human nails," a spade against the wall. With a shriek, Aegeus grasps a small box upon a table but could not force it open. The box slips from his hands, falls heavily, and bursts into pieces, showing "instruments of dental surgery intermingled with thirty-two small, white and ivory looking substances that were scattered to and fro about the floor."

There one finds, as if tattooed onto the narrative, the marks of the narcotic, desensitizing cultural shock provoked by the tyranny of the signs that impose themselves as the only reality (in this case, the written word). What is not clear, however, is the hallucinating trans-codification of the teeth into signs—a key point in the narrative that culminates in such a grotesque sequence without parallel in literature.

With clues provided by Poe himself in other texts, we come close to a solution: the letters of the alphabet/teeth. But the number of discrete signs that constitute the alphabet do not coincide with the number of discrete signs that compose a complete system of dental signs, to be known, thirty-two. D. H. Lawrence, in his 1923 study on American literature that examines in detail "Ligeia" and "The Fall of the House of Usher," dedicates a paragraph to "Berenice":

> In "Berenice" the man must go down to the sepulchre of his beloved and pull out her thirty-two small white teeth, which he carries in a box with him. It is repulsive and gloating. The teeth are the instruments of biting, of resistance, of antagonism. They often become symbols of opposition, little instruments or entities of crushing and destroying. Hence the dragon's teeth in the myth. Hence the man in *Berenice* must take possession of the irreducible part of his mistress. "*Toutes ses dents étaient des idées,*" he says. Then they are little fixed ideas of mordant hate, of which he possesses himself.[5]

Contrast that with Marshall McLuhan's commentary on the myth of Cadmus:

> The Greek myth about the alphabet was that Cadmus, reputedly the king who introduced the phonetic letters into Greece, sowed the dragon's teeth, and they sprang up armed men. Like any other myth, this one capsulates a prolonged process into a flashing insight. The alphabet meant power and authority and control of military structures at a distance.
>
> ...
>
> All this is implied in the myth about Cadmus and the dragon's teeth, including the fall of the city states, the rise of empires and military bureaucracies.[6]

Finally we must consider, besides the strange particularities of this talecastle, the fact that Aegeus's dental monomania finds its formalization in the codes of the French language. For sure, the pertinence of such statement can be corroborated in a number of ways. It could emanate from Poe's style, broadly speaking, where statements in French are common; nothing is said of the nationality of the character; the text also features a Latin citation from Tertullian; the character was intellectual and polyglot; and, lastly, the formulation derives, as a parallel, from a previous citation: "Of Mad'selle Sallé it has been well said, '*que tous ses pas étaient des sentiments.*'"[7] Something in this citation, however—"mad'selle," instead of "mam'selle," and the bizarre Miss Sallé—seems to suggest a pseudocitation, more of an invitation to humorous paronomastic games than the intent to convey real characters.

Examining the formalization of the obsession I enumerated the following: a graphic balance of design and of the alphabetic signs.

a) an anagrammatic-specular reading that suggests paronomasias by opposition: *seèdi/ses dents*;
b) the expression *des idées* evoking *desirées* ("*Des idées*—ah therefore it was that I coveted them so madly")

All things considered, I found myself still half away from the final solution. At the end, a haptic-visual reading, the eye feeling the verbo-typographic texture of the text—hence a revelation, the *eureka* of the global iconic vision: I understood the statement/dental arch lining up on the face of the page and counted the number of letters in the sentence "*que toutes ses dents étaient des idées.*" In fact, it was 32 letters / 32 teeth. And "Berenice," like Mona Lisa—"in a smile of peculiar meaning"—could as well crown the oeuvre and satisfied genius of the poet with an extra smile: "Very nice."

Decoding the semiotic key in "Berenice" reveals the structure of its encoded message and subverts the narrative, transforming it in *icon-writing*—at a level that would turn fallacious the usual semantic-content approaches, like the now-current structural analyses of narrative proposed by Tzvetan Todorov or Algirdas Julien Greimas, that are applicable perhaps to narratives led by contiguity of plot.

As it happens when solar rays fall on certain angles over a surface, revealing new reliefs and textures, the tale's new reading brings into focus vague or blurred statements and meanings since the language-object is now identified with the metalanguage, and the narrator with the author—like a theater curtain opening up to reveal the backstage area. In the initial description of the mansion of his "race of visionaries," the narrator gives special attention to the gallery of ancient paintings and to the library; the physical demise of Berenice reduces her own teeth, complete and perfect like letters spread out on the page of the succinct tale; the silence of both characters, the mysterious smile of Berenice, and the "attentive" monomania of the narrator contribute to an *external* narrative, and are indices of an *internal* narrative—just like the emphasis on typography and the monotone repetition of common words; the asphodel metaphor goes the same route—it wishes and prevents the tale to be deciphered: Aegeus's reason, "shaken from its balance only by trivial things, . . . steadily resisting the attacks of human violence, and the fiercer fury of the waters and the winds," trembled only to the touch of that flower; the digits/letters of the phrase *the teeth*, almost a palindrome that designates a dental arch, are teeth/letters and the vocal emission of its phonemes configures a smile—Berenice's smile, the author's smile . . . and of the reader, after the deciphering; the tactful amnesia of the narrator, who does not know, but intuits and fears having committed an act of horror, as terrifying as the vague and ambiguous omens he endeavored to decipher. And also: In "*que toutes ses dents étaient des idées*," the visual, typographic isomorphism, unfolds from another, at the phonic level; worth to say, the icon in question, besides a-graphic is also aphonic as in it predominates linguodental consonants (d, t).

Suddenly, the narrative atmosphere shifts from horror to humor—the horror tale was a puzzle—but the same humor recovers the horror at another level: The horror of discovering the signic nature of man.

What in the story Tertullian says about God, Poe says metalinguistically in regard to his own narrative, or yet, of his double-parallel narrative: "Tertullian's *De Carne Christi*, in which the paradoxical sentence '*Mortuus est Dei filius; credible est quia ineptum est: et sepultus resurrexit; certum est quia impossibile est*,' occupied my undivided time, for many weeks of laborious and fruitless investigation."

When the anecdotic narrative "Berenice I" ends, the narrative "Berenice II" emerges as a creature of language. A horror story becomes a tale of reason. Henceforth, "Berenice" ought to be reclassified in Poe's anthologies. In the edition prepared by Van Doren Stern (Viking Portable), the stories are classified in Fantasy, Terror, Death, Revenge, and Murder, Mystery, and Ratiocination. "Berenice" is featured among the "Tales of Death." Perhaps it should be moved to the category of Tales of Fantasy and Ratiocination, for the lack of a better one.

Usher's Malady

The lineage of poets rests upon and ends in language—his *gotha*, his crests, his epitaph. That's why they can claim a nobility that no other nobility can aspire to—be it a pseudo-gentleman of the American South, or a French petit bourgeois, like Mallarmé and Valéry, or an energetic, furious, and anguished communist poet, like Mayakovsky. Hence in Poe, many of the characters are linked to a nobility, or quasi-nobility undefined or plainly unknown.

August Bedloe is one such character, in "A Tale of the Ragged Mountains." It's the story of an avatar, and of the rupture of time-lapse: Benares in Charlottesville, Virginia, 1827. Lost in the ragged mountains in 1780, August Bedloe witnesses a mutiny of Natives against the English colonizers, gets involved, dies in combat—and returns, reembodied/disembodied, to Charlottesville to tell his story and die again. A British official named Oldeb, a friend of his doctor, Mr. Templeton, will die in that same combat. When the news of August Bedloe's passing appears in the newspaper, his name is miswritten as *Bedlo*. The narrator approaches the journal editor, who replies that it was merely a typographic mistake. The narrator concludes: "Bedlo, without the *e*, what is it but Oldeb conversed? And this man tells me it is a typographical error."

As we see, the discovery of the linguistic code transforms it into the new sacred scriptures of a new arcanum; it is not merely a game. The poet himself seems implicated in the destiny veiled and unveiled by the alphabetic code made icon: For what is *ragged*, but *edgar* backward, with an inverted *e*, and an extra *g*.

In another of his well-known tales, "The Fall of the House of Usher," the title itself is a contra-metaphor as at the end the house sinks effectively into the swamps: ". . . and the deep and dank tarn at my feet closed sullenly and silently over the fragments of the '*House of Usher*.'" Furthermore, the title features two suggestive particularities: a) *fall*, in its mirror image produces *llaf* = *laugh*, with the graphic signs stating one thing, and the phonic signs another; b) USHER, besides being formed by the pronouns *us*, *he*, *she*, *her*, also features four letters/fragments of HOUSE in a rearrangement. The rhapsody Roderick intones—"The Haunted Palace"—ends fittingly with a spectral cackle:

> . . .
>
> Through the pale door,
> A hideous throng rush out forever,
> And laugh — but smile no more.

The house not only duplicates itself in the swamp's stagnating waters, but, as if impregnated by a *sentience*, or particular sensitivity, changes itself physically according to the feelings and the fortune of its inhabitants—the inorganic translating the organic and the sensible, just like Poe's texts in relation to himself—as it happens with the quasi-sign.

This palace, *cosa mentale*—or very real, made of letters and words, dwelling of the Thinking King—is the same where Elbehnon (from Mallarmé's "Igitur") will wander in search of the absolute; it's the same prose with its "thread of light over the gravel,"[8] phono-graphic threads. For example, the encounter of the visitor-narrator with the house owner, Roderick of Usher, is anticipated by the words *rode*, and *ushered*: "Noticing these things, I *rode* over a short causeway to the house. . . . The valet now threw open a door and *ushered* me into the presence of his master."

Note that *usher* brings to mind, by similarity, *hush*. In fact, while in "Berenice" the main character suffered of an abnormal concentration of attention, Usher "suffered much from a morbid acuteness of the senses; the most insipid food was alone endurable; he could wear only garments of certain texture; the odors of all flowers were oppressive; his eyes were tortured by even a faint light; and there were but peculiar sounds, and these from stringed instruments, which did not inspire him with horror."

His sister, buried alive, returns mad from the tomb to kill him, he himself demented—MADLINE, MADMAN. It turned out they were twins. Elements common in "Berenice" are also here present: the collection of revered, strange, esoteric books; the mysterious smile on the lips of the pseudo-corpse of Madeline, perceptible anomalies, the premature burial. But Usher's malady, the dullness of perception by extreme refinement, at the same time it announces the artificial man, the signic-man—the dandy of Baudelaire and Oscar Wilde ("Life imitates art"), Jean des Esseintes, Joris-Karl Huysmans, Fernando Pessoa ("o que em mim sente está pensando" [that what in me feels is always thinking]), or McLuhan's *Homo Gutenbergi*—it encounters a pertinent formulation in the Theory of Information: The extreme differentiation of functions in an organism or in a message—that means order, and thus, a high informational degree—increases the entropic (disorder) possibilities through an increasing redundancy (norms, repetition) that tend to produce an effect of de-differentiation, like the cancer cell in relation to the highly differentiated cells in the organism, tending toward chaos, that is, total redundancy. Between chaos and chance, man strives to establish himself repeatedly, instituting a principle of survival order with, in, and through renewed language.

And it is a true pleasure, as it is rare, to conclude this Poe-analogic excursion with an observation by a Brazilian critic who managed to see what even T. S. Eliot could not decades later:

> It's not in vain that one goes to his pages to learn the secrets of artistic composition; and not one rhetorician could ever teach like him how to build and unbuild a work of art at its most structural level.[9]

"Scribble Without Alphabetic Intent"[10]

It is possible, as traditional critics have maintained, that Machado de Assis, a typographer in his youth, created an original *type* of fiction, particularly in what concerns his famous "gallery of female *types*." More probable, however, is that Assis rather committed himself to the graphic elements that compose his writings, first as a typographer and later as a journalist and author. That is, he was not a writer alienated from the medium he used—the printed word, mechanically and industrially—like the majority of automatically verbal writers who do not distinguish a Bodoni from a Garamond, or even a serif type from a non-serif type. Assis not only employed his knowledge in this sector, but typography itself impregnated the very structure of some of his most important works, including *Memórias Póstumas de Brás Cubas* (Posthumous Memoirs of Brás Cubas), from 1881. Further down I will isolate five examples of semiotic phenomena in *Brás Cubas*—five bits of information that extrapolate the alphabetic code as purely phonetic code and get saturated in typo-ideography.

It's interesting, if not strange, that poets, writers, and even linguists to this day still do not realize that the phonetic spoken code, and the alphabetic written code are two diverse codes. It is particularly notable that the same might also occur among linguists and semiologists, even as we know that Ferdinand de Saussure dedicated two chapters of his *Cours* to this subject, alarmed overall with the invasion of the purely phonetic-linguistic world by hordes of the written word. Saussure foresaw that the issue would tend to grow—in fact, the blunder that was Linguistics, as it by contamination, turned into semiology. He sensed the contradiction he couldn't avoid—that linguistic studies would end up engulfed by the written form. But he incurred in the same error in believing that the graphic image behaved like the phonetic image, which indicates that he couldn't clearly see the outlines of semiology.

Since an identical state of affairs is observable in writing, another system of signs, we shall use writing to draw some comparisons that will clarify the whole issue. In fact:

1) The signs used in writing are arbitrary; there is no connection, for example, between the letter *t* and the sound it designates.
2) The value of letters is purely negative and differential. The same person can write *t*, for instance, in different ways: The only requirement is that the sign for *t* not be confused in his script with the signs used for *l, d*, etc.
3) Values in writing function only through reciprocal opposition within a fixed system that consists of a set number of letters. This third characteristic, though not identical to the second, is closely related to it, for both depend on the first. Since the graphic sign is arbitrary, its form matters little or rather matters only within the limitations imposed by the system.
4) The means by which the sign is produced is completely unimportant, for it does not affect the system (this also follows from characteristic). Whether I make the letters in white or black, raised or engraved, with pen or chisel—all this is of no importance with respect to their signification.[11]

Even if we acknowledge his caution, in the sense that his theory refers solely to factors pertinent to the purely linguistic universe, the contradiction is unsurmountable even in this universe, and his discourse ran the risk of falling apart had he not declared: "But the tyranny of writing goes even further. By imposing itself upon the masses, spelling influences and modifies language." His example of comparing made and mad in English illustrates what he calls an aberration: "'Indirect spellings' also merit our attention. There is no double consonant in *Zettel*, Teller, etc.; German uses *tt, ll*, etc. for the sole purpose of indicating that the preceding vowel is open and short. Through a similar aberration English adds a final silent *e* to lengthen the preceding vowel: *mad, made*. The *e*, which actually affects only the preceding syllable, creates a second syllable for the eye."[12]

As in all means of communication, only quantity generates quality. The multiple and complex network of social and human relations only seems to alter significantly when those means or vehicles are featured in a significant quantity. This is a phenomenon that can easily be observed for it happens in front of our eyes. Consider the transformations going on in the cities due to the explosion of traffic; note the behavioral changes in certain regions due to the penetration of the televised image, once the number of receptacles reach a limit. At the end of the nineteenth century, and beginning of the twentieth, the written (printed) word had reached the highest point in an ascendent curve, as a hemogenic medium of mass communication, and some of its manifestations (the advertising poster, or *Un Coup des dés*, for example) indicated that a new codification world was being unveiled—the modern world of Western ideography.

Saussure was right to be alarmed by the intrusion of writing in the purely linguistic world that he endeavored to preserve—a world in which the relations happened through the direct intervention of speakers (the speaking *men*) at the very moment in which they (the speaking *men*) were about to disappear, transformed into linguistic or semiotic.

But the change wasn't being stimulated only by the advent of the printed word, as aural world was being impacted at the sonic level by the emergence of various new media. In 1877, man registered his voice with Thomas Edison's phonograph, and David Edward Hughes's microphone; in the previous year, Alexander Graham Bell had invented the telephone. The first transmission through radio, made by Guglielmo Marconi, dates back to 1896; two years later, Valdemar Poulsen made the first magnetic recordings of sounds. The first public exhibition of the Lumière brothers' *cinématographe* happened in 1895, and in less than three decades *The Jazz Singer* (1927), considered the first *talkie*, was screened to wide audiences. Throughout the 1930s, the invention of the television was at its experimental phase in laboratories in England, France, and the United States.

By the time Saussure died in 1913, recordings were beginning to be commercialized, a technology that attracted Bernard Shaw who featured the recording technology in his play *Pygmalion* (1912), drawing from ancient mythology and contemporary mass-culture phenomenon to comment on language. In a few decades, languages underwent modifications that in the past would have taken centuries.

Traditional critics in Brazil, cornered by their psychologizing and philosophizing approach, noticed the types but missed the typography, and overlooked its paronomasias, commonly known as *quibbles*, considering them not worthy of a proper style. For here we have an informational phenomenon of language elevated to aesthetic standard. In terms of Information Theory, the written word provides a less noisy channel—less subject to the entropic interference of noise—than spoken word; hence the latter higher redundancy charge than the former, with the goal to overcome the noise barrier and secure the message effective transmission; unable, de force, to infer from the phenomenon any adjunct attesting value, or lack of, to the aesthetic apparatus. This kind of approach, unmindful of language, goes against Machado de Assis's very structural method of composition, particularly in *Brás Cubas*—a method that, being indispensable, he wanted bare of any adornments (Translator's Note: In the original, "sem gravata nem suspensórios," [without a tie or suspenders]), and which was the analogic method transposed to language. Consider the following examples:

> *Parece que a miséria lhe calejara a <u>alma</u>, a ponto de lhe tirar a sensação de <u>lama</u>.*
>
> (It seems that misery hardened his soul to the point of erasing the feeling of muck.)
>
> *Tinhamos falado na prata, a velha prataria do tempo de D. João I, a porção mais grave da herança, já pelo <u>lavor</u>, já pela vetustez, já pela origem da propriedade.*
>
> (We had spoken about the silver, the old silver of D. João I time, the hefty portion of the inheritance, either for its value, antiquity, or provenance.)

The second term of the paronomasia is read *in absentia*, hypostatized as it is in the term *in presentia*, by the suggestion of similarity *lavor/valor* (labor/value)—an entire ideogram for art and the art market:

> *Agarrei-me à esperança da recusa, se o decreto viesse outra vez datado de 13; trouxe, porém, a data de 31.*
>
> (I held to the hope of refusal in case the edict come once again dated the 13th; but it featured, instead, the date of the 31st.)

A purely visual, ideogramic paronomasia, for it lacks the phonetic correspondent: thirteen/thirty-one:

> *Meu pai era homem de imaginação, escapou à tanoaria nas asas de um calembour ... entroncou-se na família daquele meu famoso homônimo, o capitão Brás Cubas ... e por esse motive é que me deu o nome de Brás.*
>
> My father was a man of imagination, ran away from tannery on the wings of a calembour ... attaching himself to the family of my famous homonym, Captain Brás Cubas ... and it is for this reason that I was named Brás.

No wonder, Machado de Assis was an admirer of Edgar Allan Poe.... But let's examine a few iconic examples, in the nonverbal sense.

1—It is through a process of casual analogy that the novel's heroine, Virgília, is introduced into the narrative at the end of Chapter XXVI through a calligram, or concrete poem, in two parts, where a double reading (in Latin and Portuguese) becomes unavoidable; ambiguity throwing out sparks that connote the phallic character and that also parallel the ideographic connotations that compose the second part and announces the arrival of Virgília (*"vinda de Virgília"*): "*vir, Virgílio, Virgília.*" The eruption of the ideogram on the page is a kind of cryptic message from Assis addressing the era's Victorian prudery (as well as his own).

2—The famous Chapter LV, "O Velho diálogo de Adão e Eva" (Adam and Eve's ancient dialogue), is rightly new in its open typo-ideographic form that fulfills the redundancy of a quasi-mythic model-situation in the sexual-amorous relationship between a man and a woman. The dialogue is composed of nonalphabetic signs such as dots, and question/exclamation marks. Statistically, the ideogram can be translated into the phonetic-digital code: reticence, and seductive dodgery from Virgília's part; insistence, begging, and protestations from Brás Cubas's part. The dialogue, of uneven distribution between its interlocutors, balances itself out, and fuses symmetrically at the end: settlement, accord, union, mutual emphatic transport. It's a sharp and subtle piece of humor that enacts and renews itself by introducing the reader's verbal repertoire in the author's quasi-verbal model.

3—The defunct author composes a handwritten unique book having in mind typographical composition, even when addressing a tombstone inscription that imitates typological kerning and layout. Always the real becoming live signs on the page, always the signs becoming closer to its objects. In the case of the tombstone, we find the text and the paratext: the tombstone icon scripted onto the page. It is a *raccourci*, an abbreviated narrative that augments the degree of surprise. It communicates that the character is not only dead, but buried, with all the formalities of decorum that the circumstance requires.

4—Chapter CXXXV, "Oblivion," is a sampling and analysis of (typographic) characters. Already in the first paragraph, in a citation translated from the English, the Portuguese expression ESQUECIMENTO is written entirely in caps (*caixa-alta*), while the original receives a slightly different treatment in small caps (*versaletes*): "*Vai em versaletes esse nome* OBLIVION! *Justo é que se dêem todas as honras a um personagem tão desprezado e tão digno, conviva da última hora, mas certo.*" (Translation: "Let's highlight in small caps the word OBLIVION. It is only right to *honor* such a despised and dignified character, our company at the last *hour, but sure*"). Currently in disuse, the small caps is a double capitalization and its meaning—to confer status—in the journalism of Assis's era is provided by the author, who in this passage, acts as a newspaper editor selecting the types for the composition. The typographic composition, hence, characterizes an information that would be lost if the word had been printed in regular type.

5—Virgília's signature, in Chapter CXLII: "*Não era a letra fina e correta de Virgília, mas grossa e desigual; o V da assinatura não passava de um rabisco sem intenção alfabética*" (Translation: "It wasn't Virgília's usually refined, straight handwriting, but rough and uneven; the V was nothing but a scribble without alphabetic intent"). To the subtle, great lascivious man that was Brás Cubas/Assis, at once awakened and repressed, it wouldn't have escaped in this V intimations of pubis, cleavage, and lap. With finesse and modesty, Assis came closer to his masters, Lawrence Sterne, and Poe, but the main lesson learned was of metalinguistic nature: At every moment, reader, author, and narrator are separated from narrative alienation through graphic and typographic accidents that makes them aware that they are reading a book, a book and nothing else—*words, words, words*. To saturate a code means to break the rules of the game, which implies at the same time, an intersemiotic and metalinguistic operation.

Ultimatum

"*ATENÇÃO! Proclamo em primeiro lugar, A Lei de Malthus da Sensibilidade: Os estímulos da sensibilidade aumentam em progressão geométrica; a própria sensibilidade apenas em progressão aritmética*," Fernando Pessoa, *Ultimatum*, 1917. (Translation: "ATTENTION! I proclaim in the first place The Malthusian Law of Sensibility: The stimuli to sensibility increases in geometric progression; sensibility itself increases only in arithmetic progression.")[13]

And there we have a *legisign* transposed onto a *qualisign*—the question at the basis of the position-opposition Art/Life, since Poe's "The Oval Portrait" to contemporary constructs such as the android.

As a postscriptum to Pessoa's *ultimatum*, I offer the following quote from Paul Valéry: "la sensibilité chez les modernes est en voie d'affaiblissement" ("sensibility, among moderns, is weakening").

Translated by Antonio Sergio Bessa

Appendix 3: "Pound Made (New) in Brazil"
Augusto de Campos

Originally published in the collection of essays *A Margem da margem* (The edge of the edge [São Paulo: Companhia das Letras, 1989]) "Pound Made (New) in Brazil" considers the early reception of the American poet by Brazilian poets, mischaracterized as a music composer by Mário de Andrade and read hesitantly by the poets of the "45 generation," until the Noigandres poets took on the task of approaching his oeuvre in more depth, in search of new solutions for the evolution of Brazilian poetry. According to Campos, concrete poetry owes a great debt to Pound particularly regarding the application of the ideogramic method as a consequent process of overcoming the linearity of the logic-discursive verse. A French version of this essay was published in *Cahiers de L'Herne* (Paris, 1965), in the first of two volumes dedicated to the work of Ezra Pound.

***

The poetry of Ezra Pound was practically ignored during the early modernist period in Brazil. An exceptional reference to his work by a noted modernist is found in Mário de Andrade's *Pequena História da Música* (Short history of music, 1944), curiously introduced not as a poet or literary critic, but as an experimental composer alongside Kurt Weil, Manoel de Falla, and Anton Webern. Perhaps Andrade knew about Pound's opera *Villon*, of which a few excerpts for tenor and bass were performed at Salle Pleyel, in Paris in 1926. Whatever the source might have been, the oblique citation of the composer Ezra Pound in Andrade's book demonstrates how poorly informed our Brazilian modernists were of the new developments in Anglo-American poetry. Worth pointing out that although Andrade did not know the poet Ezra Pound, he became smitten by *amygism* (the dilution of Pound's Imagism), as we can infer from his essay-manifesto *A escrava que não era Isaura* (The slave who wasn't Isaura, 1922), in which he included a poem by Amy Lowell. In our early modernist period, as far as we know, only Jorge de Lima attempted an approach to the poetic work of Pound.

The generation that followed, the so-called "45 generation" of poets that emerged in the postwar period, was known for the most part as a reaction to the most radical tendencies of early modernism such as the minute-poem, the joke-poem, and the anti-verse of Oswald de Andrade. On the pretext of excessive freedom and lack of rigor, the "45 generation" poets called for a return to classic models and forms that preceded modernism. On the other hand, they also reacted to the deep-rooted influence of French poetry, until then a dominating force in our literature. Such reaction proceeded, in great part, from a rising interest in Anglo-American modernist authors, particularly T. S. Eliot, and in the "new criticism." It was in that context that a small number of Brazilian poets and critics became interested in the work of Pound. The poets of the "45 generation" were also aware of the *mad poet*, accused of treason in his own country, author of a difficult and fragmentary poem titled *The Cantos*, but their approach to his work was rather superficial, opting instead for the more soothing company of Eliot, whose reverse evolution from the modernism of *The Waste Land* to the neoclassicism of *Four Quartets* and stage plays seemed to point to those poets a new path to follow.

It was around 1949 that Décio Pignatari, Haroldo de Campos, and I started to dedicate ourselves to the study of the poetry and critical work of Ezra Pound. And although we did not agree with Pound's political views, we started to actively contribute to the literary rehabilitation of the American poet, during a phase in which the rushed slogans of "treason" and "fascism" served as pretext for expunging his poetry everywhere and omitting it in his own country through what James Blish deemed relentless "rituals" from the part of American critics intent on erasing Pound's poetic legacy.[1] In 1952, we embraced as the motto of our poetic experience the word *noigandres*, of enigmatic meaning, extracted from a poem by Arnaut Daniel, the Provençal troubadour seen by Pound as the paradigm of the poet inventor. ("Noigandres, eh noigandres. / Now what the DEFFIL can that mean?" Canto XX). We also put together under this name a journal that by 1953 would launch the concrete poetry movement.[2] In addition, we maintained correspondence with Pound while he was still interned at St. Elizabeths Hospital and collaborated with American publications open to seriously study his work, such as *The Analyst*, and *The Pound Newsletter*.[3] We also set ourselves to recreate *The Cantos* in Portuguese, producing a group translation of seventeen Cantos that would be ultimately published in 1960. The chosen title *Cantares* followed a suggestion by Pound in a letter dated April 11, 1957: "if not too late can you use the title *cantares* . . . cantares de gesta being nearer the real nature of the poem than 'cantos' / it is the tale of the tribe / and had no title other than 'a poem of some length, when the 17 and 27 were done, labeled 'draft.'" Through this publication, and also through articles and manifestos on concrete poetry published in the mid-1950s, fundamental problems related to Pound's work began to be "digested" more systematically by young Brazilian poets. That included topics such as the ideogrammatic method applied to poetry and criticism; techniques related to poetic montage and the idiomatic mosaic; the survey of poet-inventors; and translation as creation. Poet Mário Faustino, tragically deceased in 1962, gave relevant contribution for the divulgation and discussion of Pound's work producing notable translations of poems from *Personae*. Faustino exemplarily applied Pound's critical methodology to militant criticism and to the didactic essay, in the spirit and style of his approach. In 1958, he produced a series of essays on Pound that constitute the most complete survey on the American poet made in Brazil. Faustino's premature death prevented him from collecting in one volume the essays that were published between 1956 and 1959 in the literary supplement of *Jornal do Brasil*.[4] From the same generation, José Lino Grunewald would also contribute translations and critical essays becoming one of the best interpreters of Pound's poetry in Brazil.

Brazilian concrete poetry owes a great debt to Pound, less as direct poetic influence—since his poetry, abolishing the discursive, moved toward a radicalization of methods far beyond the perspective of epic poetry— and more as a critical, ethical-aesthetic instigation. The great contribution that the concrete poets envisioned in Pound's work, from the point of view of evolution of poetic form, was the application of the ideogramic method as a consequent process of overcoming the linearity of the logic-discursive verse.

One of the interesting aspects that can be imputed to the studies on Pound's work made in Brazil concerns the proximity established between certain techniques used in *The Cantos*, and in *Un Coup des dés*, even though Pound, according to Eliot, ignored Stéphane Mallarmé in his essays on French poetry. The fact is that the reality of the work itself trumps the author's opinion or knowledge. And departing from this reality, it is possible to establish a parallel between the fugal, contrapuntist structure in *Un Coup des dés* and in *The Cantos*. Regardless of the different perspectives that set both authors apart, and that stylistically would become evident in their respective use of the vocabulary—Mallarmé's ambiguous word versus Pound's *mot juste*—in *dialexical* opposition, so to speak, both authors had in common the musical structuring of themes. In Mallarmé, according to his own preface to *Un Coup des dés*, "from this stripped-down mode of thought, with its retreats, prolongations, flights," the texture of the "dominant motif, a secondary, and adjacent ones," all that "joined under a strange influence, that of Music, as it is heard in a concert." In Pound, the contrapuntist structure was mentioned in a letter to his father (April 11, 1927) that outlined his scheme for the entire poem: "Rather like, or unlike subject and response and counter subject in fugue." This would be, in sum, the point of encounter in the evolution of poetic forms, between the two works, beyond the repercussions of such techniques at the level of the texts, that would explain other affinities between a poem that Paul Valéry called an "ideographic spectacle" (*Varieté II*) and what Pound conceived, in great part, as an extension of the poetic possibilities of the Chinese ideogram. Hugh Kenner, one of Pound's most competent critics, came to the same realization in *The Poetry of Ezra Pound* (1951): "The fragmenting of the aesthetic idea into allotropic images, as first theorized by Mallarmé, was a discovery whose importance for the artist corresponds to that of nuclear fission to the physicist."[5] In 1955, I published two essays ("Poesia, Estrutura," and "Poema, Ideograma") that further compared Mallarmé's and Pound's techniques. Learning about those essays, Pound did not pose any obstacles to my positions. In a letter dated April 7, 1955, addressed to "los H. & A. de Campos / NOIGANDRES," he commented with humor in his typical epistolary jargon:

> as to me an' Mallarmé getting to São Paulo, simult.
> and as to what a small segment of the race runs its KULCHUR,
> it might amuse you to know that in 1897
> an imaginary spectator might have seen a y. m. on bicycle
> rushing that copy of Cosmopolis around London, the same
> known to me later as H "Bunk" Tucker (Bunk equiv.
> oncle), my wife uncle, and cousin of Lionel Johnson.

And at the end of the same letter:

> There WAS a copy of the original issue of Cosmopolis in my ma-in-law flat, which I must have picked up and sent to Rapallo in 1938/ but I don't remember seeing it since then. Hope it hasn't be LIBERATED.

In a subsequent letter dated July 8, 1955, sent from St. Elizabeths, he reiterated:

> My wife's uncle was on Cosmopolis in? 1896 (or approx.) when they printed Jeux de Dés.

Finally, in a letter from Tirolo, Italy, dated January 2, 1959, he mentions in passing "the experiments, initiated competently by Mallarmé with a pure heart," which could be read as a reconsideration of his omitting the French poet from his *paideuma*.

Another consequence of the instigations of the ideogrammic method applied to criticism, in regard to Brazilian literature, relates to the reassessment of our literary history instigated by Pound's criterion of *invention*. The first outcome of that reassessment was the rediscovery of poet Joaquim de Sousândrade (1832–1902), whose oeuvre had been dispersed, *disjecta membra*, throughout several libraries in the country. Born in Maranhão, Sousândrade was educated in Europe, graduating in literature and engineering in Paris. A passionate republican, he was forced to leave London, where he resided for a few months, due to an article he wrote against Queen Victoria. Around 1870, he moved to New York where he lived for the span of about a decade. At the end of his adventurous life, abandoned by his wife and daughter, Sousândrade died poor and forgotten. His poetic activity started with *Harpas Selvagens* (Wild harps, 1857) and closed with *Novo Éden* (New Eden, 1893), and posthumously two manuscripts of his last writings (*Harpas de Oiro* [Golden harps]) were found. But his most important work, which upset the critics of his time, is an epic poem in thirteen cantos titled *O Guesa* (The Guesa), a project he started in Brazil in 1866 and continued adding to it throughout his stays in Europe and in the United States with several drafts published in London and New York.[6] Sousândrade's *avant la lettre* use of collage technique in *O Guesa* presents surprising affinities with Pound's *Cantos*, particularly in the episode that we named "Wall Street Inferno" according to the poet's own verse ("*E voltava do inferno de Wall Street . . .*" [And returned from the inferno of Wall Street]), in Canto X. A comprehensive comparative study of Sousândrade's *Guesa* vis-à-vis Pound was presented in *revisão de sousândrade* in 1982.[7]

O Guesa narrates in epic style the poet's voyages through Europe, Africa, and the Americas, starting in the Andes. Sousândrade takes on the persona of the *guesa*, a legendary figure extracted from the *muísca* cult, the Indigenous people from Colombia. According to the legend, a *muísca* child would be kidnapped from his parents and destined, after a long pilgrimage, to be ritually sacrificed by priests (*xeques*); after his killing by arrows, his heart would be removed in an offering to the sun, and his blood collected in sacred urns. A symbol both of the *poète maudit*, and the *bon sauvage*. From its classic armature, for the most part written in decasyllables, two long excerpts included in Cantos II and X distinguish themselves both in form and content. Built along short epigrammatic strophes and featuring different casts of *dramatis personae* in the manner of Johann Wolfgang von Goethe's Walpurgis Night episode in *Faust*, mixed to limerick, the first excerpt depicts a grotesque Sabbath in the Amazon Forest performed by a cast of characters cued from Brazilian and American history mixing Natives and corrupt missionaries. The second excerpt features an atemporal burlesque set on New York's Wall Street revolving around the ups and downs of the Ulysses S. Grant presidency. Through a collage of news gathered from contemporary newspapers, the poem echoes local political turmoil, mixed with the international news such as the proclamation of Queen Victoria as empress of India, the Franco-Prussian War, as well as the struggles between Russia and Turkey. Historic and mythologic figures appear in these episodes clashing in fantastic dialogues. The entire plot juxtaposed in nonlinear sequence following a rather analogic order, synthetic-ideogrammic.

Inserted in the body of a canto dedicated to the United States of America, (here addressed as the "young people of the avantgarde") the "Wall Street Inferno" will point to the republican contradiction, its cancer, at the center of the financial speculations, conceived as a circle in Hell. This, in our view, is where Sousândrade's cosmovision coincides with Pound's scheme developed in *The Cantos*. Setting aside the extravagant solutions Pound advocated for economic themes and the misguided political affiliations he adopted, we can identify in both poets a common and fundamental aversion to the nefarious power of money. The capacity, to echo Michel Butor apropos of Pound, to capture poetically the economic phenomenon. Thus, as Pound proclaimed *bellum perenne* on Usura, for Sousândrade the Stock Exchange and its macabre speculation frenzy becomes the symbol of a society falling apart, dazed by the avidity of money:

. . . *Pára o Guesa perlustrado.*
Bebe à taberna às sombras da muralha
Malsólida talvez, de Jericó,
Defesa contra o Indio—E s'escangalha
De Wall Street ao ruir toda New York[8]

(. . . Guesa stops, pondering.
Has a drink at the tavern by the shades of the wall
Disform perhaps, of Jericho,

Defense against the natives—And falls apart
From Wall Street as New York falls)

For Pound, the nineteenth century is the "century of Usura." According to him, the United States economic development after the Civil War, consisted of a series of maneuvers of the New York and the Chicago Stock Exchanges. Pound's concept of Usura, as we know, stems from Dante's *Inferno*. Sousândrade's inferno shares the same overwhelming atmosphere, as it opens with the invocation of the three visitors to the hellish realms—Orpheus, Dante, and Aeneas—as the Guesa (the Inca) arrives to Wall Street; paradoxically, the scene does not convey a *descent* to Hell but rather an *ascension*, for the poet started from South America and toward the United States:

*(O Guesa, tendo atravessado as ANTILHAS, crê-se livre dos
XEQUES e penetra em NEW-YORK-STOCK-EXCHANGE; a Voz
dos desertos:)*
—*Orfeu, Dante, Aeneas, ao inferno
Desceram; o Inca há de subir . . .
= Ogni sp'ranza lasciate,
Che entrate . . .*
—*Swedenborg, há mundo porvir?*

(Guesa, having crossed the Antilles, believes himself to be free from
XEQUES and enter the NEW-YORK-STOCK-EXCHANGE; the
Voice from the deserts:)
—Orpheus, Dantes, Aeneas, to inferno
Descended; the Inca must climb
= *Ogni sp'ranza lasciate,
Che entrate . . .*
—Swedenborg, is there a world to come?

(Note the typographic variety, with innovations like the use of the double dash to introduce a second character. It seems that the graphic physiognomy of newspaper made a strong impression on Sousândrade, just like it did on Mallarmé). Under the bidding war between railroad auctioneers, a saraband in which capitalists and speculators are castigated, the poem continues:

*(Xeques surgindo risonhos e disfarçados em Railroad managers
Stockjobbers, Pimpbrokers, etc., etc., apregoando)*
—*Harlem, Erie! Central! Pennsylvania!
= Milhão! cem milhões! mil milhões!*

—Young é Grant! Jackson,
Atkinson!
Vanderbilts, Jay Goulds, anões!

(Xeques arriving smiling and disguised as Railroad managers
Stockjobbers, Pimpbrokers, etc., etc., preaching)
—Harlem, Erie! Central! Pennsylvania!
= One million! A hundred million! A thousand million!
—Young is Grant! Jackson,
Atkinson!
Vanderbilts, Jay Goulds, dwarves!

The dealers, bankers, men of high finance, and venal politicians that inhabit Sousândrade's Hell belong to the same lineage as Pound's usurers. But it's not only in the conceptualization of a financial hell that the two poets resemble each other. For they also share several stylistic characteristics: The imagist technique, the synthetic-ideogrammic diction, that involve processes such as history compression, montage of colloquial or literary quotes, or of *fait-divers* of the time, idiomatic *potpourri*, fusion of personae, besides the conversational fragmentation are of the same quality of the atemporal journalism typical of *The Cantos*. In the "Wall Street Inferno" everything is dialogue matter. The characters—like the Poundian masks—take on the initiative of discourse. Dashes, single or double, signal the voices. The brief fragments of prose that antecede the strophes function as summaries of actions, or scenic instructions. It is a minimalist theater, kaleidoscopic, where everything turns vertiginously as in a gyrating stage.

See, as an example, the following strophe, in which Latin, French, and English intertwine, that alludes to the affair Beecher-Tilton, the famous scandal that involved the famous preacher Henry Ward Beecher, head of the Plymouth Church, accused of an affair with a parishioner, the wife of journalist Theodor Tilton:

(Dois renegados, católico, protestante:)
—*Confiteor, Beecherô . . . L'Épouse*
N'eut jamais d'aussi faux autel
—*Confiteor . . . Hyacinth*
Absinth,
Plymouth was barroom, was bordel!

(Two renegades, catholic, protestant:)
—*Confiteor, Beecherô . . . L'Épouse*

N'eut jamais d'aussi faux autel
—Confiteor . . . Hyacinth
Absinth,
Plymouth was barroom, was bordel!

Or this other fragment that has as theme the affair Alabama, the pirate ship empowered by the British in support of the South during the Civil War, and that placed the United States and England in a political crisis that contributed to the fall of Gladstone:

(GLADSTONE pagando à tesouraria de WASHINGTON os milhões da arbitração de GENEBRA)
— *Very smarts! Ô! Ô! Very smarts!*
Mas pôs o Alabama pra trás
Aos *puffs*-Puritanos
Cem manos!
Sobre-*rum*-nadam *fiends, rascáls;*
Post war Jews, Jesuítas, Bouffes
Que decidem de uma nação
A cancan! . . . e os [GREEK]
Homeros
De rir servem, não de lição

(GLADSTONE paying WASHINGTON's treasure the millions from the GENEVA arbitration)
— *Very smarts! Ô! Ô! Very smarts!*
But sent Alabama backwards
To the *puffs*-Puritans
A hundred hands!
Over-*rum*-flowing *fiends, rascals;*
Post war Jews, Jesuits, Bouffes
Who decide of a nation
The cancan! . . . and the [GREEK]
Homers
Good for a laugh, not for learning

Strophes that remind, for their irony and concision, a work like *Hugh Selwyn Mauberly*.

That Sousândrade reveals to be, under many aspects, a precursor of Pound should not cause surprise: It is a plausible and detectible happenstance in the realm of comparative literature, through methods of prospective archeology research that Pound found in the work of Leo

Frobenius: "Where we found these rock drawings, there was always water within six feet of the surface." To what Pound added: "That kind of research goes not only into the past and forgotten life, but points to tomorrow's water supply."[9]

Alongside other poets that resided in the United States, such as Vladimir Mayakovsky and Federico García Lorca, Sousândrade left, in 1877 a rare and visionary carnet de voyage embedded in the quilt of "Wall Street Inferno." To write so extensively about him in an essay dedicated to Ezra Pound can strike the reader as impertinent. But it is, I maintain, a very Poundian mode of homage to the American poet. To homage him, making it new. Made in Brazil.

Translated by Antonio Sergio Bessa

Appendix 4: "The Aph*freud*isiac Lacan in the Galaxy of Lalangue"
Haroldo de Campos

Written originally as an address to a group of psychoanalysts in São Paulo, the essay starts as an exploration of the importance of *style* in the work of Jacques Lacan to quickly become a reflection on the legacy of the baroque and its persistence in the work of so-called "difficult" writers such as Lacan, Stéphane Mallarmé, and James Joyce. To that tradition, Campos suggests *inscribing* his own collection of fifty prose-poems titled *galáxias*. A first version of this essay was presented in 1985, at the Biblioteca Freudiana Brasileira in São Paulo. After two further revisions, Campos presented it in its present form at the Colégio Freudiano da Bahia, and published in the journal of the Brazilian School of Psychoanalysis (*Correio 18–19*, January 1989). A French translation by Inês Oseki-Dépré was published in issue 41 of the *Revue du Litoral*, Paris, 1994.

***

An Exercise in *Stylo*graphy

In July 1985, my good friend Joseph Attié introduced me to Judith Miller in the offices of the journal *L'Âne*. On that occasion we spoke about the relationship between Lacan and Don Luis de Góngora, Lacan and the baroque, a subject that I promised to approach in an essay. On the same occasion, I was informed that *L'Âne* was planning a special issue focused on the issue of style, or more precisely, on Lacan's quoting Buffon's famous phrase "*Le style est l'homme même*" (Style is man himself). Lacan's gloss—a pact of kinship between the psychoanalyst and the classic formula, under the condition of stretching it into an interrogation (*rallier* in order to *rallonger*)—now reads: "*Le style c'est l'homme . . .; l'homme à qui l'on s'adresse?*" (Style is man . . . the man to whom we address?)[1]

Thus amplified, the adage—says Lacan—would satisfy the principle, promoted by him, according to which: "*dans la langage notre message nous vient de l'Autre*" (in language, our message comes from the Other). I immediately intervened with a new gloss—a re-gloss to the Lacanian gloss—saying: It occurs to me a *motto*, an epigraph to this projected issue of *L'Âne*:

> *Le style c'est l'homme* (Buffon)
> *Le style c'est* l'Autre (Lacan)
> *Le stylo c'est l'Ane*

In my *Witz*, my witty *jeu d'esprit*,[2] *stylo* (pen) comes to replace style, both—*style* and *stylograph* (*stylo*, for short)—related to the same Latin word *stilus*, an acute, sharp instrument, made of metal or bone, with which one would write on waxed tables. This is, coincidentally, one of the meanings of the word *estilo* in Portuguese. One is also reminded that, in the same etymological area, the diminutive form of *estilo*, *estilete*, has been lexicalized as a "kind of dagger," arriving to us *via* the Italian *stiletto*. It was thus by an act of metonym—the trespassing of signifiers—that the manual instrument of writing came to designate the scriptural mark itself: the style.

Hence: "*Le stylo c'est l'Ane.*" Ane is an abbreviation of *Analyste*, or better yet, *Âne-à-liste*, ironic wordplay with which Lacan puts into question the institutional transmission of psychoanalysis.[3] In this motto, the result of rereading Buffon, through Lacan; in this doubly witty dislocation of that famous axiom, I insinuate still another allusion: *stylo* brings us to that passage of "The Function and Field of Speech and Language in Psychoanalysis" (1953) in which Lacan affirms that "*l'analyste participe du scribe*," or, in a more extensive citation:

> We play a recording role by serving a function which is fundamental in any symbolic exchange—that of gathering what *do kamo*, man in his authenticity, calls the "lasting word." A witness blamed for the subject's sincerity, trustee of the record of his discourse, reference attesting to its accuracy, guarantor of its honesty, keeper of its testament, scrivener of its codicils, the analyst is something of a scribe. But he remains the master of the truth of which this discourse constitutes the progress.[4]

Well, this quasi-scribe, this *stylo* who is also *"maître de la verité"*—the analyst—at least from Lacan onward, ostensibly claims a *style* (from where I could perhaps continue with my game: *"Le stylo c'est le style,"* which would be the equivalent of bringing both words to its etymological matrix, thus closing the hermeneutic circle). It is Lacan himself who stresses, in "Psychoanalysis and Its Teaching," that:

> A return to Freud, which provides the material for a teaching worthy of his name, can only be produced by the pathways by which the most hidden truth manifests itself in the revolutions of culture. This pathway is the only training that I can claim to transmit to those who follow me. It is called: a style.[5]

In regard to this declaration of attitude, Catherine Backès-Clément, concerning psychoanalysis and literature, has made some pertinent observations:

> *Formation; révolution de la culture: le style, défini par Lacan, se situe d'emblée hors de sa situation littéraire, ou plutôt, il est le corrélat nécessaire de ce qui, chez Lacan, s'appelle lettre, et régénère le signifiant "littérature," qui vient de Belles-Lettres. Le style, formation "révolutionnaire" sur le plan du langage, c'est ce qui, dans la pensée de Lacan, rend possible un dépassement de la "littérature," au profit de la littéralité: puissance de la lettre, instance de la lettre dans l'Inconscient, et, comme l'indique la suite de ce titre d'un morceau des Écrits, la raison depuis Freud, genèse d'une autre rationalité.*[6]

From Góngora to Mallarmé

This preoccupation with style (or the occupation of style), from the part of a psychoanalyst does not bother the writer—the poet—since the same analyst affirms that "it is the whole structure of language that the psychoanalytic experience discovers in the unconscious"; and that "language, with its structure, exists prior to each subject's entry into it at a certain moment in his mental development" and also that "the dreamwork proceeds in accordance with the laws of the signifier"; or that "modern verse is organized according to the same law of the parallelism of the signifier, whose concert governs both primitive Slavic epic and the most refined Chinese poetry"; and finally, "it suffices to listen to poetry, which Saussure was certainly in the habit of doing, for a polyphony to be heard, and for it to become clear that all discourse is aligned along the several staves of a musical score."[7] Lacan's observations are validated by the discovery of Ferdinand de Saussure's notes on the nonlinear dance of phonic figures or "anagrams" in Latin, Vedic and Old German poetry.[8] They coincide also with Roman Jakobson's idea of paronomasia (the play of phono-semantic convergence and/or contrasts), as a key-trope in poetry. This *occupation* (in the Latin sense of *ob-capire*, "to take possession of") of the field—vacant to other less creative followers of Freud—which the word style encapsulates does not bother, I reaffirm, the poet who discovers the fragment of "The Situation of Psychoanalysis and the Training of the Psychoanalyst in 1956," in which Lacan embraces the comparison with Góngora:

> ... there is no stylistic form, however elaborate (and the unconscious abound in such forms)—not excepting erudite, conceptualist, and precious forms—that is disdained by the unconscious any more than by the author of these lines, the Góngora of psychoanalysis, as people call him, at your service.[9]

The Góngora of psychoanalysis.... Let's recapitulate: Don Luis de Góngora y Argote, the Prince of Darkness of Spanish baroque, responsible for the *culto*, or *culterano* style, synonymous with formal excess and bad taste, against which, for two centuries at least, literary scholars inveighed—a trend we now regard as "Góngoraphobia;" the author whose obscurity was reinterpreted by Dámaso Alonso—one of the rescuers of the Góngorean style in modern poetry, together with Garcia Lorca, Gerardo Diego, and Afonso Reys—as an effect of obfuscation, caused by an aesthetic radiation of luminosity. Góngora, whom the French symbolists compared to Mallarmé, thus contributing to the reassessment of his work in modern days.[10] And Lacan has also been compared to Mallarmé, known by many as *l'Obscur* (this being also the title of Charles Mauron's 1941 book on the poet), notably, in the special issue of the *Yale French Studies* dedicated to structuralism, in which Lacan's work is introduced to the English-speaking public by Jan Miel in the following terms:

> A final word about Jacques Lacan's style. As a friend or doctor to some of the leading artists and poets of this century, and himself an acute critic of literature, Dr. Lacan does not begrudge himself the advantages of a complex literary expression. His style, called Mallarmean by his own colleagues, is distinctive and at times immensely difficult—deliberately so ...[11]

The parallel traced by Miel works wonderfully since, in the tradition of Mallarmé, Lacan is also a *syntaxier* (a syntaxist), a deft manipulator of

French syntax up to the extreme limit of phrasal design, which, not by chance, allows him to observe that "symbolic determination must be considered first as a product of syntax, if one wishes to grasp its analogical effects"; and that "the symbolic order can be approached only through its own apparatus. Just as you cannot do algebra without knowing how to write, you cannot handle or parry even the slightest signifying effect without at least suspecting what is implied by writing."[12]

It is this Góngora-Mallarmé, Dr. Lacan, who inscribes in an ideal syllabus of analytical teaching "rhetoric, dialectic, grammar and poetics—the supreme pinnacle of the aesthetics of language—which would include the neglected technique of witticisms." Because "psychoanalytical experience has rediscovered in man the imperative of the Word as the law that has shaped him in its image. It exploits the poetic function of language to give his desire its symbolic mediation." From which follows that "to be able to restore to speech its full evocative value, . . . to be taught and to be learned, this technique would require a profound assimilation of the resources of a language [*langue*], especially those that are concretely realized in its poetic texts. It is well known that Freud was steeped in German literature."[13]

Freud, Writer-Inventor

On the topic of Freud as a writer, there is an often neglected, pioneering essay, "*Freud als Schriftsteller*" (1930), by the Swiss literary theoretician Walter Muschg that brings into focus aspects of Freud's rapport to language that seem to vindicate Lacan's endeavors. For Muschg, Freud's writings clearly indicate the degree of his mastery of language and singles out the beauty and persuasiveness of his formulations, its sonority and rhythmic assuredness, which are present even in book titles such as *Das Unbehagen in der Kultur*, *Das Ich und das Es*, *Jenseits des Lustprinzips*, and *Trauer und Melancholie*. In these titles, due to an "antithetical tension" that finds correspondence in the "ictus" (marked tempos) of accentuation, the ear seems to capture, in "laconic formula," something like "the law of personality (*das Gesetz der Persönlichkeit*) its refrained energy, plenitude in parsimony." It underscores the "tactical eloquence" of supremely balanced composites like *Die Traumdeutung*, or the "imagistic force" (*bildkraft*), underscored by "binary rhythm," of a designation such as *Massenpsychologie und Ich -Analyse*. "Nobody would put in doubt," comments Muschg, "that a hand so expert in beauty had allowed itself to express this way." In examples such as these we already find, according to Muschg, the paradigm for the great Freudian finds in works such as

Psychopathologie des Altagsleben, in his writing on *Witz*, or on the interpretation of dreams:

> The way he dominates the keyboard of chords, the consonance and sound associations that play internally off each other; the way he is capable to follow up the most dazzling wordplay (*Wortwitz*), the caprices of free sound; with him, a brother of Morgenstern and the Surrealists, the micro-tonal piano of language is played, and leaves in the reader a strong impression of his capacities for linguistic fantasy (*Sprachphantasie*). This chapter is followed, deservedly, by the one about the reproduction of syntactical relationships in dreams, one that all poets will receive with fascination. Only someone with a profound experience of language could write all this.[14]

From my point of view, it is this Freud, attentive to the syntactic design of language, capable of capturing the subtle web of sounds and meaning, who is at the core of Lacan's most profound inquiries; this micrologic Freud, rather than the other one, whose essays on great literary and artistic works or their creators (*Gradiva* by Wilhelm Jensen, Michelangelo's *Moses*, for instance, or the analytical essays on Fyodor Dostoyevsky and Leonardo da Vinci) are so often quoted.

It is correct, on the other hand, that Freud's attitude toward language was primarily that of a man of science, a researcher (*Forscher*), as Muschg stresses:

> As a pure researcher Freud was led to usurp the primordial word (*Urwort*) from all poets, the dream word, for himself. This primordial word came to him as the epitome (*Inbegriff*) of a scientific thematic supremely chosen, that is for sure but also note how he took hold of the power of sound to stimulate (*Lautreize*)![15]

And Muschg proceeds to enumerate the variations that Freud was capable of extracting from the word *Traum* (*Traumquelle, Traumtag, Traumwunsch, Traumrede, Traumarbeit, Traumverdichtung, Traumereizen, Traumentstellung, Traumgedanke, Traummaterial*). As to the meaning of this neologisms factory that uses the resources of agglutination in the German idiom, Muschg notes that besides their fascinating aspect, these seductive words were created as "fundamental concepts of analysis" (*anlytische Grundbegriffe*). "The magic of words is not under the whim of an impulse to corrupt but follows and serves to a certain knowledge. It is not a pleasurable free play, but the application of laws (*Gesetzgebung*)."

The same can be said of Lacan, whose primary interest is not in *le plaisir du texte*, (as in Roland Barthes's case), but rather in the function of the signifier as "fundament of the dimension of the symbolic," which "only the analytical discourse allows us to isolate." What does not stop him from claiming on the other hand, in a text dedicated to Jakobson: "I will say that the signifier is situated at the level of enjoying substance (*substance jouissante*)."[16] *Le stylo*, the "scribe" is also—and above all—the "master of truth":

> The analysis must aim at the passage of true speech, joining the subject to an other subject, on the other side of the wall of language. That is the final relation of the subject to a genuine Other, to the Other who gives the answer one doesn't expect, which defines the terminal point of the analysis.
>
> . . .
>
> That is where the subject authentically re-integrates his disjointed limbs, and recognizes, reaggregates his experience.[17]

But, in going back to Freud, the course back to the precursor is made by a radicalization of the analytical discourse. I propose to call it "aph*freud*isiac" Lacan. For what is it if not in principle an obsessive exaltation of style, elevating to the extreme potency of language that which, in Freud, was above all a mechanism of analytical reading (even when traceable in the disperse paradigms of an indubitable scriptural predisposition). Thus, if I am allowed another parallel, Lezama Lima *gongorized* Góngora, taking him ostensibly onto excess in serpentine curlicues, in his exegetic essay "*Sierpe de Don Luis de Góngora*." In this sense, it can be said, Lacan partakes of the baroque.

From Lacan to Joyce (to Return to Freud)

In the same issue of *Littérature*, in which Catherine Backès-Clément articulates the Lacanian style—a style that produces a revolution in the formation of the analyst via language, as that of the innovative writer who revolutionizes language "branding it with his style"—Lacan published one of his most complex texts, "Lituraterre." While Lacan's title proposes a humorous pun on the journal's title (*Littérature*), it also pays homage to James Joyce by mashing *literature* and *litura* (Latin for *smudge*, *scratch*, *scribble*; hence the term *liturarius*: a sketchbook of rough drafts, scribbles, blotters). Lacan admits that he found the point of departure for his subversion of the *Belles Lettres* in James Joyce, who knew how to slide, with agility, amid the mistake between the *letter* and the *litter* (the latter, by its turn, from the Latin *lectus*, meaning bed). The *literordura*, as I wrote in one of the fragments of my *galáxias*. Joyce becomes here, the Freud of *textual practice*, a paradigm for all writers who, not content with *bellettrisme*, instead of concealing the backstage of text-making, expose the production processes. Writers who, according to Backès-Clément (based on Julia Kristeva's *Sémanalyse*), make the *Es* of the text (the *It* of text, the *other scene* of its engendering, Kristeva's *genotext*) erupt in the textual *Ich* (the *phenotext*, the manifested text, open to the *genotext* like the illusory subjectivity to the Unconscious). Writers who put in practice—according to Kristeva—the Freudian precept: *Wo Es war, soll Ich werden*.

At this point, we can intervene with still another operation—that of translation. For as far as it is concerned with the materiality of language ("language is not immaterial. It is a subtle body, but body it is"[18]), translation is also an act of unveiling. It announces the arrival of the text coming into *pure language* (Walter Benjamin) dissimulated in the text of departure.

Freud's gnomic formula, an aphorism-testament from his *Neue Vorlesungen*, has been translated and retranslated by Lacan many times, but nowhere the operation is more completely elaborated than in "The Freudian Thing":[19]

> Wo Es war, soll Ich werden.
> Where the Id was, there the Ego shall be.[20]
> Le moi doit déloger la ça.[21]
> I must come to the place where that (id) was.[22]
> Donde estuvo eso, tengo que advenir.[23]
> Lá onde era isso, me é preciso chegar.[24]
> Là où fût ça, il me faut advenir.[25]
> Là où c'était *peut-on dire*, là où s'était *voudrions nous faire qu'on entendit*, c'est mon devoir que je vienne à être.[26]

This last transposition (made, according to Lacan, "counter to the principles of the economy of expression"[27]), *Wo* (*Là où*) is understood as "*lieu d'être*" (a place of *being*). *Es*, often translated as *ça* or *soi*, is translated as *c'* (the elided *c* of *c'est*), a solution that, according to Lacan, has the benefit of getting rid of the objectifying *das*, that does not exist in the original. On the other hand (since a homophonic relation is established between the German word *es* and the initial letter of the French word *Sujet*), this solution aims at the production of an unexpected reflexive verb, *s'être* (be him/herself), a verb, which "would express the mode of absolute subjectivity, insofar as Freud truly discovered it in its radical eccentricity."[28]

I hope not to exceed Lacan's act as trans(vio)lator by proposing to translate Freud's adage à la Joyce, I mean, by operating basically on the signifiers and their phonic possibilities (and reencountering at this level the signifier's economy, momentarily suspended in the re-elaboration of the "scribe/master of truth" equation). Hence, we have in Portuguese:

Lá onde iss'estava dev'eurei devir-me

(There where t'was must-I'll be-me)

My operation consists of the imbrication of *isso* (this) and *si* (him/herself), and at the same time to cause the *eu* [I] to emerge from his/her *dever* (obligation), ("moral obligation," says Lacan), from the French *devir/devenir* (*werden* [to become]), not *survenir* (to overcome), nor *advenir* (to arrive), but *venir au jour* (come to light), *devir-se* (to become [him/her]self) ("il me faut," "c'est mon devoir" as a subject / "sujet véritable de l'inconscient"). The *me*, in my formula, may appear excessive, but I meant it to correspond to Lacan's reflexive *me faut*. The advantage of my translation is to bring back the concision and cadence of Freud's aphorism, now reinstated in Portuguese. Jacques Derrida: "To relinquish materiality: such is the driving force of translation. And when that materiality is reinstated, translation becomes poetry."[29] In what I have elsewhere referred to as "transcreation," hermeneutics is encapsulated in the signifier.[30]

Es Freud mich: Rejoyce!

If I am allowed to take this game a step further, I would like to focus on a polysemic counterpoint of words à la Joyce regarding the case of fetishism, reported by Freud and recounted by Lacan, as a *signet* to illustrate the way through which Freudian analysis of the unconscious, through formulas of connecting, and substitution, surprises the signifier in its function of transference (*Übertragung*). It's the story of a bilingual (English/German) patient to whom sexual satisfaction depended on a certain shine on the nose (*Glanz auf der Nase*). Analysis revealed that, because of his Anglophonic upbringing, his feverish curiosity about the maternal phallus (this *manque à être* [lack of being]) had deviated toward a "glance at the nose" (instead of "shine on the nose," as it would be adequately expressed in the forgotten language of the subject's infancy). The commutation from the German *Glanz* into the English *glance* can be restated as a pseudo-Joycean micro-story about Sham, the penman and Ana Livia Plurabela, the Eternal Feminine—Mother-Sister-Daughter-Lover-Wife—in *Finnegans Wake*.

Tudo seducedeu num brilhance de nasolhos.[31]

From that we can now pass—by a *commodius vicus of recirculation*, as Joyce noted—to Friedrich Schleiermacher's exemplary *wit* analyzed by

Freud, whose sole distinctive character, without which the *wit* would be abolished, consists in giving the same words multiple applications:

> *Eifersucht ist eine Leidenshaft*
> *Die mit Eifer Sucht, was Leiden schafft*

The *wit* is undone (its *Aufhebung* happens) in a banal translation, where the signifier is effaced:

> Jealousy (*Eifersucht*) is a passion (*Leidenshaft*)
> that with zeal (*Eifer*) searches (*Sucht*) that which
> causes (*Schafft*, from the verb *Schaffen*) pain (*Leiden*). [32]

Given their illegibility, it is tempting to compare Joyce (the Penman, "master of language") to Lacan (*Le Stylo*, the Scribe, proposed *master of truth*). About his *Écrits*, Lacan ironically noted, in the 1973 Postface to book XI of the *Seminar*, that the volume might be bought but not read, a fact which did not surprise him, since, he thought, as they had been written not to be read:

> After all the written as the not-to-be-read was introduced by Joyce, I'd do better to say intr*a*duced (both introduced and not translated) because to deal with the word is to negotiate beyond all languages, Joyce hardly translates himself at all, so that he is equally little-to-be-read-everywhere.[33]

In "The Function of the Written," a 1973 text from book XX of the *Seminar*, Lacan revisits this theme:

> I can agree that Joyce's work is not readable—it is certainly not translatable into Chinese. What happens in Joyce's work? The signifier stuffs (*vient truffer*) the signified. It is because the signifiers fit together, combine, and concertina—read *Finnegans Wake*—that something is produced by way of meaning (*comme signifié*) that may seem enigmatic, but is clearly what is closest to what we analysts, thanks to analytic discourse, have to read—slips of the tongue (*lapsus*). It is as slips that they signify something, in other words, that they can be read in an infinite number of different ways. But it is precisely for that reason that they are difficult to read, are read awry, or not read at all. But doesn't this dimension of "being read" (*se lire*) suffice to show that we are in the register of analytic discourse? What is at stake in analytic discourse is always the following—you give a different reading to the signifiers that are enunciated (*ce qui s'énonce de signifiant*) than what they signify.[34]

In the Galaxy of Lalangue

In "The Rat in the Maze" (1973), Lacan explains what he understands for *lalangue*. Here, I would like to state my objection to a translation of this new word that has been proposed in Brazil: *alíngua*.[35] Differently of the feminine article in French (*la*), the Portuguese equivalent (*a*), when juxtaposed to a word might be confused with the prefix of negation, meaning privation (as in aphasia, apathy, agnostic, etc.). Thus, *alíngua* (a-tongue), could signify absence of language, the same way that *alíngüe* (a-tongued), would mean the opposite of *plurilíngüe* (pluri-tongued), *multilíngüe* (multi-tongued), in short, the equivalent of *deslinguado* (tongueless). But *lalangue* is the opposite of the a-language (nonlanguage), of the privation of language. It is rather an emphasized language, a language tensed by the *poetic function*, a language that serves to things other than communication.[36] Our *idiomaternal* (to use a word I coined in my poem "Ciropédia ou a educação do príncipe," from 1952), not for nothing—Lacan insists—written as one word, since it designates the "occupation (*l'affaire*) of each one of us," to the extent that the unconscious is made of *lalangue*. Hence, I prefer *Lalangue*, with *la* prefixed as the *La* we employ when we refer to a great actress, or a diva (La Garbo, La Duncan, La Monroe). It also brings to mind the word *lalia*, from the Greek *laleo*, indicating loquacity, and, via the Latin *lallare*, meaning *lullaby*; or *glossolalia*, the supernatural talent to speak unknown languages. The entire semantic area that this agglutination invokes serves to underline the fact that, if "language is, no doubt, made up of *lalangue*," if it is a "harebrained lucubration, (*élucubration*) about *lalanguage*," being sure that this "knowing how to do things (*savoir-faire*) with *lalanguage* . . . goes well beyond what we can account for under the heading of language."[37] The *idiomaternal—lalangue—affects* us with *effects*, sums up Lacan, demonstrating that he plays with mastery the game that he enunciates.

For this reason, I named the intervention of Lacan's *style* in the analyst's formation, and in the evolution of the analytical discourse from a microtonal side of Freud, an aph*freud*isiac inserted into the galaxy of *lalangue*.

Now a few words on my own *galáxias*. Writing on the conjunction Freud/Lacan/Joyce, I have often referred to *translation*, but I could as well have written in terms of a *tradition*, a kind of "tradition of rupture" (to use Octavio Paz's expression) that configures itself in the sequence of works by writers such as Joyce. In that tradition I dared to inscribe the text that I titled *galáxias* (written between 1963 and 1976, and that originally was entitled, in a more programmatic way, *livro de ensaios: galáxias* [book of essays: galaxies]). The best characterization for these galactic texts I found in 1970, when most of them were already written. In that year, in the initial pages of *S/Z*, Roland Barthes exposed his concept of the *scriptible* (writerly) text, which would be considered illegible when compared to classical texts of literature, that is, with those, by definition, legible. *Starred, plural*, the *writerly text* entailed reading as a work in itself: "the more plural the text, the less it is written before I read it," wrote Barthes, who set the (unattainable) goal of such text thus:

> In this ideal text, the networks are many and interact without any one of them being able to surpass the rest; this text is a galaxy of signifiers, not a structure of signifieds. It has no beginning, it is reversible; we gain access to it by several entrances, none of which can be authoritatively declared to be the main one; the codes it mobilizes extend as far as the eye can reach, they are indeterminable.... The systems of meaning can take over this absolutely plural text, but their number is never closed, based as it is on the infinity of language.[38]

Lacan, by his turn, in "The Field of the Other," expresses:

> In so far as the primary signifier is pure non-sense, it becomes the bearer of the infinitization of the value of the subject, not open to all meanings, but abolishing them all, which is different.... This is why it is untrue to say that the signifier in the unconscious is open to all meanings. It constitutes the subject in his freedom in relation to all meaning, but this does not mean that it is not determined in it. Far, in the numerator, in the place of the zero, the things that are inscribed are significations, dialectized significations in the relation of the desire of the Other, and they give a particular value to the relation of the subject to the unconscious.[39]

In "The Pleasure of the Text," Barthes seems to concur with Lacan: "It is not the reader's 'person' that is necessary to me, it is this site: the possibility of a dialectic of desire, of an *unpredictability* of bliss; the bets are not placed, there can still be a game."[40] The difference is that, for the critic-writer Barthes, in the game of the *plural* text there is no decision principle ruling the codes of sense, there are no criteria for *truth*. For Lacan, scribe-stylist, but above all *maître de la verité*, what matters—in the study of dreams, of the lack, of wit, of the psychopathology of everyday life—is the psychoanalytical anamnesis that has to do not with *reality*, but with *truth*, with the appearance of truth in speech, with the restitution of the subject to its true place (*Wo es war*), total speech (*parole pleine*). In short, what interests him is the divination of the human mystery, for which the game of writing (of writer-inventors like François Rabelais and Joyce) provides evidences and suggests clues.[41]

Translated by Antonio Sergio Bessa

Notes

Introduction

1. It is important from the outset to state that the analogy between poetry and architecture was not an innovation introduced by the concrete poets, as in fact they were tapping into a great tradition that sees language as physical matter. Already in *De vulgari eloquentia*, in the early fourteenth century, Dante Alighieri wrote of poetry as a construction: "we call construction a group of words put together in regulated order" (63) or "a canzone is a connected series of stanzas" (73); and he defines stanza as "a capacious storehouse (*mansio capax*) or receptacle for the art in its entirety" (73). Cf. *Dante: De Vulgari Eloquentia*, ed. and trans. Steven Botterill (Cambridge: Cambridge University Press, 1996).

2. The influence of Pound is again made apparent as the word *noigandres* was taken from Canto XX, in which the poet tells about his struggles to understand the word found in a poem by Arnaut Daniel. Pound tells of a visit to German philologist and Provençal scholar Emil Levy (1855–1918), to no avail.

3. In his introduction to *The Spirit of Romance*, Richard Sieburth calls attention to Pound's attempt (both in his *Cantos* and in *The Spirit of Romance*) to "articulate a pattern, at once historical and atemporal, of cultural beginnings and rebeginnings." Sieburth adds that Pound subscribed to the "early German Romantics' estimation of the Middle Ages as the decisive inauguration of modernity in European literature." See Ezra Pound, *The Spirit of Romance*, introduction by Richard Sieburth (New York: New Directions, 2005), vii.

4. A term Pound adapted from German scholar and ethnologist Leo Frobenius, meaning "the tangle or complex of the inrooted ideas of any period." Ezra Pound, *Guide to Kulchur* (New York: New Directions, 1970), 57.

5. A prolific poet, and world traveler, Joaquim de Sousândrade (1832–1902) is best known as the author of *O Guesa*, a pan-American epic poem influenced by romantic and Indianist ideas and that according to Augusto de Campos and Haroldo de Campos anticipated a number of modernist techniques related to collage and citation.

6. See Charles Baudelaire, "The Painter of Modern Life," in *Selected Writings on Art and Literature*, trans. and introduction P. E. Charvet (London: Penguin Books, 1992), 402. The entire passage is the following: "He is looking for that indefinable something we may be allowed to call 'modernity', for want of a better term to express the idea in question. The aim for him is to extract from fashion the poetry that resides in its historical envelope, to destil the eternal from the transitory."

7. For an analysis of the challenges faced by the emperor to represent a deeply divided population made up of European immigrants, native Brazilians, and enslaved Africans, see Lilia Moritz Schwarcz, *As Barbas do Imperador*, 2nd edition (São Paulo: Companhia das Letras, 2010).

8. See Krista Brune, "Retranslating the Brazilian Imperial Project: O Novo Mundo's Depiction of the 1876 Centennial Exhibition," *Journal of Lusophone Studies* 3, no. 2 (Fall 2018). Published by the American Portuguese Studies Association (APSA).

9. See Keila Grinberg, "The Emperor and the Abolitionist: A Brazilian Royal Visits the U.S.," *Americas Quarterly*, January 13, 2020.

10. The recording of "Pelo Telefone" in 1916 is considered by samba historians the landmark event that made popular the carnival song genre. Although its authorship has been contested over time, the song was registered solely by Donga, in Brazil's National Library. Its countrywide release is also notable as it conveys another aspect of the early stages of modernization in Brazil focusing on communication and entertainment. The song is an invitation to revelry (*folia*), and the image of the telephone is curiously used as an instrument of power. The lyrics' central line ("O chefe da polícia manda lhe avisar / que na Carioca tem uma roleta para se brincar" [The police chief asks to tell you / of a new gambling joint in Carioca]) paints a deft image of a street rascal in Rio at the beginning of the century, holding court at a bar table and managing things in his own particular way.

11. In the original: Daí que, para poder pronunciar o ineditismo dessa experiência crucial representada pelas metrópoles tecnológicas, era preciso forjar outra dicção: fluida, pontual, plástica, descontínua, multifária.

12. Oswald de Andrade, *Telefonema*, introduction and notes Vera Maria Chalmers (São Paulo: Editora Globo, 1996).

13. See Nicolau Sevcenko, "Os Maquinismos de uma cenografia móvel" [The Mechanics of a movable scenography], in *Orfeu extático na metropole: São Paulo, sociedade e cultura nos frementes anos 20* (São Paulo: Editora Companhia das Letras, 1992), 119. The entire quote is as follows: "For Alcântara Machado the urban phenomenon is but the visible point of a deeper cultural matrix. 'The malaise is more extensive than one can imagine and has its origins in the racial obsession about what is foreign.' And he sums up his thoughts with a corroding image: 'The city exudes the whiff of an international exposition.'" [In the original: "Para Alcântara Machado esse fenômeno urbano é apenas a ponta visível de uma matriz cultural mais profunda.'o mal é muito mais extenso do que se pode imaginar e tem origem na obsessão racial do que é estrangeiro.' E arremata o raciocínio com uma imagem coruscante: 'A cidade tem assim um arzinho de exposição internacional.']. Sevcenko's fascinating research about the transformations the city of São Paulo went through in the 1920s directly connects the impact of the international exhibitions on the redesign of colonial era sites.

14. The participation of workers' delegations in world exhibitions dates back to as early as 1862, and according to Benjamin, quoting Henry Fougère, their demands "gave a direction to the social movement of the Second Empire, and even, we may say, to that

of the second half of the nineteenth century." See Walter Benjamin, *The Arcades Project* (Cambridge, MA: The Belknap Press of Harvard University Press, 2002), 186–88.

15. The "Semana de arte moderna" [Week of modern art] refers to a series of exhibitions, concerts, and events organized in São Paulo in the span of three days that helped launch the careers of writers such as Oswald de Andrade, Mário de Andrade, and Raul Bopp; painters Anita Malfatti and Tarsila do Amaral; composer Heitor Villa-Lobos, among others. For a complex analysis of the event in the context of the rapid growth of the city of São Paulo, see Sevcenko, *Orfeu extático na metropole*. As it happened, the model for the Semana seemed to echo the International Exhibition of Modern Art (often referred to as the Armory Show), held in New York a decade earlier. Attended for the most part by a selective audience made up of members of the upper middle class, the events organized around the Semana seemed to lack the broad appeal that the European expositions promoted.

16. In 1973, Caetano Veloso recorded "Gilberto Misterioso," a song based on a fragment from "Wall Street Inferno," and included in the album *Araçá Azul* (Philips Records, 4:50), and in the previous year, Hélio Oiticica, produced *Agripina é Roma-Manhattan*, a short film based on another fragment from the same poem.

17. See Antonio Sergio Bessa, "Word as Object: Concrete Poetry in Brazil, circa 1953," in *Poesie-Konkret Concrete-Poetry*, ed. Anne Thurmann-Jajes (Cologne: Salon Verlag, 2012), 69–95.

18. See Antonio Sergio Bessa, "Sound as Subject: Augusto de Campos's *Poetamenos*," in *The Sound of Poetry / The Poetry of Sound*, ed. Marjorie Perloff and Craig Dworkin (Chicago: University of Chicago Press, 2009), 219–36.

19. See Antonio Sergio Bessa, "Poetics of the Un-Poetic: Semiological Disorder in Augusto de Campos' *Popcretos*," in *Augusto de Campos at 90*, guest editors K. David Jackson, Marjorie Perloff, and André Vallias, Santa Barbara Portuguese Studies, 2nd Ser., Vol. 8, 2021. https://sbps.spanport.ucsb.edu/sites/default/files/sitefiles/volume/Vol_8/10.%20Bessa.pdf

20. See Antonio Sergio Bessa, "The Concrete, the Conceptual, and the Galáxias," in *Postscript: Writing After Conceptual Art*, ed. Andrea Andersson (Toronto: University of Toronto Press, 2018), 358–71.

21. See Antonio Sergio Bessa, "Samba Lessons," in *Haroldo de Campos: Tradutor e traduzido*, ed. Andréia Guerini, Simone Homem de Mello, and Walter Carlos Costa (São Paulo, Perspectiva, 2019), 213–31.

1. Word as Object

1. Cf. Augusto de Campos, Décio Pignatari, and Haroldo de Campos, *Novas: Selected Writings of Haroldo de Campos*, ed. Antonio Sergio Bessa and Odile Cisneros (Evanston, IL: Northwestern University Press, 2007), 217.
2. Augusto de Campos et al., "Pilot Plan for Concrete Poetry."
3. Augusto de Campos et al., "Pilot Plan for Concrete Poetry," 218.
4. Augusto de Campos et al., "Pilot Plan for Concrete Poetry."
5. "Pontos—Periferia—Poesia concreta" [Points—Periphery—Concrete poetry], in Augusto de Campos, Haroldo de Campos, and Décio Pignatari, *Teoria da poesia concreta—Textos críticos e manifestos, 1950–1960* (São Paulo: Livraria Duas Cidades, 1975), 21–22. Like many other writings from the early stages of concretism, this essay is a "fusion" of two earlier texts mixed with new material. Noigandres' reediting of

their early essays culminated in 1958 in "Pilot-Plan for Concrete Poetry," a text that sums up almost a decade of their continuous engagement with the Brazilian literary establishment.

6. Augusto de Campos et al., "Pontos—Periferia—Poesia concreta," 18.

7. Augusto de Campos, "Poesia concreta," in *Teoria da poesia concreta*, 44.

8. Pound's influence on Brazilian concrete poetry started in the late 1940s when news of his arrest in Italy and subsequent confinement at St. Elizabeths was being circulated in the international media. This influence was formally acknowledged in 1952 with the release of the first issue of the journal *Noigandres*, and in 1960 a selection of translations by Augusto de Campos, Haroldo de Campos, and Décio Pignatari were published as *Cantares de Ezra Pound*; another decade would go by until *The ABC of Reading* was released in a translation by Augusto de Campos and Paulo Paes. Spanning over two decades, this brief succession of events corroborates Noigandres' sustained dialogue with the Poundian *paideuma* and its ultimate *cannibalization* into the Brazilian avant-garde. Noigandres' stringent tone in the early manifestos, one must add, also shares Pound's taste for the pedagogical as the latter's directives for Imagism suggest: "1) Direct treatment of the 'thing' whether objective or subjective; 2) To use absolutely no word that does not contribute to the presentation; 3) As regarding rhythm: to compose in the sequence of the musical phrase, not in sequence of a metronome." Cf, "A Retrospect," in *Literary Essays of Ezra Pound* (New York: New Directions, 1973), 3. Excerpts from *Literary Essays of Ezra Pound*, copyright © 1973 by The Estate of Ezra Pound. Reprinted by permission of New Directions Publishing Corp.

9. Augusto de Campos, "Poesia concreta," 45.

10. Ezra Pound, *ABC of Literature* (New York: New Directions, 1960), 37. Excerpts from *ABC of Reading*, copyright ©1934 by Ezra Pound. Reprinted by permission of New Directions Publishing Corp.

11. Pound, *Literary Essays of Ezra Pound*, 26. Excerpts from *Literary Essays of Ezra Pound*, copyright © 1973 by The Estate of Ezra Pound. Reprinted by permission of New Directions Publishing Corp.

12. Pound, *Literary Essays of Ezra Pound*.

13. Pound, *Literary Essays of Ezra Pound*.

14. Pound, *Literary Essays of Ezra Pound*, 26–27.

15. Pound, *Literary Essays of Ezra Pound*, 25.

16. The entire quote reads thus: "Sincere means without wax, *sine cera*, but there is nothing in its surface to tell us that Roman antique dealers and makers of fake expensive marble used wax for their frauds. They still use it for that purpose in Naples." Ezra Pound, "How to Write," in *Machine Art and Other Writings*, ed. Maria Luisa Ardizzone (Durham, NC: Duke University Press, 1996), 88. Excerpts from letters, drafts, and archival materials by Ezra Pound, New Directions Pub. acting as agent, copyright ©2025 by Mary de Rachewiltz and the Estate of Omar S. Pound. Reprinted by permission of New Directions Publishing Corp.

17. Pound, "How to Write."

18. Pound, "How to Write," 89.

19. Ernest Fenollosa, *The Chinese Written Character as a Medium for Poetry* quoted by Pound in Pound, "How to Write."

20. Pound, "How to Write," 90.

21. Pound, "How to Write," 102–3.

22. Pound, "How to Write," 109.

23. Reviewing Richard Sieburth's edition of Pound's *Poems and Translations* for the Library of America and of *The Pisan Cantos* for New Directions, Perloff also notes that "for all Pound's talk of image and 'radiant cluster,' phanopoeia is not this poet's métier." Marjorie Perloff, "Pound Ascendant," *Boston Review*, April/May 2004.

24. Ezra Pound, "The Renaissance," in *Literary Essays of Ezra Pound*, 215. Excerpts from *Literary Essays of Ezra Pound* copyright © 1973 by The Estate of Ezra Pound. Reprinted by permission of New Directions Publishing Corp.

25. Pound, "The Renaissance," 217.

26. Pound, "The Renaissance," 218.

27. In 1917, "In a Station of the Metro," was included in *Lustra*. Hugh Kenner writes that in 1913 Pound instructed Harriet Monroe to print the poem with irregular spaces between clusters of words ("two lines, five phases of perception"). Hugh Kenner, *The Pound Era* (Berkeley: University of California Press, 1971), 197. One might consider that in its economy of means, Pound's early experiment in typography seems closer to Noigandres' esthetics than Mallarmé's *Un coup de dés*, the poem they often regarded as a model. In its immediacy, "In a Station of the Metro," embodies Oswald de Andrade's ideal of "compressed minutes of poetry" that Noigandres so admired. Excerpts from *Personae* copyright © 1926 by Ezra Pound. Reprinted by permission of New Directions Publishing Corp.

28. Ezra Pound, *A Memoir of Gaudier Brzeska* (New York: New Directions, 1970), 86–89. Excerpts from *Gaudier-Brzeska*, copyright ©1980 by New Directions Publishing Corp. Reprinted by permission of New Directions Publishing Corp.

29. Kenner, *The Pound Era*, 187.

30. Ralph Bevilaqua, "Pound's 'In A Station of the Metro': A Textual Note," *English Language Notes* 8, no. 4 (June 1971).

31. J. L. Austin, *Sense and Sensibilia*, Reconstructed from the manuscript notes by G. J. Warnock (New York: Oxford University Press, 1964), 2.

32. Austin, *Sense and Sensibilia*, 56.

33. Austin, *Sense and Sensibilia*, 58.

34. Austin, *Sense and Sensibilia*, 101.

35. Austin, *Sense and Sensibilia*, 107.

36. Austin's insistence on precision in philosophical language, we must acknowledge, does not entirely translate into Pound's call for precision in poetry, an area where subjectivity has the final word (pun intended). On the issue of subjectivity, Austin writes: "I am not disclosing a fact about *myself*, but about petrol, when I say that petrol looks like water." That is clearly not the same case in terms of poetry. Austin, *Sense and Sensibilia*, 43.

37. "Phanopoeia" was originally published in *The Little Review*, November 1918, and later collected in *Umbra*. Excerpts from *Umbra* copyright © 1920 by Ezra Pound. Reprinted by permission of New Directions Publishing Corp.

38. Daniel's canzones were translated to the Portuguese by Augusto de Campos in *Verso—Reverso—Controverso* [Verse—Reverse—Controversial] (São Paulo: Editora Perspectiva, 1979). The lines in question were rendered thus: "Vejo vermelhos, verdes, blaus, brancos, cobaltos / Vergéis, plainos, planaltos, montes, vales."

39. Ezra Pound, *Cantos* (New York: New Directions, 1998), 230. Excerpts from *The Cantos of Ezra Pound*, copyright © 1971 by Ezra Pound. Reprinted by permission of New Directions Publishing Corp.

40. In "*Yeux Glauques*," from the collection *Lustra*, 1915, inspired by a painting of the same title by the pre-Raphaelite painter Sir Edward Burne-Jones, Pound defines this particular eye color as "Thin like brook water / With a vacant gaze"; not simply green or emerald, but according to Hugh Kenner, the quality one finds in the owl's eye and that can also be applicable to the flickering quality of leaves in olive trees, willows, and grape vines; in Kenner's words: "to shine and then not to shine, glint, rather than shine." Kenner, *The Pound Era*, 45. Excerpts from *Personae* copyright © 1926 by Ezra Pound. Reprinted by permission of New Directions Publishing Corp.

41. *Brododaktylus* refers to a quality of pink hues related to the fingers of goddess Eos, the Latin Aurora, who in the morning lifts the veil of the night and announces the sunrise. Excerpts from *The Cantos of Ezra Pound*, copyright © 1971 by Ezra Pound. Reprinted by permission of New Directions Publishing Corp.

42. Augusto de Campos, "The Concrete Coin of Speech," in *Teoria da Poesia Concreta*, 119.

43. Augusto de Campos, "The Concrete Coin of Speech," 121.

44. Wendy Steiner, *The Colors of Rhetoric: Problems in the Relation Between Modern Literature and Painting* (Chicago: University of Chicago Press, 1982), 1.

45. Jean Starobinski, *Enchantment: The Seductress in Opera* (New York: Columbia University Press, 2008), 166.

46. Steiner, *The Colors of Rhetoric*, 1.

47. Augusto de Campos, "The Concrete Coin of Speech," 122.

48. Aderaldo Ferreira Araújo (1878–1967), born in the northeast state of Ceará, became blind at age eighteen after an accident in the railroad where he was employed; hence the appellation Cego Aderaldo (Aderaldo, the Blind). After the death of his parents Aderaldo became itinerant, singing to huge crowds in street fairs in small towns in the hinterland.

49. Augusto de Campos, "Um Dia, um dado, um dedo," in *Verso reverso controverso* (São Paulo: Editora Perspectiva, 1978), 257–62.

50. In his introduction to *Outro*, Campos also commented on Timothy Leary's vision of a new cultural landscape shaped by cybertechnology. "The information-age cyberperson will not sit for 150 minutes trapped in Cimino's wonderfully operatic mind or Coppola's epic intensities. For many of us, the best stuff we see on a movie screen are the trailers. A new art form is emerging the production of 3-minute teasers about coming attractions. Electronic haikus!" Cf. Timothy Leary, "Imagineering," in *Chaos & Cyber Culture* (Berkeley, CA: Ronin Publishing, 1994), 15.

51. Cf. Walter Benjamin, "One Way Street," in *Selected Writings, Volume 1, 1913—1926*, ed. Marcus Bullock and Michael W. Jennings (Cambridge, MA: The Belknap Press of Harvard University Press, 2004), 456.

2. Sound as Subject

1. Décio Pignatari, "Poesia concreta: organização" [Concrete poetry: organization], in Augusto de Campos, Décio Pignatari, and Haroldo de Campos, *Teoria da poesia concreta—Textos críticos e manifestos, 1950–1960*, 2nd ed. (São Paulo: Livraria Duas Cidades, 1975), 86. (Unless otherwise noted, all translations are by the author.) Coincidentally, Mário de Andrade, in *Pequena história da música* [Short history of music], lists the "composer" Ezra Pound in the same breath as Webern: "Also in trios, quartets and quintets a most interesting generation has bloomed, employing the most unusual

and curious group of soloists (Kurt Weill, Falla, Ezra Pound, and Anton Webern)." Augusto de Campos concludes that Andrade might have heard of the performance of *Le Testament* at the Salle Pleyel in 1926. Augusto de Campos, *Música de invenção* (São Paulo: Editora Perspectiva, 1998), 27.

2. Décio Pignatari, "Poesia concreta: organização," 87.

3. Haroldo de Campos, "Olho por olho a olho nu," in Augusto de Campos et al., *Teoria da poesia concreta*, 48.

4. Rodrigo Naves, "Minha relação com a tradição é musical" [My relation with tradition is musical], in Haroldo de Campos, *Metalinguagem & outras metas*, 4th ed. (São Paulo: Editora Perspectiva, 1992), 257–58.

5. Ferdinand de Saussure, *Course in General Linguistics*, trans., introduction, and notes by Wade Baskin (New York: McGraw-Hill, 1966), 66.

6. Flora Süssekind, "(Quase audível)—Nota sobre 'ão," in *Sobre Augusto de Campos*, ed. Flora Süssekind and Júlio Castañon Guimarães (Rio de Janeiro: 7 Letras, 2004), 153.

7. "Poesia e música," Haroldo de Campos interviewed by Luís A. Milanese, in Haroldo de Campos, *Metalinguagem & outras metas*, 285.

8. Augusto de Campos, *O Balanço da bossa—e outras bossas*, fifth edition (São Paulo: Editora Perspectiva, 2003); *Música de Invenção* (São Paulo: Editora Perspectiva, 1998); *Música de Invenção 2* (São Paulo: Editora Perspectiva, 2016).

9. Introduction to *Poetamenos*, in Augusto de Campos et al., *Teoria da poesia concreta*, 15.

10. Glenn Gould, mimeograph distributed with program for New Music Associates concert, Toronto, October 3, 1953 (rescheduled to January 9, 1954), http://www.uv.es/~calaforr/Webern/gould.htm.

11. The entire quote is worth citing: "Anton Webern, miniaturist par excellence, *Klangfarben* melodist per occasion, Mahler's spiritual descendant-an artist whose mature works, and in particular, of course, his only solo composition, the *Variations, op. 27* are occupied with Mondrian-like geometric concerns which bypass timbral considerations, whose adolescent opus, the one-movement *Quintet for Piano and Strings*, is only slightly more open to keyboard opportunity than is Mahler's *Quartet*, and whose make-work transcription tasks for his teacher Arnold Schoenberg (the *Orchestral Lieder, op. 8*; the *Chamber Symphony, op. 9*; etc.) adopt an every-note-that-can-be-there-will-be-there stance." Cf. "Korngold and the Crisis of the Piano Sonata," in *The Glenn Gould Reader*, ed. and introduction by Tim Page (New York: Alfred A. Knopf, 1989), 201.

12. In the original: "A música é para mim uma 'nutrição de impulso' indispensável. Como a poesia, no dizer de Pound, está mais próxima da música e das artes plásticas do que da própria literatura, acho natural que assim seja. Sem Webern, Mondrian e Maliévitch, eu não teria formulado o *Poetamenos* (também devedor, é óbvio, de Mallarmé, Pound, Joyce e Cummings)," *Revista Cult*, São Paulo, 1998, no. 17.

13. Webern used this diagram as the basis for his *Concerto, op. 24,* and it was ultimately inscribed on his gravestone, it can be translated as "Arepo, the harvester, holds the wheels at work," and there is much speculation as to what it really represents.

14. In his 1934 *Concerto for Nine Instruments,* for example, all the pitch material is derived only from the three-note series B-Bb-D and its three mirror forms (retrograde, inversion, retrograde inversion).

15. Highly influenced by atonal music, Herbert Eimert (1897–1972) was one of the founders, in 1951, of the Studio für elektronische Musik des Westdeutschen Rundfunks,

in Cologne, which he directed until 1962, when he was succeeded by Karlheinz Stockhausen.

16. Augusto de Campos, *Música de Invenção*, 96.

17. Augusto de Campos, *Música de Invenção*, 95.

18. In a symposium organized on March 29, 2023, at Casa das Rosas, São Paulo, to commemorate the seventieth anniversary of the first edition of *Poetamenos*, poet André Valias noted the correspondence between the number of poems in Campos's collection and the number of sides on a die. In the same gathering, João Queiroz, professor of cognitive semiotics at the Juiz de Fora University, also commented on the possible parallel between the six poems in *Poetamenos* and the six bagatelles written by Anton Webern.

19. Augusto de Campos, *Balanço da bossa e outras bossas*, 213.

20. Theodor W. Adorno, *Alban Berg: Master of the Smallest Link* (Cambridge: Cambridge University Press, 1991), 14.

21. A literal translation reads, "A sound that does not sound / in the air that is not / almost as a person."

22. Eduardo Sterzi, "Todos os sons, sem som," in *Sobre Augusto de Campos*, 105.

23. Sterzi, "Todos os sons, sem som," 107.

24. It can perhaps be argued that this shift was part of an international phenomenon, since innovations related to the projection of voice in bossa nova shared a sense of kinship with musicians like Chet Baker, for instance, and even Fred Astaire. The *canto-falado* style subsequently found near-perfect vehicles in two films by Jacques Demy, done in collaboration with the composer Michel Legrand: *Les Parapluies de Cherbourg* (1964) and *Les Demoiselles de Rochefort* (1967).

25. Walter Garcia, *Bim Bom—A Contradição sem conflitos de João Gilberto* (São Paulo: Editora Paz e Terra, 1999), 81–82.

26. The role of the machine in concrete poetry is addressed by Haroldo de Campos in "Poesia concreta—linguagem—comunicação," in Augusto de Campos et al., *Teoria da poesia concreta*, 70. In English, "Concrete Poetry—Language—Communication," in Haroldo de Campos, *Novas: Selected Writings*.

27. Garcia, *Bim Bom*, 122.

28. Garcia, *Bim Bom*, 126.

29. Garcia, *Bim Bom*, 127.

30. Garcia, *Bim Bom*, 171.

31. Cf. the final poem in "Bestiário—para fagote e esôfago": "and / this / the / official / cate / gory / of the / bard / with / whom/—soon he's dead—/the / august / bust / fair enough / embattles." (My translation).

32. Gary Tomlinson, *Metaphysical Song* (Princeton, NJ: Princeton University Press, 1999), 47.

33. Sterzi, "Todos os sons, sem som," 112.

34. The influence of Rodrigues's songbook on the work of Augusto de Campos remains to be fully appreciated, but the fact that Campos dedicated three essays in *Balanço da bossa* to Rodrigues (which includes an attempt to compile the composer's complete discography) gives a measure of the sense of reverence he had for the great *sambista* from Porto Alegre.

35. Augusto de Campos, *Balanço da bossa*, 315–16.

36. Although Campos does not describe the event in detail, their encounter most likely happened in 1963 during the Curso de introdução ciência e arte [Introductory session on science and art], in Porto Alegre, in which Haroldo de Campos was

in charge of the literary content, presenting conferences on Sousândrade, Oswald de Andrade, João Cabral de Melo Neto, and on concrete poetry.

37. Augusto de Campos's admiration for Lupicínio Rodrigues is cleverly memorialized in his translation of John Donne's "The Apparition," in which he uses a famous line by Rodrigues ("nos braços de um outro qualquer") as a solution for Donne's "And thee, feigned vestal, in worse arms shall see." For a detailed reading of Campos's unorthodox "recreations" of Donne, see Ana Helena Souza, "'A Urdidura subjacente': Recriações de poemas de John Donne," in *Sobre Augusto de Campos*, 268–84.

38. Augusto de Campos, *Balanço da bossa*, 222–23.

39. Prominent among these references are an anonymous Provençal song from Galicia and lines from Luís de Camões ("Esperança de um só dia" [Hope of a single day]), as well as from the Parnassian poet Luis Guimarães Junior ("Oh, se me lembro, e quanto" [Oh, do I recall it, and how]).

40. In the French anthology of Campos's work organized by Jacques Donguy the author performs a formidable "unpacking" of the word mutation going on in *Poetamenos*. In the section that follows, I use many of Donguy's solutions, as well as information given to me directly by Augusto de Campos. Cf. Augusto de Campos, *Anthologie-Despoesia*, préface et traduction Jacques Donguy (Nîmes: Al Dante, 2002), 16–29.

41. Augusto de Campos, "O Rei Menos o Reino," in *VIVA VAIA—Poesia 1949–1979* (São Paulo: Ateliê Editorial, 2001), 10.

42. Cf. Marques da Cruz, *História da Literatura* (São Paulo: Editora Cia. Melhoramentos, 1924).

43. Camões's sonnet "Sete anos de pastor" refers to the biblical story of Jacob, who labored seven years in order to marry Rachel. Campos quotes from the first line in the second stanza:

Sete anos de pastor Jacó servia
Labão, pai de Raquel, serrana bela;
mas não servia ao pai, servia a ela,
e a ela só por prêmio pretendia.

Os dias, na esperança de um só dia,
passava, contentando-se com vê-la;
porém o pai, usando de cautela,
em lugar de Raquel lhe dava Lia.

Vendo o triste pastor que com enganos
lhe fora assim negada a sua pastora,
como se a não tivera merecida;

começa de servir outros sete anos,
dizendo:—Mais servira, se não fora
para tão longo amor tão curta a vida.

44. The word *azeredo* indicates an orchard of *azeiros* (Prunus lusitanica), a tree of the Rosaceae family.

45. Apropos of "lygia fingers," Donguy writes, "Idéogramme lyrique de la féminité et de la félinité, avec la syllabe 'ly' qui assume le caractère d'une cellule thématique"

[Translation: "lyrical ideogram of femininity and of felinity, with the syllable 'ly' that takes the role of a thematic cell"]. Augusto de Campos, *Anthologie-Despoesia*, 8.

46. Francis Bacon, *De dignitate et augmentis scientiarum*, II, xiii, trans. Robert Leslie Ellis and James Spedding. Quoted in John Hollander, *The Figure of Echo: A Mode of Allusion in Milton and After* (Berkeley: University of California Press, 1981), 11, fn. 4. I thank Fernando Pérez Villalón for bringing to my attention Hollander's notion of the acoustic image, a subject of central interest in the poetics of concretism.

47. Hollander, *The Figure of Echo*, 10.

48. Hollander, *The Figure of Echo*.

49. Marjorie Perloff, *Differentials: Poetry, Poetics, Pedagogy* (Tuscaloosa: The University of Alabama Press, 2004), 41–42.

3. Mechanics of Composition

1. Mallarmé's ambiguous use of the word *instrument* brings up the analogy between writing and music, however, he is also considering the progress of the printing apparatus, whose production of new formats like daily newspapers and advertisement posters were quickly transforming the city environment. He ponders, for example, on the implication that large sheets as opposed to thick stacks of pages, and the new folding and rhythms will have on the ancient ritual of reading: "Folding is, with respect to the page printed whole, a quasi-religious indication: the large sheets are less striking than the thick stacks of pages, which offer a tiny tomb for the soul." Cf. Stéphane Mallarmé, "The Book as Spiritual Instrument," in *Divagations*, trans. Barbara Johnson (Cambridge, MA: Belknap Press, 2007), 227. It is worth considering that as early as 1930 poet Bob Brown decried the "existing medievalism" of the book and proposed a reading machine apt to keep up with the speed of his era. Cf. *The Readies*, ed. and intro. Craig Saper (New York: The Roving Eye, 2014).

2. Cf. *The Wedge*, in *The Collected Poems of William Carlos Williams—Volume II 1939-1962*, ed. Christopher McGowan (New York: New Directions, 1988), 54. In a letter to Ezra Pound dated April 15, 1949, Williams wrote that *The Wedge* was "gathered together during the war under the incentive provided me by various GIs who wanted a book of my poems, so their letters said, that they could carry in their pockets." Cf. Mary Ellen Solt, *Dear Ez: William Carlos Williams Letters to Ezra Pound* (Bloomington, IN: The Private Press of Fredric Brewer, 1985), 42.

3. The Merriam-Webster Dictionary defines a *simple machine* as "any of various elementary mechanisms formerly considered as the elements of which all machines are composed and including the lever, the wheel and axle, the pulley, the inclined plane, the wedge, and the screw."

4. Cf. "Poetry and Abstract Thought," in Paul Valéry, *The Art of Poetry*, trans. Denise Folliot and intro. T. S. Eliot (New York: Pantheon Books, 1958).

5. Haroldo de Campos first approached Williams's work in 1958 in his essay "William Carlos Williams: Altos e baixos" commending "the Williams of certain short poems, master of a sharp cutting technique in constant negotiation with graphic space—no longer neutral, but to some extent an active element in the structure of his poems—through which language (often just a phrase, a fragment unraveling like a reel) is scanned in sensitive stresses (*ictos*): a language that retains the inflection of colloquial speech albeit minimized, reduced to a notation of color, sound, form, environment, hence the spatial rhythm that goes against the morose habits of reading, through

unexpected highlights and pauses, generating new articulations." Campos mentioned a visit he paid to Dr. Williams's house in Paterson, New Jersey, in fragment 27 of the *galáxias*.

6. Décio Pignatari, "Forma, função e projeto geral" [Form, function and general project], in *Teoria da poesia concreta: Textos críticos e manifestos 1950—1960*, 2nd edition (São Paulo: Livraria Duas Cidades, 1975), 109. It's worth noting that Pignatari's essay was first issued through the magazine *AD* (Arquitetura e Decoração), at the time a vehicle for progressive ideas in support of the broad construction spree promoted by the Kubitschek government.

7. Cf. Paula Gorenstein Dedecca, "Visão do outro e autoimagem" [Vision of the other and self-image], in *Sociabilidade, crítica e posições arquitetônico, as revistas especializadas e o debate do moderno em São Paulo (1945–1965)* (Master of Architecture and Urbanism dissertation, Universidade de São Paulo, 2012), 152.

8. In his 1957 essay "Concrete Poetry—Language—Communication," Haroldo de Campos cast an incisive look into the mechanics of "terra" in view of the emerging experiments with *musique concrète* in Europe. More to point, Campos examined the poem's structure as it relates to the process of feedback in cybernetics and quoted at length from *Minds and Machines* by W. Sluckin. He sums up the poem's structure thus: "The word terra would be the generator of the complex that embodies the poem: terra—erra—ara terra—rara terra—erra ara terra—terra ara terra [earth/hearth—err—tend the earth—rare earth—err tend the earth—earth tends earth]: these are the thematic elements that originate from this nucleus, besides the expression 'terra a terra' (down to earth), that follow throughout like a virtual phonetic chorus." See Haroldo de Campos, "Concrete Poetry—Language—Communication," in *Novas: Selected Writings*, 238.

9. In this regard, it is worth mentioning Roland Greene's distinction of Spanish and Portuguese narratives of the colonization in the Americas. The first, he writes, "concerns the feats of singular figures often told from their first-person vantage," while the latter (the Portuguese in Brazil) "are centered on the place itself." The land, Greene writes evoking Pero Vaz de Caminha, "is named not for Christ or for the king but for the cross, in a lovely passage that witnesses the name Terra de Vera Cruz—the word *terra* becoming with its second iteration in the delicately rhyming last phrase ('aaterra / a tera / davera'), part of a name that nonetheless preserves something of the place's unnamed past as simply 'land.' " At the end of the chapter, Greene cites Pignatari's "terra" to bring the reader "back to where we began, with its iteration of that word in Vaz de Caminha's letter." And he adds: "Like the naming that carried traces of the land's unnamed condition, Pignatari's 'terra' preserves the undisclosed place itself and the discovered but unattainable *terra roxa*. The diagonal clearing that runs across the poem is perhaps the brief, doomed interval between these two states of what came to be called Brazil—or, what might amount to the same thing, the mark of European Christian civilization, of the Vera Cruz, on the terrestrial surface." See Roland Greene, " 'For Love of Pau Brasil'—Objectification in Colonial Brazil," in *Unrequited Conquests: Love and Empire in the Colonial Americas* (Chicago: University of Chicago Press, 1999), 77–134.

10. See Vladimir Mayakovsky, "Agitation and Advertising," quoted in Victor Margolin, *The Struggle for Utopia: Rodchenko, Lissitzky, Moholy-Nagy, 1917–1946* (Chicago: University of Chicago Press, 1997), 113–14. NEP refers to Lenin's New Economic Policy: "whereby the state temporarily abandoned the drive for total nationalization of the

economy and allowed the private sector a greater role." Margolin, *The Struggle for Utopia*, 48.

11. In addition to the influence of Russian revolutionary tactics, it must be acknowledged that "beba coca cola" owes a debt to Oswald de Andrade's 1928 *Manifesto Antropofágico*, which called for the cannibalization of foreign culture. In its devouring and regurgitation of the brand Coca-Cola (decomposed into shreds of glass and drool), "beba coca cola" follows on the path opened by Andrade. The poem ought to be seen as an anti-advertisement, a subversive boomerang aimed at capitalist ideology.

12. Walter Benjamin, *The Arcades Project*, trans. Howard Eiland and Kevin McLaughlin (Cambridge, MA: The Belknap Press of Harvard University Press, 1999), 170.

13. Décio Pignatari, "nova poesia: concreta," in *Teoria da Poesia Concreta*, 41–43.

14. The advertising campaign produced for the Shell Oil Company by João Carlos Magaldi in collaboration with the agency Ogilvy & Mather consisted of five thirty-second videos featuring the three participants of the pop group Mutantes released countrywide. In addition, there were graphic materials for magazine circulation.

15. See Moacy Cirne, "Duas ou três coisas sobre o poema/processo," in *Revista Ponto 2* (Rio de Janeiro, 1968).

16. For more information on poema/processo, see my essay "A Guerra de palavras" [The War of Words], in *Poema/Processo, uma vanguarda semiológica*, ed. Gustavo Nóbrega (São Paulo: WMF Martins Fontes, 2017), 234–43. This essay, together with several contributions by poets connected to poema/processo, was published in a special issue dedicated to the movement by OEI # 66, Stockholm, September 27, 2014, 520 pages.

17. Luiz Ângelo Pinto and Décio Pignatari "Nova linguagem, nova poesia" [New Language, New Poetry], in *Teoria da Poesia Concreta*, 159–60.

18. Décio Pignatari, *Semiótica & Literatura*, 6th edition (São Paulo: Ateliê Editorial, 2004), 16–20.

19. Pignatari, *Semiótica & Literatura*, 89.

20. Pignatari, *Semiótica & Literatura*, 30.

21. Tristão de Alencar Araripe Júnior, "Raul Pompéia: O Ateneu e o romance psicológico." Essay originally published in twenty-one parts in *Novidades*, Rio de Janeiro, from December 6, 1888 to February 8, 1889. In *Obra Crítica de Araripe Júnior–Volume II, 1888–1894*, ed. Afrânio Coutinho (Rio de Janeiro: Ministério da Educação e Cultura–Casa de Rui Barbosa, 1960), 125–77.

22. Araripe Júnior, "Raul Pompéia," 156. In this regard, Pompeia's mechanistic vision of a character "victim of a contagion, who every moment is invaded by whatever is salient or percussive in other characters surrounding him," is reminiscent of Nathalie Sarraute's idea of *tropism*, which she developed in novels like *Le Planétarium*.

23. Araripe Júnior, "Raul Pompéia," 158.

24. Araripe Júnior, "Raul Pompéia," 161.

25. Tristão de Alencar Araripe Júnior, "Movimento literário do ano de 1893," in *Obra Crítica de Araripe Júnior–Volume III, 1888–1894*, ed. Afrânio Coutinho (Rio de Janeiro: Ministério da Educação e Cultura–Casa de Rui Barbosa, 1960), 138.

26. Décio Pignatari, "Recordaflexões brasileiras (de um diário de bardo, a bordo da espaçonave *El Durasno*)" [Brazilian Memoir-reflections (from the diary of a bard on board of the spaceship El Durasno)], in *Polem*, 1974, ed. Duda Machado. In the original: "A linguagem está embutida no código genético ADN. Quer dizer: a linguagem é uma mutação na espécie humana (Darwin, Freud, Monod). O homem está virando

signo noosférico e nosferático, como já vinham dizendo Poe, Peirce, Mallarmé e Pignatari." The word pun Noosphere/Nosferatu might refer to the short, underground 1970 film *Nosferato no Brasil* by Ivan Cardoso and featuring Tropicália lyricist/poet Torquato Neto. Ivan Cardoso, *Nosferato no Brasil*, 1970, black and white, and color, 25 minutes, filmed in Super 8. The odd, humorous pairing of the concept of the Noosphere and the fictional figure of the vampire Nosferatu, denoted Pignatari's openness to a new moment in Brazilian culture spearheaded by the eclectic style of Tropicália. Like Neto's lyrics, Pignatari's text delivers a kaleidoscopic mix of historical references, and personal musings, with raw emotion. References to Darwin and Freud are perhaps not surprising, but the mention of Jacques Lucien Monod (1910–1976) suggests that Pignatari's interest in codes and information was leading him to exciting sources such as Monod's 1971 book *Chance and Necessity: Essays on the Natural Philosophy of Modern Biology*, which explores the genetic code and its ability to reproduce and transmit information.

27. Pignatari compares Gouveia to Orson Welles and the subject of his film Charles Foster Kane: "Delmiro Gouveia was the Welles/Kane of the first wave of industrialism in Brazil."

28. The entire entry reads thus: "Santos-Dumont was our first designer, and one of the greatest in the world. His *14 bis* airplane was an industrial design masterpiece. Mondrian before Mondrian. Mies van der Rohe before Mies. The heavenly abodes."

29. Sérgio Buarque de Holanda, "O Homem máquina," article originally published in *A Cigarra*, March 1921. See Sérgio Buarque de Holanda, *Escritos Coligidos*, vol. 1, 1920–1949, organized by Marcos Costa (São Paulo: Editora UNESP, Fundação Perseu Abramo, 2011), 15–18. In the article, Buarque de Holanda dreads the possibility that in the near future the "thinking machine" that Ramon Llull sketched out in the *Ars Magna* would be built by modern man out of "nuts and bolts, powered by electricity or steam." It is worth noting that in 1937, Jorge Luis Borges briefly also addressed Llull's *Ars Magna* to summarily conclude that "the thinking machine does not work." As a conclusion he offered the following: "As an instrument of philosophical investigation, the thinking machine is absurd. It would not be absurd, however, as a literary and poetic device. Discerningly, Fritz Mauthner notes that a rhyming dictionary is a kind of thinking machine." See Jorge Luis Borges, "Ramon Llull's Thinking Machine," in *Selected Non-Fiction*, ed. Eliot Weinberger and trans. Esther Allen (New York: Penguin Publishing, 2000).

30. First articulated by the French philosopher Teilhard de Chardin and further developed by Ukrainian biogeochemist Vladimir Vernadsky, the *noosphere* indicated a new evolutionary stage informed by human consciousness. Departing from this concept, the poem offers a phantasmagoric vision of a mechanized city, when the first experiments in aviation were happening, promoted by pioneers such as Octave Chanute (1832–1910), Gabriel Voisin (1880–1978), Clément Ader (1841–1925), Louis Blériot (1872–1935), and the brothers Orville (1871–1948) and Wilbur Wright (1876–1912).

31. Julio Plaza, "Reflections of and on Theories of Translation," in *Dispositio* VI, no. 17–18: 45–91. Department of Romance Languages, University of Michigan.

32. In "From Avant-Garde to Digital: The Legacy of Concrete Poetry," Marjorie Perloff refuted Caroline Bayard's assertion that concrete poetry is "bedeviled by a lingering Cratylism—the doctrine put forward by Plato that the sound and visual properties of a given word have mimetic value, and that, by extension, concrete poetry equates 'graphic-typographical form with semantic function.'" See Perloff,

Unoriginal Genius: Poetry by Other Means in the New Century (Chicago: University of Chicago Press, 2010), 50–75. In the same essay, Perloff quotes Kenneth Goldsmith's impression of listening to a presentation by Décio Pignatari in New York in 2001: "I was stunned. Everything he was saying seemed to predict the mechanics of the internet in so many respects: delivery, content, interface, distribution, multi-media, just to name a few. Suddenly it made sense: like de Kooning's famous statement: 'History doesn't influence me. I influence it,' it's taken the web to make us see just how prescient concrete poetics was in predicting its own lively reception half a century later. I immediately understood that what had been missing from concrete poetry was an appropriate environment in which it could flourish. For many years, concrete poetry has been in limbo: it's been a displaced genre in search of a new medium. And now it's found one."

33. George Steiner, "The Distribution of Discourse," in *On Difficulty and Other Essays* (New York: Oxford University Press, 1978), 63. And on page 65: "Vygotsky held that in their ontogenetic development thought and speech have different roots. In the linguistic growth of the child, he found a pre-intellectual stage; correspondingly, there is a pre-linguistic stage in thought development. Up to a certain point in time, the two follow different and independent lines. It is when these lines converge that thought becomes verbal and speech rational."

34. "noosfera" was first published in the *Suplemento Literário de Minas Gerais*, on October 13, 1973, and later in the journals *Polem* (1974) and *Qorpo Estranho* (1976). The layout of those first publications were disapproved by Pignatari, who invited Omar Khouri in 1984 to design the definitive version.

4. Poetics of the Unpoetic

1. Luiz Costa Lima, "O Campo de uma experiência antecipadora," in *revisão de sousândrade*, third edition, ed. Augusto de Campos and Haroldo de Campos (São Paulo: Editora Perspectiva, 2002), 461–503.

2. Cf. T. S. Eliot, "Dante," in *Selected Essays 1917–1932*, fourth printing (New York: Harcourt, Brace and Company, 1938), 199–237. Of particular importance for our argument is the following passage: "Dante's is a *visual* imagination. It is a visual imagination in a different sense from that of a modern painter of still life: it is visual in the sense that he lived in an age in which men still saw visions. It was a psychological habit, the trick of which we have forgotten, but as good as any of our own. We have nothing but dreams, and we have forgotten that seeing visions—a practice now relegated to the aberrant and uneducated—was once a more significant, interesting, and disciplined kind of dreaming."

3. Richard Sieburth, "In Pound We Trust: The Economy of Poetry/The Poetry of Economics," *Critical Inquiry* 14, no. 1 (Autumn, 1987): 142–72.

4. Eugene Vance, "Chaucer's *House of Fame* and the Poetics of Inflation," *Boundary 2* 7, no. 2 (Winter, 1979): 17–38. Revisions of the Anglo-American Tradition: Part 1 (Winter, 1979).

5. Claude Lévi-Strauss, *The Savage Mind* (Chicago: University of Chicago Press, 1966), 20.

6. Following the end of World War II, the growing reach of the press in Brazil was responsible for popularizing avant-garde debates such as the concrete/neo-concrete polemics through the creation of weekly cultural supplements to major newspapers.

Those supplements in time gave way to fully-fledged publications like the journal *Invenção*, which started as a weekly page in *Correio Paulistano* (1960–1961). In the next decade an ambitious editorial project was set afoot aimed at disseminating high culture and knowledge through affordable fascicles available throughout the country at newsstands. Alongside the proliferation of photonovelas, comics, and weekly glossies, a widespread readership had access to collections such as *Grandes Compositores da Música Universal* [Great composers of universal music, 1968–1970] based on the Italian series issued by Fratelli Fabbri. Other series comprised encyclopedic collections on visual arts masters, playwrights, and philosophers. For more on this subject see my essay "Environment, Object, Action: Graphics by Other Means in the New Century," in *Trienal Poli/Gráfica de San Juan: El Panal/The Hive* (San Juan: Instituto de Cultura Puertoriqueña, 2012), 82–103.

7. It is worth noting that in "Esquema geral da Nova Objetividade," Hélio Oiticica makes a passing reference to Cordeiro's *Popcretos* noting that Cordeiro's "proposition fuses the semantic to the work's structural aspect. For him, the disintegration of the physical object is also semantic disintegration, for the construction of a new meaning." [In the original: *"proposição na qual o lado estrutural (o objeto]) funde-se ao semântico. Para ele a desintegração do objeto físico é também desintegração semântica, para a construção de um novo significado"*]. And although he does not reference Campos's series of poems, his analysis could also be applicable. For the complete text, see *Escritos de Artistas: Anos 60/70*, organized by Glória Ferreira and Cecilia Cotrim (Rio de Janeiro: Jorge Zahar Editor, 206), 154–68.

8. For the poem "SS," Campos provided the following entry: "the ambiguous SSemantics of acronyms. The pope. The gestapo. The supreme soviet. The monokini [sans soutien]. The physiognomy of letters. From abstract symbol to iconic sign, vice-versa. 2 months of rage in the newspapers. clippings. packings. the talk of the tribe. details-detritus of reality. the liberty in letters. the brazilian anthropophagic chaos redestroyed by the titlemania of a anarchitect" [*"a ambígua SSemântica das SSiglas. o papa, o Gestapo, o soviete supremo, o monoquini, a fisiognomia das letras. de simbolo abstrato e signo icônico, vice-versa. 2 meses de raiva nos jornais. recortes. revólucros. geSSy, eSSo, modeSS. a fala da tribo. detalhes-detritos da realidade. a liberdade em letras. o caos antropofágico brasileiro redestruído pela manchetomania de um anarquiteto."*]

9. See Dante Alighieri, *Paradiso* 14: "*Dal centro al cerchio, e sì dal cerchio al centro movesi l'acqua in un ritondo vaso, secondo ch'è percosso fuori o dentro: ne la mia mente fé sùbito caso questo ch'io dico, sì come si tacque la gloriosa vita di Tommaso, per la similitudine che nacque del suo parlare e di quel di Beatrice . . .*" [From rim to center, center out to rim, so does the water move in a round vessel, as it is struck without, or struck within. What I am saying fell most suddenly into my mind, as soon as Thomas's glorious living flame fell silent, since between his speech and that of Beatrice, a similarity was born].

10. Jaques Donguy compiled a helpful index of all the elements in "ôlho por ôlho" that also includes other public figures such as Fidel Castro, Pelé, Miguel Arraes, Sammy Davis Jr, John F. Kennedy, Sophia Loren, Shirley MacLaine, Juscelino Kubitschek, Bertrand Russell, Françoise Hardy, Brigitte Bardot, and Elizabeth Taylor. Augusto de Campos, *Anthologie: despoesia*, preface and trans. Jacques Donguy (Paris: Al Dante, 2002), 78.

11. The phrase refers to a public statement issued by Arraes as he left prison and embarked to exile in Algeria.

12. João Bandeira, "O país num PSIU!" [The country in a PSST!], in *Serrote #25* (São Paulo: Instituto Moreira Salles, 2017), 149.

13. The poem's final layout was designed by Francelizio Barra, and in addition to its several designs de Campos also produced a typewritten version that is more in keeping with the machine-poem model.

14. The last two issues of *Invenção* devoted generous attention to Haroldo de Campos's *galáxias*, and featured ample documentation of the *Popcretos* exhibition and poems. Issue 4 presented a selection of *galáxias* introduced by a helpful explanatory note ("dois dedos de prosa"), and included a special section on the exhibition *Popcretos* with texts by Augusto de Campos and Waldemar Cordeiro ("Arte Concreta Semântica"). *Invenção, Revista de Arte de Vanguarda*, no. 4, December 1964. The journal's final issue featured four collage poems by Augusto de Campos: "SS," "anti-ruído," "psiu!," and "luxo," as well as "Profilograma 1—Pound-Maiakóvski," which overlapped portraits of the two poets by Gaudier-Brzeska and Rodchenko. *Invenção, Revista de Arte de Vanguarda*, no. 5, December 1966–January 1967. Coincidentally this last issue registered the early reception of Sousândrade abroad: "Sousândrade's Stock," in *The Times Literary Supplement*, London, June 24, 1965; "*Sousândrade nous provoques encore*," by Pierre Furter, *Journal de Genève*, Literary Supplement; "Crisi del linguaggio e avanguardie letterarie in Brasile," by Luciana Stegagno Picchio, *Paragone*, no. 190, Milano; "Notícia de Sousândrade," by Ángel Crespo and Pilar Gómez Bedate, in *Revista de Cultura Brasileña*, no. 12, Madrid. *The Times Literary Supplement*'s article notes: "Writing in elliptical verses, multilingual, and inflected by limerick Sousândrade creates a montage of political events of the day, newspapers' articles literary references to convey an ironic vision of the birth of modern North America." The juxtaposition of these new bodies of work from the Campos brothers in *Invenção 4* is intriguing as it stresses how often they approached similar problems to arrive at different solutions. Consider one of the *galáxias* published in this issue ("no jornalário . . ." [by the newsstand . . .]), about which Haroldo affirmed: "as *galáxias* não são apenas feitas de epifanias, mas também de antiepifanias. O 'raro' e o 'reles.' Momentos de paraíso e momentos de inferno. Como a vida. Como a história" [the *galáxias* aren't made solely of epiphanies, but of anti-epiphanies as well. The "rare" and the "vulgar." Paradisical moments and infernal moments. Like life. Like history]. We could suggest a symmetry of sorts between these two bodies of work as they are both informed by a collagistic practice of piecing together residues of *life* and *history*. Last but not least, we might also take into account Pignatari's essays on semiotic that were published in *Invenção*, as well as his own experiments on advertising. In this pivotal moment in the group's journey, we can still find a cohesive dialogue between their different explorations.

15. Augusto de Campos, "Pound Made (New) in Brazil," in *A Margem da margem* (São Paulo: Companhia das Letras, 1989), 99–112. The essay offers a comprehensive look at Noigandres' correspondence with Pound while at St. Elizabeths, and also with Pound scholar Hugh Kenner, who writes in a letter dated May 11, 1955: "I envy the existence of newspapers that publish articles about such topics," referring to articles Augusto de Campos published in *Diário de São Paulo*.

16. Cf. Augusto de Campos, "Errâncias de Sousândrade," in Joaquim de Sousândrade, *O Guesa* (São Paulo: Selo Demônio Negro, 2009).

17. In Canto XLII Pound narrates the creation in 1472 of Monte dei Paschi, ("a mount, a bank, a fund, a bottom a credit institution"), guaranteed by Cosimo I de Medici based on tax revenue on grazing land outside Sienna. Pound saw in this

establishment the "true bases of credit, to wit the abundance of nature and the responsibility of the whole people." Pound admitted no mystery about his cryptic method and mused that it would be more intelligible to the general reader as history becomes better understood. Cf. Ezra Pound, *Guide to Kulchur*, Eleventh Printing (New York: New Direction, 1970), 194. Excerpts from *The Cantos of Ezra Pound*, copyright © 1971 by Ezra Pound. Reprinted by permission of New Directions Publishing Corp. Excerpts from *Gaudier-Brzeska*, copyright ©1980 by New Directions Publishing Corp. Reprinted by permission of New Directions Publishing Corp.

18. In *Vanguarda e subdesenvolvimento* [Avant-garde and underdevelopment, 1969], Ferreira Gullar posed the question of whether a concept of avant-garde conceived in Europe or in the United States would be applicable in an underdeveloped country, and suggested that in Brazil the *new* (whether ideas or technologies) contradictorily meant "freedom and submission." By omitting the connection foreign authors and ideas maintained with their specific national and cultural circumstances, Gullar wrote, the Brazilian avant-garde became victim to a formalist exercise. Issued ten years after the publication of the Manifesto Neoconcreto, *Vanguarda e subdesenvolvimento* seemed to bring to a close the constructivist era in Brazil, in which Gullar had played a major role as poet and polemicist. Gullar's synchronic and geographic reading of the avant-garde becomes problematic when we consider works such as Sousândrade's whose anticipatory nature is difficult to determine.

19. See Sousândrade, *O Guesa*, 280.

20. Although other contemporary artists endeavored to work along the same lines, *Popcretos* seems to conveys a more complex understanding of "montage and the idiomatic mosaic." Consider for example Rogério Sganzerla, *Documentário* (1966, black and white, 10:04 minutes). The film follows two friends roaming through downtown São Paulo looking for a suitable film to watch on a lazy afternoon. Their promenade past newsstands and cinema houses allows Sganzerla to document that precise moment in Brazil and abroad through a collage of images of comics, film posters, and newspaper headlines. In an early scene, for example, one character glosses over *O Jornal da Tarde*, showing to the camera its main headline: "SUBVERSÃO ESTA VOLTANDO" [Guerrila is back]; later images focus on covers of *MAD* magazine and comics as well as film posters featuring Jean-Luc Godard, Samuel Fuller, and Orson Welles.

21. Lucien Goldmann, *The Hidden God: A Study of Tragic Vision in the* Pensées *of Pascal and the Tragedies of Racine*, trans. Philip Thody (New York: Verso, 2016), 201.

5. Disruption of Style

1. Haroldo de Campos, "O A*freud*isíaco Lacan na Galáxia de Lalingua—Freud, Lacan e a escritura," *Correio, Revista da Escola Brasileira de Psicanálise*, no. 18–19, (Belo Horizonte, Minas Gerais): 136–62.

2. The setting for this conversation was the offices of *L'Âne, Le Magazin freudien*, distributed by Editions du Sevil, Paris. In a footnote, Campos explains that the title for the journal was given by Lacan himself, punning on the word "analyst" as "âne-á-liste" ("ass with a list"). The journal, however, bears the subtitle: "Analyse nouvelle expérience."

3. For a complete English translation of the "Overture," see Jacques Lacan, *Écrits: The First Complete Edition in English*, trans. Bruce Fink, in collaboration with Héloïse Fink and Russell Grigg (New York: W. W. Norton, 2006), 3–5.

4. Roland Barthes, *S/Z*, trans. Richard Miller (New York: Hill and Wang, 1974), 5–6.

5. From the cycle *As Disciplinas*, written in 1952 and published in *Xadrez de Estrelas—percurso textual 1949–1974* (São Paulo: Editora Perspectiva, 1976). Translation: "The Poem proposes itself: system / of rancorous premises / evolution of figures against the wind / star chess." Cf. Haroldo de Campos, *Novas: Selected Writings*, 13.

6. Even in purely visual terms, and despite the fact that since in the "Pilot Plan for Concrete Poetry," the reference to "writing as constellation" is often attributed to Mallarmé, a case can be made that Vieira's "chess" analogy is more adequate to describe Campos's poetry. Early concrete poems like the micro-collection "O Âmago do Ômega," with their vertical and horizontal axes that establish multiple word relations and suggest multiple reading possibilities, resemble a chess board rather than constellations. The high volume of quotations in those poems, furthermore, adds a dialogical element that is at the core of board games.

7. In the Catholic Church liturgical calendar, *sexagésima* indicates the second Sunday before Ash Wednesday, a time for atonement in preparation for Lent. Vieira delivered his sermon at the Royal Chapel in Lisbon in 1655

8. Antonio Vieira, "Sermão da Sexagésima," in *Sermões—Tomo 1*, organized by Alcir Pécora (São Paulo: Hedra, 2014), 29–52.

9. Cf. Haroldo de Campos, "ora, direis, ouvir galáxias?," in *galáxias* (São Paulo: Editora 34, 2004), 119. This text also was originally written as liner notes for the CD *isto não é um livro de viajem—16 fragmentos de galáxias* (Rio de Janeiro, Editora 34, 1992), featuring sixteen fragmentos read by the author.

10. Fernando Pessoa greatly admired Vieira's style and acknowledged his influence in several works. In *Livro do Desassossêgo*, for instance, writing under the pseudonym of Bernardo Soares, Pessoa admitted that a page by Vieira, in the "cold perfection of its syntactic engineering," caused him to "tremble like a branch in the wind, in the passive delirium of something moved." In that same volume, in a thrilling passage in which he confesses being "nobody . . . the prolix commentary of a book yet to be written," Pessoa added this curious "description of an ideal": "the sensibility of Mallarmé within Vieira's style." Cf. Fernando Pessoa, *Livro do Desassossego* (Rio de Janeiro: Livraria Brasiliense, 1986), 156–57. Viera is also the subject of one of the poems in *Mensagem*, 1934, Pessoa's sole collection published in life. "Defesa e Ilustração da Língua Portuguesa" is an essay by Pessoa published posthumously: Cf. Fernando Pessoa, *A Lingua portuguesa*, org. Luísa Medeiros (São Paulo: Companhia das Letras, 1997), 51–73.

11. In Vieira, "Sermão da Sexagésima." Note that the style proposed by Vieira differs from the "mosaic style" proposed and embraced by Marshall McLuhan in *The Gutenberg Galaxy*: "The present volume has employed a mosaic pattern of perception and observation up til now." Cf. McLuhan, "The Galaxy Reconfigured, or the Plight of Mass Man in an Individualistic Society," in *The Gutenberg Galaxy* (Toronto: University of Toronto Press, 1992), 265.

12. Roland Barthes, *S/Z*, 14. While Barthes might not have read Vieira's sermons, he was, nonetheless, clearly aware of Jesuit rhetoric. In his essay "Style and its Image," the relation between content and form is conveyed in terms of an opposition between "Aristotelian (later Jesuit) rhetoric and Platonic (later Pascalian) rhetoric." Cf. *The Rustle of Language*, trans. Richard Howard (Berkeley: University of California Press, 1989), 91. If *galáxias* is indeed the "ideal text" that Barthes asked for, one wonders how it would respond to an analysis based on the system of codes employed in *S/Z*.

13. Vieira, "Sermão da Sexagésima."

14. I quote, here and elsewhere, Lane Cooper's complete translation of Buffon's essay published in *The Writer's Art by Those Who Have Practiced It*, ed. Rollo Walter Brown (Cambridge, MA: Harvard University Press, 1932), this quotation, p. 278.
15. Brown, *The Writer's Art by Those Who Have Practiced It*, 278.
16. Brown, *The Writer's Art by Those Who Have Practiced It*, 281.
17. "Seminar" is derived from the Latin word *seminarium*, meaning "seed plot," a term traditionally associated with the training of priests. In the context of the present discussion, Lacan's seminars must be considered as following in this tradition. "Seme," on the other hand, derives from the Greek word *sêma* and denotes a distinguishing mark, a sign, or a signal.
18. Roland Barthes, *S/Z*, 17
19. Vieira, "Sermão da Sexagésima."
20. Haroldo de Campos, "Do Epos ao epifânico (Gênese e elaboração das *galáxias*)," in *Metalinguagem e outras metas*, 4th edition (São Paulo: Perspectiva, 1992), 271.
21. Cf. "Entrevista: Haroldo de Campos por Armando Sergio Prazeres, Irene Machado and Yvanna Fechine," in *Galáxia: Revista transdisciplinar de comunicação semiótica, cultura* (Transdisciplinary review of communication, semiotics and culture), no. 1, Pontifícia Universidade de São Paulo, 2001.
22. James Joyce, *Stephen Hero*, ed. John J. Slocum and Herbert Cahoon (New York: New Directions, 1955), 211.
23. "Não mais, Musa, não mais, que a lira tenho / Destemperada, e a voz enrequecida," *Os Lusiadas*, X, cxlv ["No more, Muse, no more, my lyre is / out of tune, and my throat is hoarse"], *The Lusíads*, trans. Landeg White (Oxford: Oxford World's Classics, 1997), 226.
24. Cf. Canto XIII, vv. 19–20, in *Dante's Paradiso*, trans. and comment John D. Sinclair (New York: Oxford University Press, 1961), 188.
25. The figure of the "Moura Torta," literally meaning "crippled fairy," belongs to the Portuguese fabulary and denotes an evil character who often sets a plot in motion.
26. Haroldo de Campos, *galáxias*, 119.
27. Haroldo de Campos, "Do Epos ao epifânico (Gênese e elaboração das *galáxias*)," 269–77.
28. Toward the end of the first movement, Berg introduces a theme based on the Carinthian folk song "Ein Vogel auf'm Zwetschenbaum," and he later, at the end of the second movement, repeats it. The Bach chorale "Es ist genug," from the Cantata *O Ewigkeit, du Donnerwort* (BWV 60), introduces the adagio section in the second movement.
29. Roland Barthes, *The Pleasure of the Text*, trans. Richard Miller (New York: Hill and Wang, 1975), 64.
30. In the first chapter of *Tristes Tropiques*, Claude Lévi-Strauss inveighs against the trend of travelogues that "fill the bookshops," and goes on to deliver one of the most spectacular expeditionary accounts of the twentieth century. Perhaps as a nod to Lévi-Strauss, the eighth fragment of *galáxias* affirms from the start: "this is not a travelogue."
31. Haroldo de Campos, *A Educação dos Cinco Sentidos* (São Paulo: Brasiliense, 1985), 113–14.
32. Cf. Ezra Pound, *Cantares*, trans. Augusto de Campos, Décio Pignatari, and Haroldo de Campos (Rio de Janeiro: Ministério de Educação e Cultura, 1960).
33. "Noigandres, eh noigandres, / "Now what the DEFFIL can that mean!" See Canto XX, in *The Cantos of Ezra Pound* (New York: New Directions Books, 1996), 90.

34. For the full translation of this fragment see Haroldo de Campos, *Novas: Selected Writings*, 124–25. In it, I opted for the first solution (*surrounded*, instead of *spinner*), to convey the image of the *cantador* as a wanderer, immersed in nature, at the mercy of God.

35. Inês Oseki-Dépré, "Translation as Creation and Criticism: *Galáxias* as Text and Theory of Translation," in *Haroldo de Campos: A Dialogue with the Brazilian Concrete Poet*, ed. K. David Jackson (Oxford: Center for Brazilian Studies, 2005), 107–18.

36. Interesting to note that references to dead languages (*linguamorta*), and to Pessoa's "defense and illustration" of the Portuguese language are already found in Campos's 1952 poem "Ciropédia, ou a educação do príncipe," in *Xadrez de estrelas—percurso textual 1949–1974* (São Paulo: Editora Perspectiva, 1976), section 10.

37. Cf. António José Saraiva, *O Discurso Engenhoso* (São Paulo: Perspectiva, 1980).

38. Cf. "Anthropophagous Reason: Dialogue and Difference in Brazilian Culture," in Haroldo de Campos, *Novas: Selected Writings*, 177

39. For an insightful, well-informed account of Oiticica's relationship with Haroldo de Campos, and the latter's influence on Oiticica's work, see Frederico Coelho, *Livro ou Livro-me—Os Escritos Babilônicos de Hélio Oiticica (1971–1978)* (Rio de Janeiro: Editora da Universidade do Estado do Rio de Janeiro, 2010). Of special interest to the present subject is Coelho's commentary on Salomão's "groovy promotion"— packets with clippings from Brazilian newspapers and art magazines that Salomão mailed to Oiticica in New York in the early 1970s—which gives us insight into the kind of textual operations going on at the time. Although "groovy promotion" was meant solely to convey an unfiltered picture of events going on in Brazil at the time, Salomão's procedure of selecting, cutting, and layering appealed to Oiticica as a model for the "ideal text." Style in these works, like in the *galáxias*, is densely layered, interwoven, and referential.

6. Poetry and Modernity in the New World

1. Haroldo de Campos, "The Ex-centric's Viewpoint: Tradition, Transcreation, Transculturation," in K. David Jackson, *Haroldo de Campos: A Dialogue with the Brazilian Concrete Poet* (Oxford: Centre for Brazilian Studies, University of Oxford, 2005). The volume gathers a collection of essays by several authors presented at two conferences at the Universities of Oxford and Yale in honor of Haroldo de Campos on his seventieth birthday. The conference at Oxford held at Wadham College on October 13–14, 1999, was followed by the Yale symposium held at the Whitney Humanities Center on the October 17–19, 1999.

2. Piero Boitani, "The Last Voyage," in *Haroldo de Campos: A Dialogue with the Brazilian Concrete Poet*, 219.

3. The name of Lisboa derived from the Latin Olisippo and became Ulixbona in the sixth century when the region was under Visigoth rule; many see in the name variations in references to Ulysses and Odysseus.

4. Haroldo de Campos, *Sobre Finismundo: A Última viagem* (Rio de Janeiro: Sette Letras, 1996), 22.

5. Haroldo de Campos, *Depoimentos de oficina* (São Paulo: Unimarco Editora, 2002), 56–57.

6. Campos, *Sobre Finismundo*, 35.

7. Campos, *Sobre Finismundo*, 35.

8. Michael North, *The Dialect of Modernism: Race Language and Twentieth Century Literature* (New York: Oxford University Press, 1994), 77.

9. A compilation of oral folk tales collected from African Americans from the southern United States, *Uncle Remus* was originally seen as capturing the Deep South slave dialect (Gullah). For an e-book version of the original publication see Project Gutenberg at http://www.gutenberg.org/files/22282/22282-h/22282-h.htm.

10. For an informative overview of the subject see Ezra Pound, *The Pisan Cantos*, ed., annotated, and intro. Richard Sieburth (New York: New Directions, 2003), ix–xliii. Sieburth notes, for instance, that "having been abroad, diasporically [*sic*] removed from the daily textures of American speech," Pound's "initial three weeks of enforced silence" in Pisa, "represented the first time in years he was actually forced to shut up and listen to the world around him. (…) Overhearing or half-glimpsing his African-American 'companions in misery.'" Sieburth also notes that Pound admired the "blues-based poetry of Langston Hughes," and in a footnote he comments that, "as Pound is working on the Pisans in the summer of 1945, Charlie Parker, Dizzy Gillespie and Max Roach are inventing be-bop on 52nd Street."

11. North, *The Dialect of Modernism*, 97.

12. Noel Rosa and Vadico, "Conversa de botequim" (Bar talk), 1935.

13. Campos, *Sobre Finismundo*, 24.

14. Although of obscure origin, the etymological roots of the word *malandro* points to the Latin (*malus*: bad, wrong), as well as the Provençal (*landrin*: lazy, vagabond), and the Ancient Greek (*mélas*: black, dark).

15. In an interview published in *Sobre Finismundo*, 35, Haroldo de Campos acknowledged that the poem has a "*logopoeic*, synthetic design, to be seen and read."

16. With a series of great hits such as "Ronda," "Na boca da noite," and "Volta por cima," Vanzolini (1924–2013) created a distinctive São Paulo lyric that captured the melancholy of the individual trapped in the concrete city. Like Campos's Ulysses, Vanzolini was also a factotum, a Harvard-trained zoologist with important contributions to the field.

17. Cf. Jorge Caldeira, *A Construção do samba* (São Paulo: Mameluco, 2007), 86.

18. Cf. Alec Marsh, "Letting the Black Cat Out of the Bag: A Rejected Instance of 'American-Africanism' in Pound's *Cantos*," *Paideuma: Modern and Contemporary Poetry and Poetics* 29, no. 2 (Spring & Fall 2000): 125–42. Special issue: *Ezra Pound and African American Modernism*. Published by National Poetry Foundation.

19. Marsh, "Letting the Black Cat Out of the Bag."

20. Caldeira, *A Construção do samba*, 84.

21. I am referring here to the influence of authors like José de Alencar, whose allegorical novels romanticized the relationship among natives, slaves, and colonizers and served as the basis for early modernists like Mário de Andrade and Raul Bopp in their assessment of tradition.

22. Caldeira, *A Construção do samba*, 88. To make his point, Caldeira quotes from Roberto Schwarz's definition of Pau Brazil poetry: "Its raw material is obtained through two operations: the juxtaposition of elements characteristic of colonial Brazil and of bourgeois Brazil and the elevation of the product—disjointed by definition—to a distinguished allegory of the country." To which Caldeira adds: "Whether for Oswald [this juxtaposition] meant the 'prefiguration of a post-bourgeois humanity,' for Noel, the critical jingoism produced by this kind of collage would be seen in a less optimistic form." Cf. Roberto Schwarz, *Que horas são* (São Paulo: Companhia das Letras, 1988), 12.

23. Schwarz, *Que horas são*, 87.

24. Campos, *Novas: Selected Writings*, 157–77.

25. Antonio Candido, "Dialética da malandragem—Caracterização das *Memórias de um sargento de milícias*" [Dialectics of Roguery—Characterization of the novel

Memórias de um sargento de milícias], in *Revista do Instituto de Estudos Brasileiros*, no. 8 (São Paulo: USP, 1970), 67–89.

26. *Memórias de um sargento de milícias* [*Memoirs of a Militia Seargent*] was first published in 1852 in installments in a Rio newspaper, and for over a century it was considered an aberration in Brazilian literature. The novel charts the progress of Leonardo, a troubled youth growing up amid a corrupt and amoral society that through a series of adventures ends up in the military. Faced with the challenge to justify Almeida's picaresque style vis-à-vis the romantic aesthetic prevalent at the time, Candido concocted his "dialectic of roguery" theory to depict a unique conjunction of forces in Brazilian society and culture.

27. Candido, "Dialética da malandragem," 67–89.
28. Candido, "Dialética da malandragem," 67–89.
29. Candido, "Dialética da malandragem."
30. Caldeira, *A Construção do samba*, 84.
31. Cf. Sieburth, "The Sound of Pound," http://writing.upenn.edu/pennsound/x/text/Sieburth-Richard_Pound.html.
32. In the same essay, Sieburth notes that a recording made by Pound in 1939 is "monotonous in its 'epic' or 'bardic' style of medieval chant—whose archaic sing-song, melismatic mode of delivery often seems at odds with the 'modernity' (or the 'factuality') of Pound's subject matter."
33. Sieburth, "The Sound of Pound."
34. For an English translation of "Claustrofobia," see Haroldo de Campos, *Novas: Selected Writings*, 15–16.
35. The codified way the concrete poets approached the subject of the city is best exemplified by poems like "nossos dias com cimento" from *Poetamenos* (1953), which telegraphically convey an urban scene of beggars amid formal fragments; or even more abstract compositions such as "cidadecitycité" (1963), and "luxo-lixo" (1965).
36. For the English translation, "Ode (Explicit) in Defense of Poetry on St. Lukács's Day," see Haroldo de Campos, *Novas: Selected Writings of Haroldo de Campos*, 98–101. Worth noting that when poet and translator Chris Daniels was working on his translation, the line "*esses trigênios vocalistas*" (these three vocalist genii, a pun on Trigêmeos Vocalistas, a musical group composed of three brothers popular in 1940s São Paulo) caused particular concern as it referred to a little-known moment in Brazilian popular culture. After several trials, Daniels came up with an ingenious solution: "we free kings," which refers to the title of jazz musician Rahsaan Roland Kirk's 1961 album that included a variation of the nineteenth-century Christmas carol "We Three Kings."
37. Nicolau Sevcenko, *Orfeu extático na metrópole: São Paulo, sociedade e cultura nos frementes anos 20* (São Paulo: Companhia das Letras, 1992), 18.
38. Cf. Paul Valéry, "Leonardo Poe Mallarmé," in *The Collected Works of Paul Valéry*, volume 8, ed. Jackson Mathews, trans. Malcolm Cowley and James R. Lawler (Princeton, NJ: Princeton University Press, 1972), 193. Valéry's insightful remark emerges in the process of a brief assessment of French poetry: "French poets are generally little known and appreciated abroad. We are more readily given the advantage in prose; but poetic power is sparingly and reluctantly allowed us. The order and the kind of strictness that have ruled our language since the seventeenth century, our particular accentuation, our strict prosody, our taste for simplification and immediate clarity, our fear of overstatement and bathos, a sort of modesty of expression and an abstract tendency of mind have created a poetry which differs considerably from that of other nations

and to which foreigners most often remain insensitive. La Fontaine seems to them insipid. Racine is forbidden ground: his harmonies are too subtle, his design too pure, his language too elegant and finely shaped for those who lack an intimate and native knowledge of our tongue. Even Victor Hugo's name has scarcely spread beyond France except for his novels. But with Baudelaire, French poetry at last has gone beyond our frontiers. It has come to be read throughout the world; it has taken its place as the true poetry of modernity; it has provoked imitation, it has nurtured many minds."

39. Sevcenko, *Orfeu extático na metrópole*, 259.

40. Sevcenko, *Orfeu extático na metrópole*, 264–65.

41. See Haroldo de Campos, "são paulo," in *Entremilênios*, organized by Carmen de Arruda Campos (São Paulo: Editora Perspectiva, 2010), 129–37.

42. Claude Lévi-Strauss, *Tristes Tropiques*, trans. John and Doreen Weightman (New York: Atheneum: 1984), 95.

43. Mário Pedrosa, "Brasília, a cidade nova," in *Acadêmicos e modernos: Textos escolhidos III*, organized by Otília Arantes (São Paulo: Editora da Universidade de São Paulo, 1998), 411–22.

44. Marjorie Perloff, "From Avant-Garde to Digital: The Legacy of Brazilian Concrete Poetry," in *Unoriginal Genius: Poetry by Other Means in the New Century* (Chicago: University of Chicago Press, 2010), 56.

45. Haroldo de Campos, "Poesia e modernidade: Da morte da arte à constelação. O poema pós-utópico," in *O Arco-íris branco* (São Paulo: Imago, 1996), 269.

Appendix 1: The Noigandres / Ezra Pound Correspondence

1. Excerpts from letters, drafts, and archival materials by Ezra Pound, New Directions Pub. acting as agent, copyright ©2025 by Mary de Rachewiltz and the Estate of Omar S. Pound. Reprinted by permission of New Directions Publishing Corp.

Appendix 2: "Deciphering Semiotics"

1. Roman Jakobson, "Linguistics and Poetics," in *Language in Literature*, ed. Krystyna Pomorska and Stephen Rudy (Cambridge, MA: The Belknap Press of Harvard University Press, 1987), 86.

2. Edgar Allan Poe, "A Few Words on Secret Writing," in *Edgar Allan Poe: The Dover Reader*, ed. Janet B. Kopito (New York: Dover Publication, 2014), 508.

3. Edgar Allan Poe, "The Gold Bug," in *Poetry, Tales, and Selected Essays*, with notes by Patrick F. Quinn and G. R. Thompson (New York: The Library of America, 1996), 587.

4. Jakobson, "Language in Operation," in *Language and Literature*, 54.

5. D. H. Lawrence, *Studies in Classic American Literature* (New York: Thomas Seltzer, 1923), 110.

6. Marshall McLuhan, *Understanding Media: The Extensions of Man* (New York: McGraw Hill, 1965), 82.

7. Edgard Allan Poe, "Berenice," in *Poetry, Tales, and Selected Essays*, 231.

8. Here Pignatari quotes from Manuel Bandeira's pioneering essay on Mallarmé. The entire sentence is: "Poesia não é senão a expressão musical, superaguda, emocionante, de um estado de alma; as palavras se iluminam de reflexos recíprocos como um virtual rastilho de luzes sobre pedras." [Poetry is nothing but the musical expression, supersharp, thrilling, of a state of being; words lit themselves of reciprocal reflexes like

a thread of light over the gravel]. Manuel Bandeira, "O Centenário de Mallarmé," in *Seleta de Prosa*, organized by Júlio Castañon Guimarães (Rio de Janeiro: Nova Fronteira, 1997), 509.

9. Tristão de Alencar Araripe Júnior, *Obra Crítica*, vol. III, organized by Afrânio Coutinho (Rio de Janeiro: Casa de Rui Barbosa, 1960), 466.

10. The subtitle quotes from Machado de Assis's *Memórias Póstumas de Brás Cubas*, chapter CXLII. The entire quote:
"Não era a letra fina e correta de Virgília, mas grossa e desegual; o V da assinatura não passava de um rabisco sem intenção alfabética; de maneira que, se a carta aparecesse, era mui difícil atribuir-lhe a autoria" [It wasn't Virgília fine and correct handwriting, but rough and unequal; simply signed V, it was nothing but a scribble without alphabetic intent; in such way that, if the letter showed up, it would be hard to attribute its authorship]. In Machado de Assis, *Memórias Póstumas de Brás Cubas*, chapter CXLII, in *Obra completa em quatro volumes*, vol. 1, organized by Aluizio Leite, Ana Lima Cecilio, and Heloisa Jahn (Rio de Janeiro: Editora Nova Aguilar, 2008), 747.

11. Ferdinand de Saussure, *Course in General Linguistics*, ed. Charles Bally and Albert Sechehaye in collaboration with Albert Riedlinger, trans., intro., and notes Wade Baskin (New York: McGraw Hill, 1966), 119–20.

12. Saussure, *Course in General Linguistics*, 29–31.

13. Originally published under the pseudonym Alvaro de Campos, "Ultimatum" is included in *The Selected Prose of Fernando Pessoa*, ed. and trans. Richard Zenith (New York: Grove Press, 2022), 47.

Appendix 3: "Pound Made (New) in Brazil"

1. See James Blish, "Rituals on Ezra Pound," *The Sewanee Review* LVIII, no. 2 (April–June 1950): 185–226.

2. Noigandres no. 1 to 4 (1952–1958), no. 5, an anthology from verse to concrete poetry (1962), São Paulo, edited and published by the authors.

3. *The Analyst*, ed. Robert Mayo, Northwestern University, 1953–1957; *The Pound Newsletter*, ed. John Edwards, University of California, 1954–1956.

4. Faustino's essays were ultimately collected in *Mário Faustino: Poesia-Experiência* (São Paulo: Editora Perspectiva, 1976).

5. Hugh Kenner, *The Poetry of Ezra Pound*, new preface by the author, foreword by James Laughlin (Lincoln: University of Nebraska Press, 1985), 262.

6. Joaquim de Sousândrade, *O Guesa*, printed by Cooke & Halsted (London: The Moorfield Press, ca. 1888).

7. Augusto and Haroldo de Campos, *revisão de sousândrade* (São Paulo: Editora Invenção, 1964). Reedited with new materials by Editora Nova Fronteira, 1982.

8. Preamble to the "Inferno" section in Canto X of *O Guesa*.

9. Ezra Pound, *Guide to Kulchur* (New York: New Directions, 1970), 57.

Appendix 4: "The Aph*freud*isiac Lacan in the Galaxy of Lalangue"

1. Translation: "Shall we adopt the formulation—the style is the man—if we simply add to it: the man one addresses?" Cf. Jacques Lacan, "Overture to this Collection," in *Écrits*, trans. Bruce Fink in collaboration with Héloïse Fink and Russel Grigg (New York: W.W. Norton, 2006), 9.

2. We find the word *Witz* in one of Freud's most fascinating works: *Der Witz und seine beziehung zum Unbewusstsen*, 1905. Although *Witz* has been translated into French as "*mot d'esprit*," in "The Instance of the Letter in the Unconscious," Lacan affirms that "*esprit*" is, in fact, the equivalent of the German word. He poses objection, nevertheless, to its English translation as "*wit*," a concept he finds overburdened by intellectual discussion that has lost its "essential virtue" to the word "humour," which by its turn has a distinct meaning; "*pun*," on the other hand, is "too narrow." James Strachey, in fact, in the Standard Edition, used "*joke*" instead of "*wit*" (the term used in the first English translation, by A. A. Brill, 1916), for understanding that "*wit*" refers only to the more refined and intellectual jokes. The concept, it's worth mentioning, had particular theoretical relevance during the Romantic period in Germany (hence Freud's use of Schleiermacher).

3. Apuleius's philosophical allegory of the Asinus Aureus, according to Bakhtin (in his book on Rabelais), is soaked in the carnivalesque tradition of popular comedy. In the present context, though, the caricatured metamorphosis responds to a specific satirical goal. In the first issue of *L'Âne* (1981), an editor's note explained that the magazine title had been proposed by Lacan as a substitute to the simple designation "L'Analyste." The play of words in "L'Âne-á-liste," [The ass with a list], according to Elizabeth Roudinesco, *Historia da psicanálise na França*, vol. 2, 1925–1985 (São Paulo: J. Zahar, 1988), refers to the "lists of instructors." But also to the "electoral lists," thus alluding to the power struggle that ended up with the dissolution, by Lacan, of the École Freudienne de Paris, which he had founded in 1964. Lacan's wordplay ends up extrapolating its context and irradiates an ironic light on the struggles within the Parisian establishment, particularly in regard to the analyst's formation, and the relationship between psychoanalysis and power.

4. Lacan, *Écrits*, 258.

5. Lacan, *Écrits*, 383. In 1842, it is important to notice, Marx, in his rebellion against the Prussian censorship, used Buffon's maxim to emphasize his right to freedom of expression: "*Mein Eigentum ist die Form, sie ist meine geistige Individualitat. Le style c'est l'homme. Und wie!*" [Form is my property, my spiritual individuality. Style is man himself. And how!]

6. Translation: "Training; culture revolution: style, as defined by Lacan, is situated outside of its literary situation, or rather, it is the necessary correlation of what Lacan calls *letter*, and that regenerates the signifier *literature* out of the *Belle Lettres*. Style, a revolutionary formation at the level of language, is what, according to Lacan, makes possible to overcome literature in profit of "literality": the power of the letter, the agency of the letter in the unconscious, and, as the sequence of a title in one of the texts in *Écrits* indicates, reason after Freud ('la raison depuis Freud'), genesis of another rationality." Cf. Catherine Backès-Clément, "La stratégie du langage," *Littérature* 3 (October 1971): 11–29.

7. All quotes from "The Instance of the Letter in the Unconscious." Cf. Jacques Lacan, *Écrits*, 412–41.

8. Lacan's attitude toward Saussure changed after the unveiling of his unpublished works, by Jean Starobinski, on the unresolved question of the "anagrams." In this regard see my essay "The Ghost in the Machine—Saussure and the Anagrams," (translated by Craig Dworkin, in Haroldo de Campos, *Novas: Selected Writings*). In "Knowledge and Truth," the relation between anagrammatic reading and the dream-work is

established thus: "Analysis came to announce to us that there is knowledge that is not known, knowledge that is based on the signifier as such. A dream does not introduce us into any kind of unfathomable experience or mystery—it is read in what is said about it, and one can go further by taking up the equivocation therein in the most anagrammatic sense of the word ('equivocations'). It is regarding that aspect of language that Saussure raised the question whether the strange punctuation marks he found in the Saturnine verses were intentional or not. That is where Saussure was awaiting Freud. And it is where the question of knowledge is raised afresh." *The Seminar of Jacques Lacan, Book XX*, trans. with notes by Bruce Fink (New York: W.W. Norton, 1998), 96.

9. Cf. Jacques Lacan, "The Situation of Psychoanalysis and the Training of the Psychoanalysts in 1956," in *Écrits*, 390–91.

10. As to the question of Góngora in the history of literature, particularly from the point of "reception theory," see my essay "The Disappearance of the Baroque in Brazilian Literature," trans. Antonio Sergio Bessa, in Haroldo de Campos, *Novas: Selected Writings*.

11. *Yale French Studies—Structuralism*, double issue 36–37, October 1966 (New Haven, CT: Yale University Press), 110. Printed for YFS by Eastern Press, New Haven.

12. Lacan, "The Situation of Psychoanalysis and the Training of Psychoanalysts in 1956," 391–93.

13. Jacques Lacan, "The Function and Field of Speech and Language in Psychoanalysis," in *Écrits*, 238–64.

14. Translator's note: My translation of Muschg's text was based on Campos's Portuguese translations. For the original text, see Walter Muschg, "Freud als Schriftsteller," in *Deutsche Essays—Prosa aus zvei Jahrhunderten*, ed. Ludwig Rohner (Munich: Deutscher Taschenbuch Verlag, 1972).

15. Muschg, "Freud als Schriftsteller."

16. Jacques Lacan, "To Jakobson," in *The Seminar, Book XX*, 24

17. Jacques Lacan, "The Introduction of the Big Other," in *The Seminar, Book II*, trans. Sylvana Tomaselli (New York: W. W. Norton, 1988), 246–47.

18. Jacques Lacan, "The Function and Field of Speech and Language in Psychoanalysis," 248

19. See Jacques Lacan, "The Freudian Thing, or the Meaning of the Return to Freud," in *Écrits*, 334–63.

20. Lacan criticized the English translation thus: "Freud said neither das Es, nor das Ich." See Lacan, "The Freudian Thing, or the Meaning of the Return to Freud," 347.

21. "One can but wonder what demon inspired the author of the extant French translation, whoever it was, to render it as 'Le moi doit déloger le ça' ('The ego must dislodge the id'). It is true that one can savor in it the tone of an analytic quarter in which people know how to carry out that sort of operation it evokes." Lacan, "The Freudian Thing, or the Meaning of the Return to Freud," 363.

22. English translation of "The Instance of the Letter in the Unconscious," *Yale French Studies* 36–37 (1966): 142.

23. Spanish translation, in Jacques Lacan, *Lectura estructuralista de Freud*, trans. Tomás Segovia (Mexico: Siglo Veintiuno Editores, 1971).

24. Brazilian translation, in Jacques Lacan *Escritos*, trans. Inês Oseki Dépré (São Paulo: Editora Perspectiva), 255.

25. Jacques Lacan, "L'Instance de la lettre dans l'inconscient," in *Écrits*, 524.

26. Jacques Lacan, "La Chose Freudienne," in *Écrits*, 417–18.
27. Lacan, "The Freudian Thing, or the Meaning of the Return to Freud," 347.
28. Lacan, "The Freudian Thing, or the Meaning of the Return to Freud."
29. In making this assertion, in "Freud and the Scene of Writing," in *Writing and Difference*, trans. Alan Bass (Chicago: University of Chicago Press, 1978), 210, Derrida was not referring to the possibility of a creative translation, an operation that also privileges the "poetic function" of language. The problem of translation has also occupied Derrida in "*Des tours de Babel*," an essay that elaborates Benjamin's theory of translation.
30. The authors of *Traduire Freud* (André Bourguignon, Pierre Colet, and Jean Laplanche), reject the idea of a Lacanian translation for the new French text of the *Complete Works*, as being a "detour." They opt for a translation that would leave the text "open to interpretation, and not closed within a certain ideology." Thus, they arrive at the following solution: "Où ça était, je (moi) dois (doit) devenir." Judicious as it might be this argumentation does not seem to have the power to invalidate Lacan's use of translation as a recourse of exegesis.
31. Translator's note: Campos's witty scenario is a super-composite of references in which Freudian and Joycean references collide. The sentence can be read alternately as: "Everything succeeded in a glance of eyes / All the seduction was in the shine on the nose."
32. In a "creative transposition" (Jakobson)—a "trans-poeticizing" (Umdichtung, to use Benjamin's expression), or a "trans-creation," as I call it—in which the signifier has primacy, the *Witz* keeps the phonic semantics of its "language material" (Sprachmaterial, according to Freud): O CIÚME causa uma DOR / que aSSUME com gUME / o seu CAUSADOR. [JEALOUSY causes PAIN / assaulting with a KNIFE / the one who CAUSED it.
33. Excerpt quoted in Luke Thurston, *James Joyce and the Problem of Psychoanalysis* (Cambridge: Cambridge University Press, 2004), 69.
34. Jacques Lacan, "The Function of the Written," in *Écrits*, 37.
35. Translator's note: The English version of this text, (*The Seminar, Book XX*, 137–46), translates *lalangue* as llanguage. In the present essay I opted to keep Lacan's original spelling for its resonance to de Campos's wordplay.
36. Although Lacan agrees with Jakobson in matters related to linguistics and poetry ("Not that I don't agree with him about it quite fully when it comes to poetry," in *The Seminar, Book XX*, 14–15), he prefers to demarcate the proper sphere of analytical discourse (the problem of foundation/subversion of the subject and of the structure of the unconscious) by coining a neologism: *linguisterie*.
37. Lacan, "The Rat in the Maze," in *The Seminar, Book XX*, 139.
38. Roland Barthes, *S/Z*, trans. Richard Miller (New York: Hill and Wang, 1974), 5–6.
39. Cf. "The Field of the Other," in *The Seminar of Jacques Lacan Book XI*, trans. Alan Sheridan (New York: W. W. Norton, 1981), 252.
40. Roland Barthes, *The Pleasure of the Text*, trans. Richard Miller (New York: Hill and Wang, 1975), 4.
41. It is to Rabelais, Joyce's multifaceted precursor, that Lacan's text ultimately remits, finding in him the anticipation of the ethnographic discoveries through which to glimpse into the substantial decoding of the human mystery.

Index

Aboutboul, Elliot, 113
Ader, Clément, 185n30
Adorno, Theodor, 30, 180n20
Aeschylus, 103
Agresti, Olivia Rosseti, 118, 121
Albers, Josef, 135
Alcântara Machado, Antonio de, 4, 174n13
Alencar, José de, 193n21
Alighieri, Dante, 12, 35, 67, 69, 72, 88, 92, 98, 157, 173n1, 186n2, 187n9, 191n24
Allen, Esther, 185n29
Almeida, Manuel Antônio de, 105, 194n26
Almeida, Paulo Augusto de, 57
Alonso, Dámaso, 164
Amaral, J. V., 127, 133
Amaral, Tarsila do, 175n15
Andersson, Andrea, 113, 175n20
Andrade, Mário de, 24, 105, 110, 151, 178-79n1
Andrade, Oswald de, 4, 99, 104, 152, 175n15, 181n36, 184n11
Antheil, George, 135
Apollinaire, Guillaume, 9, 10, 106
Apuleius, 197n3
Arantes, Otília, 195n43
Araripe Junior, Tristão de Alencar, 58, 59-60, 61, 184n21, 196n9
Ardizzone, Maria Luisa, 176n16

Aristotle, 190n12
Arraes, Miguel, 73, 187n10-11
Arruda Campos, Carmen de, 90, 195n41
Astaire, Fred, 180n24
Attié, Joseph, 81, 161
Austin, J. L., 14, 15, 177n36
Avalle, D'Arco Silvio, 98
Ayer, A. J., 15,
Azeredo, Lygia, 32, 44-45. *See also* Lygia

Bach, Johann Sebastian, 27, 89, 135, 191n28
Backès-Clément, Catherine, 163, 167-68, 197n6
Bacon, Francis, 42, 182n46
Baker, Chet, 180n24
Bakhtin, Mikhail, 197n3
Bally, Charles, 196n11
Bandeira, João, 73, 113, 188n12
Bandeira, Manuel, 109, 195-96n8
Bardot, Brigitte, 187n10
Barra, Francelizio, 188n13
Barros, Geraldo de, 46, 57
Barros, Lenora de, 113
Barthes, Roland, 25, 82-86, 166, 172, 190n4, 190n12, 191n18, 199n38
Bartók, Béla, 105
Baskin, Wade, 179n5, 196n11
Bass, Alan, 199n29

Baudelaire, Charles, 2, 102, 108, 139, 144, 174n6, 195n38
Bayard, Caroline, 63, 185n32
Beecher, Henry Ward, 158
Bell, Alexander Graham, 3, 147
Benjamin, Walter, 4, 22, 55–56, 108, 111, 168, 174–75n14, 178n51, 184n12, 199n29, 199n32
Bense, Max, 90, 91
Berg, Alban, 30, 89, 180n20, 191n28
Berkeley, George, 15, 133
Bessa, Antonio Sergio, 175n1, 198n10
Bevilaqua, Ralph, 14, 177n30
Bill, Max, 48, 56, 135
Bishop, Elizabeth, 110
Blake, William, 74
Blériot, Louis, 185n30
Blish, James, 152, 196n1
Bodart, Roger, 122
Boitani, Piero, 98, 192n2
Bopp, Raul, 175n15, 193n21
Borges, Jorge Luis, 98, 185n29
Bosch, Hieronymus, 69–70
Botterill, Steven, 173n1
Boulez, Pierre, 23, 28, 48, 89, 131
Bourguignon, André, 199n30
Brâncusi, Constantin, 135
Brecht, Bertolt, 108
Brill, A. A., 197n2
Broodthaers, Marcel, 78
Brown, Bob, 182n1
Brown, Rollo Walter, 191n14
Brune, Krista, 3, 174n8
Buarque de Holanda, Sérgio, 61, 185n29
Buddha, 133
Buffon, Georges-Louis Leclerc, 81–82, 85–86, 162
Bullock, Marcus, 178n51
Burne-Jones, Edward, 16, 180n40
Butor, Michel, 77–78, 156

Cabral de Melo Neto, João, 90, 181n36
Cahoon, Herbert, 191n22
Caldeira, Jorge, 102, 104, 193n22
Calder, Alexander, 49
Camões, Luis de, 40, 43, 88, 98, 116–17, 181n43
Campos, Álvaro de, 196n13

Campos, Augusto de, 6–11, 16, 18–22, 25–26, 28–32, 34–36, 40, 44–45, 65–80, 92, 108, 113, 115, 116, 120, 122, 132, 136, 151, 154, 173n5, 175n19, 176n8, 177n38, 178n50, 179n8, 180n34, 181n40, 186n1, 187n8, 188n14, 191n32
Campos, Haroldo de, 2, 7–8, 17, 24–25, 77, 81–96, 97–111, 113, 115–37, 152, 154, 161, 173n5, 175n21, 176n8, 178–79n1, 179n3, 180n26, 182n5, 183n8, 188n14, 189n1, 190n5, 191n20, 192n1, 193n15, 194n36, 195n41, 196n7
Campos, Raquel, 113
Candido, Antonio, 57, 60, 104–5, 193–94n25, 194n26
Cardoso, Ivan, 184–85n26
Carlos, Erasmo, 34
Carlos, Roberto, 34
Carpentier, Alejo, 98
Carroll, Lewis, 24
Cartola (Angenor de Oliveira), 109
Castañon Guimarães, Julio, 195–96n8
Castro, Fidel, 187n10
Castro, Inês de, 126
Castro, Willys de, 17
Cavafy, Constantine P., 95
Cego Aderaldo (Aderaldo Ferreira de Araujo), 21, 178n48
Chanute, Octave, 62, 185n30
Charvet, P.E., 174n6
Chaucer, Geoffrey, 186n4
Cimino, Michael, 178n50
Cirne, Moacy, 57, 184n15
Cisneros, Odile, 175n1
Coelho, Frederico, 192n39
Colet, Pierre, 199n30
Cooper, Lane, 191n14
Coppola, Francis Ford, 178n50
Cordeiro, Waldemar, 16, 21, 68, 187n7
Cosela, Damiano, 68
Cosimo I de Medici, 188n17
Costa, Marcos, 185n29
Costa, Walter Carlos, 113, 175n21
Costa Lima, Luiz, 66, 67, 79, 186n1
Cotrim, Cecilia, 187n7
Coutinho, Afrânio, 104, 184n21, 196n9
Crespo, Ángel, 188n14

Cullen Bryant, William, 121
Cummings, E. E., 10, 27, 117, 126, 127, 179n12

Daniel, Arnaut, 15, 17, 152, 173n2, 177n38
Daniels, Chris, 194n36
Darío, Rubén, 98
Darwin, Charles, 60, 184–85n26
Davis Jr., Sammy, 187n10
Demy, Jacques, 180n24
Derrida, Jacques, 169, 199n29
Dias Pino, Wlademir, 57
Dickinson, Emily, 35, 44
Diego, Gerardo, 164
Dinis I, King of Portugal, 91
Donga (Ernesto Joaquim Maria dos Santos), 174n10
Donguy, Jacques, 38, 40, 181n40, 181–82n45, 187n10
Donne, John, 35, 93, 181n37
Dorfles, Gillo, 135
Dostoyevsky, Fyodor, 166
Douglass, Frederick, 3
Drummond de Andrade, Carlos, 109
Duchamp, Marcel, 20, 44–45, 68
Duncan, Isadora, 171
Duve, Thierry de, 45
Dworkin, Craig, 113, 175n18, 197–98n8

Edison, Thomas, 147
Eiland, Howard, 184n12
Eimert, Herbert, 28, 179–80n15
Eisenstein, Sergei, 18, 24, 49
Eliot, T. S., 61, 67, 93, 100, 102, 145, 152, 153, 182n4, 186n2
Ellis, Robert Leslie, 182n46

Falla, Manoel de, 151, 178–79n1
Fano, Guido Alberto, 23
Faustino, Mário, 115, 129–30, 153, 196n4
Fechine, Yvanna, 191n21
Fenollosa, Ernest, 11–12, 18, 24, 126
Ferlinghetti, Lawrence, 131
Ferreira, Glória, 187n7
Fiaminghi, Hermelindo, 57
Fink, Bruce, 189n3, 196n1, 197–98n8
Fink, Héloïse, 189n3, 196n1
Fleishman, Lazar, 114

Fleming, William, 122
Folliot, Denise, 182n4
Forssell, Lars, 121, 125
Foucault, Michel, 67
Fougère, Henry, 174–75n14
Freud, Sigmund, 8, 60, 81, 94, 133, 161, 163, 165–72, 184–85n26, 189n1, 197n2, 198n20, 199n30
Frobenius, Leo, 133, 159–60, 173n4
Fuller, Samuel, 189n20
Furter, Pierre, 188n14

Gama, Vasco da, 98
Garbo, Greta, 171
Garcia, Walter, 33, 34, 180n25
García Lorca, Federico, 160, 164
García Marquez, Gabriel, 98
Gaudier-Brzeska, Henri, 13, 177n28, 188n14
Ghil, René, 58
Gil, Gilberto, 93–94, 107
Gilberto, João, 25, 33, 34, 180n25
Gillespie, Dizzy, 193n10
Ginsberg, Allen, 110
Giovannini, Giovanni, 125
Gladstone, William Ewart, 159
Goacher, Dennis, 118
Godard, Jean-Luc, 189n20
Goethe, Johann Wolfgang von, 88, 156
Goldmann, Lucien, 67, 80, 189n21
Goldsmith, Kenneth, 64, 185–86n32
Goldwater, Barry, 70
Gómez Bedate, Pilar, 188n14
Gomringer, Eugen, 56, 90, 91, 127, 131
Góngora, Luis de, 82–83, 161, 163–66, 167, 198n10
Gorenstein Dedecca, Paula, 183n7
Goulart, João, 79
Gould, Glenn, 27, 179n11
Gould, Jay, 158
Gourmont, Remy de, 82, 133
Gouveia, Delmiro, 61, 185n27
Grant, Ulysses S., 156, 158
Greene, Roland, 183n9
Greimas, Algirdas Julien, 142
Grigg, Russel, 196n1
Grinberg, Keila, 3, 174n9
Grünewald, José Lino, 115, 153

Guedes, Fernando, 126–27
Guerini, Andréia, 113, 175n21
Guimarães Junior, Luis, 43, 181n39
Guimarães Rosa, João, 91, 97
Gullar, Ferreira, 16, 17, 18, 189n18

Hardy, Françoise, 187n10
Harris, Joel Chandler, 100
Harris, Wilson, 98
Heidegger, Martin, 133
Hemingwey, Ernest, 90, 93
Hesse, Eva, 118, 125
Hoch, Hanna, 6
Hollander, John, 41, 42, 182n46
Homem de Mello, Simone, 113, 175n21
Homer, 99–99, 102, 159
Hoover, John Edgar, 118
Horace, 100–2
Howard, Richard, 190n12
Hughes, David Edward, 147
Hughes, Langston, 193n10
Hugo, Victor, 194–95n38
Huysmans, Joris-Karl, 144–45

Iwasaki, Ryozo, 127

Jackson, Andrew, 158
Jackson, Kenneth David, 113, 115, 175n19, 192n1
Jahn, Heloisa, 196n10
Jakobson, Roman, 137–38, 163–64, 195n1, 199n32, 199n36
Jameson, Fredric, 97–98, 110
Jennings, Michael W., 178n51
Jensen, Wilhelm, 166
João I, King of Portugal, 148
Job, Book of, 86
Johnson, Barbara, 182n1
Johnson, Lionel, 120, 154
Johnson, Lyndon, 70
Joyce, James, 1–2, 5, 11, 24, 27, 82, 87, 107, 117, 127, 161, 167–72, 179n12, 191n22, 199n31

Kane, Charles Foster, 185n27
Kasper, John, 130
Kennedy Jr., John F., 187n10
Kenner, Hugh, 14, 91, 118, 120, 154, 177n27, 178n40, 188n15, 196n5

Khouri, Omar, 186n34
Kirk, Rahsaan Roland, 194n36
Kitasono Katué, 125, 131, 135
Koellreutter, Hans-Joachim, 29
Kooning, Willem de, 185–86n32
Kopito, Janet B., 195n2
Korngold, Erich Wolfgang, 27, 178n11
Kristeva, Julia, 167–68
Kubitschek, Juscelino, 183n6, 187n10

La Fontaine, Jean de, 194–95n38
Lacan, Jacques, 8, 81–82, 85–86, 89, 94–95, 161–72, 189n2, 191n17, 196n1, 197–98n8, 198n21, 199n36
Laplanche, Jean, 199n30
Laughlin, James, 196n5
Lawrence, D. H., 140, 195n5
Lay, Thomas, 114
Le Corbusier (Charles-Édouard Jeanneret), 1
Leary, Timothy, 178n50
Leibniz, Gottfried Wilhelm, 12
Leite, Aluizio, 196n10
Leonardo da Vinci, 58, 166, 194n38
Lévi-Strauss, Claude, 110, 191n30
Levy, Emil, 173n2
Li Po, 12
Lima Cecilio, Ana, 196n10
Lissitzky, El, 183–84n10
Loren, Sophia, 187n10
Lowell, Amy, 152
Lowell, Robert, 110
Lukács, György, 108, 194n36
Luke, Gospel of, 84
Lull, Ramon, 185n29
Lygia, 36, 39, 40, 41. *See also* Azeredo, Lygia

Macedo, Joaquim Manuel de, 106
Machado de Assis, Joaquim Maria, 63, 145, 148–49, 196n10
Machado, Duda, 184–85n26
Machado, Irene, 191n21
MacLaine, Shirley, 187n10
Magaldi, João Carlos, 184n14
Magellan, Ferdinand, 98
Mahler, Gustav, 179n11
Maldonado, Tomás, 57
Malevich, Kazimir, 27

Malfatti, Anita, 175n15
Mallarmé, Stéphane, 5, 10, 22, 24–25, 35, 46, 58, 63, 82, 86, 89, 111, 120, 122, 125, 127, 131, 133, 134, 139, 144, 153–55, 157, 161, 163, 164–65, 177n27, 179n12, 182n1, 184–85n26, 190n6, 194n38, 195–96n8
Marconi, Guglielmo, 147
Margolin, Victor, 183–84n10
Marker, Chris, 44
Marques da Cruz, José, 181n42
Marsh, Alec, 103, 193n18
Martello, Pier Jacopo, 92
Martinelli, Niccolò, 135
Martins, Ruben, 55
Marx, Karl, 61, 197n5
Matisse, Henri, 135
Mauron, Charles, 164
Mauthner, Fritz, 185n29
Mayakovsky, Vladimir, 49, 51–52, 56, 134, 143, 160, 183–84n10
Mayo, Robert, 196n3
McCarthy, Joseph, 118
McGowan, Christopher, 182n2
McLaughlin, Kevin, 184n12
McLuhan, Marshall, 91, 141, 144, 190n11, 195n6
Mendes, Odorico, 93–94, 99
Michelangelo, 166
Miel, Jan, 164
Mies van der Rohe, Ludwig, 61, 185n28
Miller, Judith, 81, 161
Miller, Richard, 190n4, 191n29, 199n38
Miranda, Carmen, 106
Moholy-Nagy, László, 183–84n10
Mondrian, Piet, 16, 27, 61, 179n11, 185n28
Monod, Jacques Lucien, 60, 184–85n26
Monroe, Harriet, 177n27
Monroe, Marilyn, 171
Monteverdi, Claudio, 34
Moraes, J. J. de, 87, 89
Moritz Schwarcz, Leila, 174n7
Morse, Samuel, 137
Müller-Wille, Klaus, 6
Muschg, Walter, 165–66, 198n14

Nachbaur, Fredric, 114
Naves, Rodrigo, 24, 179n4
Neame, Alan, 135
Neutra, Richard, 47

Nóbrega, Gustavo, 184n16
Nogueira Lime, Maurício, 52
North, Michael, 100, 192n8, 193n11
Novalis, 111

Oiticica, Hélio, 5, 91, 95–96, 175n16, 192n39
Oliveira, Eduardo Jorge de, 113
Ordonez, Antonio, 90
Oseki-Dépré, Inês, 93, 161, 192n35, 198n24
Oteiza, Jorge, 90

Paes, Paulo, 176
Page, Tim, 179n11
Palatnik, Abraham, 46
Parker, Charlie, 193n10
Pascal, Blaise, 189n21
Paulinho da Viola, 109
Paz, Octavio, 2, 91, 111, 171
Pedro I, King of Portugal, 126
Pedro II, Emperor of Brazil, 2, 3
Pedrosa, Mário, 110, 195n43
Peirce, Charles Sanders, 57, 58, 60, 61, 77, 184–85n26
Pereira de Castro, Gabriel, 98
Pérez-Villalón, Fernando, 182n46
Peri, Jacopo, 34
Perloff, Marjorie, 12, 15, 44, 110, 113, 175n18, 177n23, 182n49, 185–86n32, 195n44
Pessoa, Fernando, 84, 94, 98, 103, 139, 144, 150, 190n10
Picabia, Francis, 47
Pignatari, Décio, 6, 8, 23–24, 47–64, 73, 76–77, 92, 108, 113, 115, 125–27, 137, 152, 175n1, 176n8, 178n1, 179n2, 183n6, 184–85n26, 185n27, 186n34, 188n14, 195–96n8
Pignatari, Serena, 113
Pina Martins, J. V. de, 121
Pinto, Luiz Ângelo, 57, 184n17
Plato, 185–86n32, 190n12
Plaza, Julio, 61, 80, 185n31
Poe, Edgar Allan, 58, 60, 63, 137–43, 149, 150, 184–85n26, 194–95n38, 195n2
Pomorska, Krystyna, 195n1
Pompeia, Raul, 58, 61, 184n21
Poulsen, Valdemar, 147

Pound, Ezra, 1–2, 5, 7–8, 10–16, 24, 25, 27, 35, 44, 49, 65, 67, 77–79, 91–93, 99–103, 106, 113, 115–136, 151–60, 173n2, 176n8, 177n27, 178n40, 179n12, 182n2, 188n15, 188–89n17, 191n32, 193n10, 194n32, 195n1, 196n9
Pound, Omar S., 115, 119, 123–24, 176n16, 195n1
Prazeres, Armando Sergio, 191n21

Queiroz, João, 180n18
Quincey, Thomas de, 82
Quinn, Patrick F., 195n3

Rabelais, François, 172, 197n3, 199n41
Rachewiltz, Mary de, 90, 115, 118, 119, 123–25, 136, 176n16, 195n1
Racine, Jean, 194–95n38
Regina, Elis, 34
Reis, Mário, 34
Reys, Alfonso, 164
Ribeiro Couto, Rui, 109
Ribeiro de Moraes, Leo, 47
Ricardo, Cassiano, 77
Riedlinger, Albert, 196n11
Rimbaud, Arthur, 11, 35
Roach, Max, 193n10
Rodchenko, Alexander, 51–52, 56, 183–84n10, 188n14
Rodrigues, Lupicínio, 35, 180n34, 181n37
Rohner, Ludwig, 198n14
Roller, Niels, 6
Rosa, Guimarães, 91
Rosa, Noel, 34, 100–1, 103, 109, 193n12
Roudinesco, Elisabeth, 197n3
Rousseff, Dilma, 74
Rousselot, Jean-Piere, 106
Rudy, Stephen, 195n1
Russell, Bertrand, 187n10

Sacilotto, Luis, 17
Salomão, Waly, 95, 192n39
Santos-Dumont, Alberto, 61, 185n28
Sapir, Edward, 18
Saraiva, António José, 95, 192n37
Sarduy, Severo, 26
Saussure, Ferdinand de, 25, 145–46, 147, 163–64, 179n5, 196n11, 197–98n8

Saussy, Haun, 114
Scheiwiller, Vanni, 125, 132
Schlözer, Boris de, 135
Schoenberg, Arnold, 34–35, 80, 89, 179n11
Schleiermacher, Friedrich, 169–70
Schwarz, Roberto, 193n22
Schwitters, Kurt, 6, 68
Sechehaye, Albert, 196n11
Segovia, Tomás, 198n23
Sevcenko, Nicolau, 3, 4, 108–9, 174n13, 175n15, 194n37, 195n39
Sganzerla, Rogério, 107, 189n20
Shakespeare, William, 91
Shaw, George Bernard, 147
Sheridan, Alan, 199n39
Sieburth, Richard, 67, 78, 106, 173n3, 177n23, 186n3, 193n10, 194n32
Sinclair, John D., 191n24
Slocum, John J., 191n22
Sluckin, W., 183n8
Soares, Bernardo, 190n10
Solt, Mary Ellen, 182n2
Sousândrade, Joaquim de, 2, 3, 5, 65, 66–67, 73, 77–79, 155–60, 180–81n36, 188n14, 189n18, 196n5
Souza, Ana Helena, 181
Spedding, James, 182n46
Spoerri, Daniel, 68
Spring, Declan, 113
Starobinski, Jean, 20, 178n45, 197–98n8
Stegagno Picchio, Luciana, 188n14
Stein, Gertrude, 5
Steiner, George, 64, 186n33
Steiner, Wendy, 20, 178n44
Stern, Philip Van Doren, 143
Sterne, Lawrence, 150
Sterzi, Eduardo, 32, 34, 180n22
Stockhausen, Karlheinz, 23, 91, 179–80n15
Strachey, James, 197n2
Stravinsky, Igor, 29, 131, 134
Süssekind, Flora, 25, 179n6

Talleyrand-Périgord, Charles-Maurice de, 133
Taylor, Elizabeth, 187n10
Teilhard de Chardin, Pierre, 185n30
Tertullian, 141–42
Thiers, Adolphe, 133

Thompson, G. R., 195n3
Thurmann-Jajes, Anne, 113, 175n17
Thurston, Luke, 199n33
Tilton, Theodor, 158
Todorov, Tzvetan, 142
Tomaselli, Sylvana, 198n17
Tomlinson, Gary, 34, 180n32
Torquato Neto, 107, 110, 184–85n26
Tucker, Henry "Harry," 120, 154

Vadico, (Oswaldo Gogliano), 100–1, 193n12
Valente, José de Assis, 106
Valéry, Paul, 35, 47, 58, 60, 108, 139, 143, 150, 182n4, 194–95n38
Valias, André, 113, 180n18
Vance, Eugene, 67, 186n4
Vanderbilt, Cornelius, 158
Vanzolini, Paulo, 102, 193n16
Varèse, Edgard, 135
Vaz de Caminha, Pero, 183n9
Vegetius, 59
Veloso, Caetano, 5, 30, 35, 175n16
Verde, Cesário, 22
Vernadsky, Vladimir, 185n30
Victoria, Queen, 155–56
Vieira, António, 83–89, 95–96, 190n7, 191n19

Villa-Lobos, Heitor, 175n15
Virgil, 99
Voisin, Gabriel, 185n30
Volpi, Alfredo, 19
Voss, Johan Heinrich, 93
Vygotsky, Lev, 64, 186n33

Wait, Christopher, 113
Walcott, Derek, 98
Wanderléia, 34
Warnock, G. J., 177n31
Watt, William, 126
Webern, Anton, 26–30, 33–35, 80, 131, 135, 151, 178–79n1, 179n11
Weil, Kurt, 151, 178–79n1
Weinberg, Eliot, 185n29
Welles, Orson, 185n27, 189n20
White, Landeg, 191n23
Wilde, Oscar, 144
Williams, William Carlos, 36, 46–47, 48, 182n2
Wright, Orville, 185n30
Wright, Wilbur, 185n30

Xenakis, Iannis, 29

Zenith, Richard, 196n13
Zola, Émile, 58

Antonio Sergio Bessa is a scholar of concrete poetry and the author of *Öyvind Fahlström: The Art of Writing* (2008). He has edited several volumes on concrete poetry including Haroldo de Campos's *Novas: Selected Writings* (with Odile Cisneros, 2007), and *Mary Ellen Solt: Toward a Theory of Concrete Poetry* (2010).

VERBAL ARTS: STUDIES IN POETICS

Lazar Fleishman and Haun Saussy, series editors

Kiene Brillenburg Wurth, *Between Page and Screen: Remaking Literature Through Cinema and Cyberspace*
Jacob Edmond, *A Common Strangeness: Contemporary Poetry, Cross-Cultural Encounter, Comparative Literature*
Christophe Wall-Romana, *Cinepoetry: Imaginary Cinemas in French Poetry*
Marc Shell, *Talking the Walk and Walking the Talk: A Rhetoric of Rhythm*
Ryan Netzley, *Lyric Apocalypse: Milton, Marvell, and the Nature of Events*
Ilya Kliger and Boris Maslov (eds.), *Persistent Forms: Explorations in Historical Poetics*. Foreword by Eric Hayot
Ross Chambers, *An Atmospherics of the City: Baudelaire and the Poetics of Noise*
Haun Saussy, *The Ethnography of Rhythm: Orality and Its Technologies*
Andrew Hui, *The Poetics of Ruins in Renaissance Literature*
Peter Szendy, *Of Stigmatology: Punctuation as Experience*. Translated by Jan Plug
Ben Glaser and Jonathan Culler (eds.), *Critical Rhythm: The Poetics of a Literary Life Form*
Craig Dworkin, *Dictionary Poetics: Toward a Radical Lexicography*
Harald Weinrich, *Tempus: The World of Discussion and the World of Narration*. Translated by Jane K. Brown and Marshall Brown
Liesl Yamaguchi, *On the Colors of Vowels: Thinking through Synesthesia*
Antonio Sergio Bessa, *Noigandres: Poetry Made New in Brazil*
Simone Stirner, *Poetic Grief: Form and Remembrance after National Socialism*